A TREASURY

OF MILITARY HUMOR

Edited by

James E. Myers

THE LINCOLN-HERNDON PRESS, INC.
818 South Dirksen Parkway
Springfield, Illinois 26703

Published by Lincoln-Herndon Press, Inc.
818 S. Dirksen Parkway
Springfield, Illinois 62703
217-522-2732

Printed in the United States of America

LIBRARY OF CONGRESS CATALOGUING-IN-PUBLICATION DATA

ISBN 0-942936-16-7: $10.95
Library of Congress Catalogue Card Number 89-084759
Second Printing

Cover illustration by
Richard Ferguson
Squires Advertising Agency, Inc.
Springfield, Illinois

Typography by
Donna's House of Type, Inc.
Springfield, Illinois

TABLE OF CONTENTS

INTRODUCTION

It is a truism that the American soldier jokes about, or finds funniness in, that which most concerns and endangers him. This ability to enjoy the light of laughter in the dark of war, sustains the GI in his determination to win. As in peace, humor lightens the burden of life.

Consider the joke told about the GI, prone and belly deep in mud, shells bursting all around him, whose sergeant yells at him to "get your ass lower, man! Down! Down! Lower!" The GI responds, "I can't get no lower cause my damned shirt buttons are in the way."

The GI is powerless to do much about his uncertain and often precarious situation or those who command him in it. But he can take a crack at his superiors, using humor (discretely!) that puts officers and non-coms down a bit and, in the process, makes the GI feel better, more in command of his life.

Also, he pokes fun at food, uniforms, weapons, battle, civilians . . . all those areas of his life about which he is powerless — except through the power of humor.

This ability to make a joke out of adversity has sustained the American soldier for 128 years — the years that are considered in this collection of military humor — from the Civil War until today.

Inevitably, part of GI humor is bawdy. But to a soldier, the genitals, defecation, sex are as much a part of his life and conversation as are guns and butter. Not to include the GI dirty stories would be to hide an essential aspect of that which makes Americans the superior soldiers they are.

Further, if we consider the loss of life, limb and mind from our wars, we understand that there is no need for normal proprieties, decorous language and thought. War is not concerned with genteelness, refined words and phrases, or gracious living. War IS hell and soldier humor reflects his condition, his environment and his life.

You will note terms and their definitions, as they have been created and spoken by the American soldier. Each war spawned new terms to describe more appropriately the condition or object in view. The poetic imagination, coupled with the traditional GI's amusement with officers, non-coms, situations and objects that confront him, has birthed some of the most delightful, inventive and poetic language extant. True, it is a language unknown to Daniel Webster and his dictionary, but GI words and phrases are, nevertheless, felicitous and precisely descriptive of the GI's world.

So here they are, with their jokes, art, cartoons, stories and language of the American soldier's life as a victorious fighting, joking, laughing American. His wise and indispensable sense of humor has seen the GI through terrible times in our several wars, and onto victory. These men and women soldiers are the best of Americans.

About the editor: James E. Myers was a reserve second lieutenant in March of 1941, when he entered on active duty in the Air Force. After the bombing of Pearl Harbor, he was shipped overseas to the China-Burma-India (CBI) Theatre of Operations. He served in central India and in Assam for two-and-a-half years. Then he was rotated to the United States for another year of duty, before he was released to civilian warfare!

The war years were the most useful and significant years of his life. He hopes that this compilation of GI humor indicates his high respect and affection for the American soldier and the American way, our system that created and formed our superb fighting men and women.

THE HUMOR

OF THE CIVIL WAR

1861-1865

Figures from the Statistical abstract of the United States, page 336, 1988, list the number of battle deaths of the Union forces at 140,000 with 282,000 wounded. and this was only the Union loss. The Confederate loss is estimated at 133,821 battle deaths. Compare these losses with World War II – 292,000 battle deaths and 671,000 wounded. The battle deaths in Korea were 34,000 with 103,000 wounded. the battle loss in Vietnam was 47,000 with 153,000 wounded.*

The above figures indicate the comparative and enormous cost of life and limb of our Civil War and give us insight to the fighting man's need for humor.

This relief, respite from the agony of a war between Americans, was particularly acute for Abraham Lincoln. The anguish of the Presidency comes through to us as we read his jokes and funny stories. It was a time to try mens' souls.

The humor in this chapter illustrates how the soldiers and their Commander-in-Chief coped with that time of anguish, our Civil War.

*From The Statistical Abstract of the United States, 1988.

Our military procurement agencies have always been subject to the criticism of taxpayers, the citizenry. Here, that great satirist, Orpheus C. Kerr (Orpheus Seeker) lambasts the army in terms familiar today... only he wrote in 1862!

THE LATEST IMPROVEMENTS IN ARTILLERY
By Orpheus C. Kerr (Orpheus Seeker)

WASHINGTON, D.C., August—, 1861.

By invitation of a well-known official, I visited the Navy-Yard yesterday, and witnessed the trial of some newly-invented rifled cannon. The trial was of short duration, and the jury brought in a verdict of "innocent of any intent to kill."

The first gun tried was similar to those used in the Revolution, except that it had a larger touch-hole, and the carriage was painted green, instead of blue. This novel and ingenious weapon was pointed at a target about sixty yards distant. It didn't hit it, and as nobody saw any ball, there was much perplexity expressed. A midshipman did say that he thought the ball must have run out of the touchhole when they loaded up – for which he was instantly expelled from the service. After a long search without finding the ball, there was some thought of summoning the Naval Retiring Board to decide on the matter, when somebody happened to look into the mouth of the cannon, and discovered that the ball hadn't gone out at all. The inventor said this would happen sometimes, especially if you didn't put a brick over the touch-hole when you fired the gun. The Government was so pleased with this explanation, that it ordered forty of the guns on the spot, at two hundred thousand dollars apiece. The guns to be furnished as soon as the war is over.

The next weapon tried was Jink's double back-action revolving cannon for ferry-boats. It consists of a heavy bronze tube, revolving on a pivot, with both ends open, and a touch-hole in the middle. While one gunner puts a load in at one end, another puts in a load at the other end, and one touch-hole serves for both. Upon applying the match, the gun is whirled swiftly round on a pivot, and both balls fly out in circles, causing great slaughter on both sides. This terrible engine was aimed at the target with great accuracy; but as the gunner has a large family dependent on him for support, he refused to apply the match. The Government was satisfied without firing, and ordered six of the guns at a million dollars apiece. The guns to be furnished in time for our next war.

The last weapon subjected to trial was a mountain howitzer of a new pattern. The inventor explained that its great advantage was, that it required no powder. In battle it is placed on the top of a high mountain, and a ball slipped loosely into it. As the enemy passes the foot of the mountain, the gunner in charge tips over the howitzer, and the ball rolls down the side of the mountain into the midst of the doomed foe. The range of this terrible weapon depends greatly on the height of the mountain and the distance to its base. The Government ordered forty of these mountain howitzers at a hundred thousand dollars apiece, to be planted on the first mountains discovered in the enemy's country.

These are great times for gunsmiths, my boy; and if you find any old cannon around the junk-shops, just send them along.

There is much sensation in nautical circles arising from the immoral conduct of the rebel privateers; but public feeling has been somewhat easier since the invention of a craft for capturing the pirates, by an ingenious Connecticut chap. Yesterday he exhibited a small model of it at a cabinet meeting, and explained it thus:

"You will perceive," says he to the President, "that the machine itself will only be four times the size of the Great Eastern, and need not cost over a few millions of dollars. I have only got to discover one thing before I can make it perfect. You will observe that it has a steam-engine on board. This engine works a pair of immense iron claps, which are let down into the water from the extreme end of a very lengthy horizontal spar. Upon approaching the pirate, the captain orders the engineer to put on steam. Instantly the clamps descend from the end of the spar and clutch the privateer athwartships. Then the spar swings around over the deck, and the pirate ship is let down into the hold by the run. Then shut your hatches, and you have ship and pirates safe and sound.

The President's gothic features lighted up beautifully at the words of the great inventor; but in a moment they assumed an expression of doubt, and says he:

"But how are you going to manage, if the privateer fires upon you while you are doing this?"

"My dear sir," says the inventor, "I told you I had only one thing to discover before I could make the machine perfect, and that's it."

● 𝍵 ● 𝍵 ● 𝍵 ● 𝍵 ●

Brown-Spit Baby – A child born to enlisted soldiers, usually tough as a mule's spirit, and weaned on chewin' tobacco.

A RECONNOITERER.
You were sent as a scout to try to discover,
If the enemy's troops were crossing the river,
But your eyes are engaged with the girl on the fence,
While the dog does the duty of *reckon-i-scents.*

Some wonderful titles for the liquid most enjoyed by soldiers anytime, anyplace, anywhere. Here's what Civil War soldiers called it: The ardent, Oil of Gladness, Oh do be joyful, Nockum stiff, How-come-you-so, Tanglefoot, Condensed corn . . . And, if you returned to camp drunk on Ardent, well, you were said to have "brought a brick along".

Buck-and-Gag – A form of punishment for drunkeness that placed a stick under the knees of the offender who was seated on the ground with his knees held tight against his chest. His arms were placed under the stick and tied there in front of his shins. To further harass him, a tent peg or stick was placed cross-wise in his mouth and tied behind his head! Now THAT was punishment!

Rocky Mountain Canary – A burro, so-called because of its melodious hee-haw!

Paleface – A new recruit.

General Ulysses S. Grant was asked which of the many war songs he liked best. He mentioned that he was a poor person to ask such a question because, "I know only two tunes. One of them is Yankee Doodle. The other isn't."

• 𝕩 • 𝕩 • 𝕩 • 𝕩 •

President Lincoln was disgusted with the endless delaying tactics of General McClellan. The general continually refused to engage in battle with the rebels. And McClellan was equally scornful of President Lincoln. Hence, when McClellan sent a nasty telegram to the President, "We have captured six cows. What shall we do with them," President Lincoln wired back "As to the six cows captured - milk them."

• 𝕩 • 𝕩 • 𝕩 • 𝕩 •

Perhaps the most famous story of the Civil War is the one where President Lincoln is approached by a delegation of early prohibitionists who demanded that General Grant be relieved of his command because of his well-known love for liquor.

The President paused thoughtfully for a moment and then said, "If you can tell me where Grant gets his whiskey, I'll buy a barrel of it for everyone of my generals."

• 𝕩 • 𝕩 • 𝕩 • 𝕩 •

Another story illustrates the friction between President Lincoln and General McClellan over the latter's refusal to engage in hard combat with the rebels. In fact, McClellan seemed to make no progress in the field at all, threatening by inaction to prolong the war indefinitely. The President wrote the following letter:

> My Dear McClellan:
> If you are not using the army, I should like to borrow it for a short while.
> Yours respectfully,
> Abraham Lincoln

• 𝕩 • 𝕩 • 𝕩 • 𝕩 •

If General Lee was wearing the Confederate gray uniform with gold buttons, what was General Grant wearing?
His Union suit.

• 𝕩 • 𝕩 • 𝕩 • 𝕩 •

Bluebelly – A Union soldier. When it came from a Confederate soldier saying: "You blue-bellied Yankee so-and-so," it was grounds for immediate action!

Wagon Dogs – The goldbrick! The kind of soldier who plays sick or hurt so that he can stay on the wagon trains (away from danger) where goods can be had for the stealing!

WHEN DIOGENES, SEEKING AN HONEST MAN, MET A CIVIL WAR VETERAN

"What were you in the war?" he asked.
"A private," the old soldier answered.
And Diogenes blew out his lamp and went home.

• 𝑖 • 𝑖 • 𝑖 • 𝑖 •

Finally, President Lincoln relieved McClellan and sent General Hooker to replace him. The vigorous Hooker charged into action, reporting to the President as follows: "Headquarters in the saddle!"

President Lincoln reported to his cabinet that "General Hooker has his headquarters where his hindquarters ought to be."

• 𝑖 • 𝑖 • 𝑖 • 𝑖 •

A favorite Lincoln story is one that he told about two Quaker ladies who were arguing about Jefferson Davis, president of the Confederacy, and President Lincoln.

"I believe that Mr. Jefferson will win this war," said the one lady.

"And why dost thee think so?"

"Because Mr. Jefferson is a praying man."

"But so is Abraham a praying man."

"Yes. I know. But the Lord will think Abraham is only joking."

• 𝑖 • 𝑖 • 𝑖 • 𝑖 •

A brusque, pompous lady charged into President Lincoln's office one day. "Mr. President," she said, "I demand that my son be given a commission as a major, at least. I ask this not as a favor but as a right because my grandfather fought at Lexington, my father fought at New Orleans and my husband was killed at Monterey.

"Dear Madam," the President remarked smoothingly, "It seems to be that your family has done enough for this nation. It is now time to give somebody else a chance."

• 𝑖 • 𝑖 • 𝑖 • 𝑖 •

Soldier's Wife – A sewing kit filled with the necessary items to allow a soldier to repair his own clothes. Sometimes named a *housewife*.

A CANDIDATE FOR MILITARY PROMOTION.

I was tired of the ranks, and promoted I'd be,
I tho't the shoulder straps would look finely on me,
But when I applied, it was only to find,
The promotion before just hurt me behind.

● 🛇 ● 🛇 ● 🛇 ● 🛇 ●

Owls – Desertion. It was said of a man who fled undercover of night, "the owls caught him."

Pinetop Whiskey – A vicious whiskey said to be mellowed by drowning raw meat in it for several weeks.

Bust Head – A variety of sweetened booze that was aged with meat. After a night of bust head booze, your head felt busted!

See The Elephant – To have experienced a trying experience, e.g., combat, and feel a lot wiser and cautious, as a result! It sometimes meant to quit the fight and retreat.

Anything To Preserve The Union – Today we'd say *That's the way the cookie crumbles,* or, *That's the way of the world. Make the best of it.*

Leather Gun – The penis!

Butcher's Bill – Casualty list.

• 🪖 • 🪖 • 🪖 • 🪖 •

During the Civil War, Washington had more than enough gossip mongers in high and low places. One of them approached William H. Seward, Secretary of State, and asked: "Sir, could you give me your notions of the latest developments in this war? And just where do you think the Army will strike next?"

"Madam," replied Seward, "Let me assure you that if I did not know, I would be most pleased to tell you."

• 🪖 • 🪖 • 🪖 • 🪖 •

A Confederate cavalry officer who hailed from the Arkansas Ozarks, was heard directing his men to mount their horses. His command: "Prepare fer tu git on them critters!" His second command: "Git!"

• 🪖 • 🪖 • 🪖 • 🪖 •

After the surrender of the Confederate troops at Appomattox, many of the former soldiers from the South were happy to take any available job. Many hired out as farm hands.

A South Carolina farmer hired some of these men and women and, when asked what kind of workers they were, he replied, "Well, take a look at that bunch of men working over yonder. Them boys was privates in the war and they make mighty fine workers.

"But," he went on, "Look at that other bunch just beyond them good workers. They were captains and they ain't so bad."

"What about about those men behind us?" the farmer was asked.

"Them men was colonels, ever' last one of 'em. And they don't do much and don't do it fer long. But I tell ya one thing . . . I ain't about to hire no generals!"

• 🪖 • 🪖 • 🪖 • 🪖 •

The Civil War was a brutal, deadly conflict. Today we can scarcely imagine the extent of the wounded and dead, right here in our own nation and among our fellow citizens. It was a heart-rendering experience for all Americans, and for Abraham Lincoln, it was truly a time to try men's souls, his own more than most. And he resorted to humor to relieve his anxiety and deep sadness. "I laugh that I may not cry. That's all. That's all," he said when scolded for joking at a cabinet meeting. And humor *was* a crucial factor in keeping him steady in pursuit of the victory so essential to the survival of the United States of America.

A member of President Lincoln's bodyguard came to him one day to complain about the inactivity and obvious lack of need in their work. "The men would rather be at the front, Sir," the bodyguard told him.

President Lincoln remarked that the requests reminded him of a farmer friend back in Illinois who said he could never understand why the Lord put the curl in a pig's tail. It was neither useful nor ornamental, but he reckoned that the Almighty knew what he was doing when he put it there.

"Now soldier, I don't think I need bodyguards, so we do agree on that. But Mr. Stanton, the Secretary of War, thinks I do and it is his department. If you go to the front he'll only send others to replace you and I reckon being here is pleasanter and safer than being there."

● 𝖎 ● 𝖎 ● 𝖎 ● 𝖎 ●

It so happened that, for a time, General J.C. Fremont was without a command. In discussing the matter, President Lincoln said they did not know where to place General Fremont and that the situation reminded him of the old man who advised his son to take a wife. "All right," replied the son. "Whose wife shall I take?"

● 𝖎 ● 𝖎 ● 𝖎 ● 𝖎 ●

President Lincoln was criticized for issuing another draft call for needed soldiers. He said the criticisms put him in mind of a provost marshall who, in describing Confederate methods of conscription, told this story.

"I listened a short time since to a butternut-clad individual who had made good his escape, expatiate most eloquently on the rigidness with which the conscription was enforced south of the Tennessee River. His response to a question of a citizen went something like this:

"Do they conscript close over the river (in the South)?"

"Stranger, I should think they did! *They take every man who hasn't been dead more than two days!*"

"If this is correct, the Confederacy has at least a ghost of a chance left."

● 𝖎 ● 𝖎 ● 𝖎 ● 𝖎 ●

[E.W. Andrews, the assistant adjutant-general, who had to accompany Lincoln to Gettysburg in place of a general who was suffering boils:] After cordially greeting us and directing us to make ourselves comfortable, the President, with quizzical expression, turned to Montgomery Blair (then Postmaster-General), and said:

"Blair, did you ever know that fright has sometimes proved a sure cure for boils?"

"No, Mr. President. How is that?"

"I'll tell you. Not long ago, when Colonel ——, with his cavalry, was at the front, and the Rebs were making things rather lively for us, the colonel was ordered out on a *reconnaissance.* He was troubled at the time with a big boil where it made horseback riding decidedly uncomfortable. He hadn't gone more than two or three miles when he declared he couldn't stand it any longer, and dismounted and ordered the troops forward without him. He had just settled down to enjoy his relief from change of position when he was startled by the rapid reports of pistols and the helter-skelter approach of his troops in full retreat before a yelling rebel force. He forgot everything but the yells, sprang into his saddle, and made capital time over fences and ditches till safe within the lines. The pain from his boil was gone, and the boil too. The colonel swore that there was no cure for boils so sure as fright from rebel yells. The secession had rendered to loyalty *one* valuable service at any rate."

● ♙ ● ♙ ● ♙ ● ♙ ●

Hog Ranch – That institution that is common to almost any army in the world, ancient or modern – the whorehouse!

Hooker – The available resident of the above-mentioned "hog ranch". The name may come from General Joseph Hooker who is said to have entertained his share of these cuties of the evening.

● ♙ ● ♙ ● ♙ ● ♙ ●

WE ARE THE BOYS OF POTOMAC'S RANKS

Here is an amusing recital of the adventures and mishaps of the Army of The Potomac under several of its earlier commanders. It was sung in the Third Corps in the fall of 1863 to the tune of "When Johnny Comes Marching Home."

Burnside's "Mud March" was also commemorated in the following verse which is called "The Soldier's Prayer":

Now I lay me down to sleep,
In mud that's many fathoms deep,
If I'm not here when you awake
Just hunt me with an oyster rake.

We are the boys of Potomac's ranks,
Hurrah! Hurrah!

We are the boys of Potomac's ranks,
We ran with McDowell, retreated with Banks,
And we'll all drink stone blind–
Johnny, fill up the bowl.

We fought with McClellan, the Rebs, shakes, and fever,
    Hurrah! Hurrah!
We fought with McClellan, the Rebs, shakes, and fever,
But Mac joined the navy on reaching James River,
And we'll all drink stone blind–
Johnny, fill up the bowl.

They gave us John Pope, our patience to tax,
    Hurrah! Hurrah!
They gave us John Pope, our patience to tax,
Who said that out West he'd seen naught but *graybacks,* *
And we'll drink stone blind–
Johnny, fill up the bowl.

He said his headquarters were in the saddle,
    Hurrah! Hurrah!
He said his headquarters were in the saddle,
But Stonewall Jackson made him skedaddle–
And we'll all drink stone blind–
Johnny, fill up the bowl.

Then Mac was recalled, but after Antietam,
    Hurrah! Hurrah!
Then Mac was recalled, but after Antietam,
Abe gave him a rest, he was too slow to beat 'em,
And we'll all drink stone blind–
Johnny, fill up the bowl.

Oh, Burnside, then he tried his luck,
    Hurrah! Hurrah!
Oh, Burnside, then he tried his luck,
But in the mud so fast got stuck,
And well all drink stone blind–
Johnny, fill up the bowl.

*Southern soldiers were called "Graybacks" by Union troops. But so were lice (cooties!). This is a snide suggestion by General Pope that the enemy ran from him!

Then Hooker was taken to fill the bill,
  Hurrah! Hurrah!
Then Hooker was taken to fill the bill,
But he got a black eye at Chancellorsville,
And we'll all drink stone blind–
Johnny, fill up the bowl.

Next came General Meade, a slow old plug,
  Hurrah! Hurrah!
Next came General Meade, a slow old plug,
For he let them get away at Gettysburg,
And we'll all drink stone blind–
Johnny, fill up the bowl.

Irish Promotion – A demotion!

Irish Theater – The common, everyday guardhouse!

Irish Turkey – Hash.

Irish Musket – A club.

Conferring with two other generals about G.B. McClellan's inertia President Lincoln said he desired an expression of their opinion about the matter. It was his opinion if something were not done and that soon, the bottom would fall out of the whole thing. He intended if General McClellan did not want to use the army to propose to borrow it from him, for "If McClellan can't fish, he ought to cut bait at a time like this."

Some time in the early part of the war a clergyman said in his presence that he "hoped the Lord was on our side."

"I am not at all concerned about that," replied Mr. Lincoln. "For I know that the Lord is always on the side of the right, but it is my constant anxiety and prayer that I and this nation should be on the Lord's side."

Excessive paperwork, the endless making of and passing on of documents, is the most boring of all government duties, and the military is no exception. Some think that the military invented the game of paperwork! But, lest the reader thinks that this plague of flowing paper is a new, contemporary aber-

ration in the art of communication, there follows an example of the ageless plague – and it comes from the mouth of a Civil War soldier.

RED TAPE IS NOTHING NEW IN THE ARMY

While here I applied for a furlough. Now, reader, here commenced a series of red tapeism that always had characterized the officers under Braggism. It had to go through every officer's hands, from corporal up, before it was forwarded to the next officer of higher grade, and so it passed through every officer's hands. He felt it his sworn and bound duty to find some informality in it, and it was brought back for correction according to his notions, you see. Well, after getting the corporal's consent and approval, it goes up to the sergeant. It ain't right! Some informality, perhaps, in the wording and spelling. Then the lieutenants had to have a say in it, and when it got to the captain, it had to be read and re-read, to see that every "i" was dotted and "t" crossed, but returned because there was one word that he couldn't make out.

Then it was forwarded to the colonel. He would snatch it out of your hand, grit his teeth, and say, "D –n it," feel in his vest pocket and take out a lead pencil, and simply write "app." for approved. This would also be returned, with instructions, that the colonel must write "approved" in a plain hand, and with pen and ink. Then it went to the brigadier-general. He would be engaged in a game of poker, and would tell you to call again, as he didn't have time to bother with those small affairs at present. "I'll see your five and raise you ten." "I have a straight flush." "Take the pot." After reading carefully the furlough, he says, "Well, sir, you have failed to get the adjutant's name to it. You ought to have the colonel and adjutant, and you must go back and get their signatures."

After this, you go to the major-general. He is an old aristocratic fellow, who never smiles, and tries to look as sour as vinegar. He looks at the furlough, and looks down at the ground, holding the furlough in his hand in a kind of dreamy way, and then says, "Well, sir, this is all informal."

You say, "Well, General, what is the matter with it?"

He looks at you as if he hadn't heard you, and repeats very slowly,

"Well, sir, this is informal," and hands it back to you.

You take it, feeling all the while that you wished you had not applied for a furlough, and by summoning all the fortitude that you possess, you say in a husky and choking voice, "Well, general (you say the "general" in a sort of gulp and dry swallow), what's the matter with the furlough?" You look askance, and he very languidly re-takes the furlough and glances over it, orders his Negro boy to go and feed his horse, asks his cook how long it will be before dinner, hallooes at some fellow away down the hill that he would like for him to call at 4 o'clock this evening, and tells his adjutant to sign the furlough. The adjutant tries to be smart and polite, smiles a smile both child-like and bland, rolls up his shirt-sleeves, and winks one eye at you, gets astraddle of a camp-stool, whistles a little stanza of schottische, and with a big flourish of his pen, writes the major-general's name in small letters, and his own–the adjutant's–in very large letters, bringing the pen under it with tremendous flourishes, and writes approved and forwarded.

You feel relieved. You feel that the anaconda's coil had been suddenly relaxed. Then you start out to the lieutenant-general; you find him. He is in a very learned and dignified conversation about the war in Chili. Well, you get very anxious for the war in Chili to get to an end. The general pulls his side-whiskers, looks wise, and tells his adjutant to look over it, and, if correct, sign it. The adjutant does not deign to condescend to notice you. He seems to be full of gumbo or calf-tail soup, and does not wish his equanimity disturbed. He takes hold of the document, and writes the lieutenant-general's name, finishes his own name while looking in another direction – approved and forwarded.

Then you take it up to the general; the guard stops you in a very formal way, and asks, "What do you want" You tell him. He calls for the orderly; the orderly gives it to the adjutant, and you are informed that it will be sent to your colonel tonight, and given to you at roll-call in the morning. Now, reader, the above is a pretty true picture of how I got my furlough.

● 🯄 ● 🯄 ● 🯄 ● 🯄 ●

The Act of the Emancipation Proclamation, freed the Negroes. It became law on January 1, 1863, and found the black population of the slave states not sure at all as to what the Union expected of them. Some blacks who escaped were returned to the Confederacy. Later, refuge was granted but blacks then did not serve in the Union army.

It was about this time when a Union officer struck up a conversation with an old Negro he met on the road. "Tell me, Uncle," asked the soldier, "I wonder if you realize that this awful war is coming about on your account?"

"Sho' do, suh. I've heerd 'em say it offen."

"Well, you'd like to be free, wouldn't you?"

"Yassuh. I sho' nuff would."

"That bein' the case, Uncle, how come you are not in the army yourself?"

"Suh - an' ah speaks respectful-like-suh, did you evuh see two dawgs afightin' ovuh a bone?"

"Of course. Many times."

"Well, suh, did you evuh take notice as to whethuh the bone was afightin' back?"

● ♟ ● ♟ ● ♟ ● ♟ ●

When President Lincoln was told that General Stoughton had been captured by the rebels at Fairfax, a capture that was shameful, he remarked: "I don't so much mind the loss of the brigadier as I do the loss of the horses. For I can make a much better brigadier in five minutes, but the horses cost a hundred and twenty-five dollars apiece."

● ♟ ● ♟ ● ♟ ● ♟ ●

A newspaper correspondent in search of some exciting news about the fighting, asked the President if he had heard anything new from General Grant. President Lincoln replied that he had not, that Grant was like the man that climbed the pole and then pulled the pole up after him, leaving no trace!

● ♟ ● ♟ ● ♟ ● ♟ ●

President Lincoln was making the rounds of a hospital accompanied by a young lady. In the course of the visit, the pretty girl asked a soldier just where he had been hit. "At Antietam," he replied. "But just where did the bullet hit you?" the lady asked. "At Antietam." Again she repeated the question and got the same answer: "At Antietam."

She gave up but asked President Lincoln to continue the inquiry as she moved on down the line of beds. He did this, got an answer from the wounded soldier, then caught up with her just as she was leaving the room. He took both her hands and, with a twinkle in his eye, said, "My dear girl, the ball that hit him, would not have injured you."

● ♟ ● ♟ ● ♟ ● ♟ ●

During a conversation on the approaching election, in 1864, a remark was made to President Lincoln that defeat was impossible for him in running for his second term, unless it be General Grant's capture of Richmond and subsequent nomination of Grant at the forthcoming Chicago Republican convention. "Well," said the President, "I feel very much like the man who said he didn't want to die particularly, but if he had got to die, that was precisely the disease he would like to die of!"

● 🪖 ● 🪖 ● 🪖 ● 🪖 ●

Ah! what is the matter, my trooper so gay,
    While to this young lass you are kneeling?
Your head, it is soft – as for heart you have none.
    Your butt alone seems to have feeling.

● 🪖 ● 🪖 ● 🪖 ● 🪖 ●

President Lincoln was a superb joke teller, seeming to find a story to illustrate almost any point he wanted to make. There was the time a Senator Wade said to him, "Mr. President, unless we adopt a proposition to emancipate the colored man, we will all go to the devil. Why at this moment in time we are not a mile away from hell."

"That could be," replied the President. "And, by some curious arrangement of facts, that is just about the distance from where you stand to the Capitol, where you gentlemen are in session."

● 🪖 ● 🪖 ● 🪖 ● 🪖 ●

Ward Lamon was a good friend of President Lincoln, having traveled the 8th Judicial Circuit with him in Illinois. They shared a law office in Danville, Illinois. When Lincoln left for Washington to take his office as President, his bodyguard was Ward Lamon. Later he made him Marshall of the District of Columbia. But one day Lamon got into a street fight and hit a belligerent. The man was unconscious for hours and whether he would die or not was problematical.

"I am surprised at you, Ward," said the President. "You should have known better than to use your fist when a club would have accomplished the same end and much more gently."

● 🪖 ● 🪖 ● 🪖 ● 🪖 ●

There's a certain type of story that's told in every war, it seems, and the Civil War was no exception. It seems that Stonewall Jackson found a man named Miles to be a superb bridge builder. Bridges were damaged by floods or destroyed by the enemy so often that Miles became a most valuable asset. One day, as the Union troops retreated, they burned a vital bridge behind them and Jackson needed it rebuilt to go in pursuit. He called for Miles and told him that he had to go to work night and day with his men and get foundations ready for a bridge. His engineers would soon furnish the plan for the work.

The next day, Jackson hunted up Miles and asked if the engineers had given him their finished plans for rebuilding the bridge.

"General," Miles drawled, "we done got the foundation built but I cain't tell ya whether them pictures is done or not."

● 🪖 ● 🪖 ● 🪖 ● 🪖 ●

They tell the story of a Confederate colonel who on a tough retreat, was leading his men as fast as he could. But the Yankees were close behind and, occasionally, a rebel kid would stop to fire at the enemy. Finally, the colonel yelled, "Boys, quit shootin' at those fellers. It just makes 'em all the madder!"

● 🪖 ● 🪖 ● 🪖 ● 🪖 ●

General Grant was bad-mouthing a certain army officer on his staff, but one of his officers came to the defense of the man, saying that the officer deserved a break. "After all, he's been on ten campaigns and fought in them all."

"So has that mule," said General Grant, "but he's still a jackass."

● 🪖 ● 🪖 ● 🪖 ● 🪖 ●

And the South, too, had the same kind of officers. Witness General Stonewall Jackson's remark, when he was told that a certain officer never known for his bravery or diligence, had been wounded and would not be able to continue on duty. "Wounded?" muttered Jackson, "Well, all I can say is it must have been an accidental discharge of his duty."

• ⚔ • ⚔ • ⚔ • ⚔ •

General Lee saw one of his soldiers moving back from the combat zone and at high speed. The general caught up with the man and yelled, "You should be at the front, soldier, where you belong while the battle is going on."

"Sir, I got to tell you I been there already and, Sir, I also got to tell you that it ain't no place where a self-respecting man ought to be!"

• ⚔ • ⚔ • ⚔ • ⚔ •

Abraham Lincoln told the following story about himself.

It seems that during the Blackhawk War, Lincoln was elected captain of his company, a company that knew little about the official commands for a soldier. Lincoln knew as little as any. And so, when the company had marched in proper order until stopped by a stake-and-rider fence in front of them and a gate too small to allow the company to march through it, Lincoln did what any officer might consider doing if he did not know the proper command. Captain Lincoln said, "The company is dismissed for two minutes. Then it will fall in on the other side of the fence."

• ⚔ • ⚔ • ⚔ • ⚔ •

The recruit complained to his sergeant that he was in pain from a splinter set deep in his finger.

"Ye should have more sinse," was the harsh comment of Sergeant Patrick O'Toole, "than to scratch your head!"

• ⚔ • ⚔ • ⚔ • ⚔ •

President Lincoln was angry with General McClellan for his failure to move ahead, to be aggressive in the war. "General McClellan's tardiness and unwillingness to fight the enemy or follow up advantages gained," the President remarked to friends gathered in his office, "reminds me of a man back in Illinois who knew a few law phrases but whose lawyer lacked aggressiveness. The man finally lost his patience and, springing to his feet, vociferated: 'Why don't you go at him with a fi.fa., a demurrer, a capias, a surrebutter, or a ne exeat, or something; or a nundam pactum or a non est?'

"Well," President Lincoln went on, "I wish McClellan would go at the enemy with something – I don't care what. General

McClellan is a pleasant and scholarly gentleman. He is an admirable engineer, but he seems to have a special talent for operating a stationary engine."

● ⚔ ● ⚔ ● ⚔ ● ⚔ ●

A visitor to West Point stopped before a monument dedicated to soldiers fallen in the Civil War. But only Union Army soldiers were engraved on the stone. "Why is it that only soldiers from the Union are listed?" a visitor asked.

"That, my dear sir," said a cadet, "is a signal tribute to Confederate marksmanship!"

● ⚔ ● ⚔ ● ⚔ ● ⚔ ●

Believe it or not, there were cowards on both sides during the Civil War. Here's a poem about them:

In every army, great and small,
    There is a set of patent *blowers,*
Who of the work make out to shirk all,
    And of their valiant deeds are *crowers.*
But let a battle once commence,
    Away they travel for some tree or fence;
You find their brains too soon addled,
    And you've but to see that they've *skedaddled.*

● ⚔ ● ⚔ ● ⚔ ● ⚔ ●

Side Arms – Salt and Pepper!

EATING GOOBER PEAS

The air of this old Confederate song, quite as much as its amusing lines, is revealing. "Goober peas" are peanuts. Georgians are sometimes called "goober grabbers."

un - der-neath the   trees,   Good-ness, how de - li - cious,

eat-ing goo-ber peas!   Peas! Peas! Peas! Peas!   eat -ing goo - ber

Chorus

peas!   Good-ness, how de - li - cious,   eat-ing goob-er peas!

When a horseman passes the soldiers have a rule,
To cry out at their loudest, "Mister here's your mule";
But another pleasure enchantinger than these,
Is wearing out your Grinders, eating goober peas!
Chorus

Just before the battle the Gen'ral hears a row,
He says, "The Yanks are coming, I hear their rifles now."
He turns around in wonder, and what do you think he sees?
The Georgia Militia, eating goober peas!
Chorus

I think my song has lasted almost long enough,
The subject's interesting, but rhymes are mighty rough;
I wish this war was over, when free from rags and fleas,
We'd kiss our wives and sweethearts, and gobble goober peas!
Chorus

● 𝑖 ● 𝑖 ● 𝑖 ● 𝑖 ●

Shadow Soup: Weak chicken soup. The men described it as made from a chicken hung so that its shadow would fall on the boiling soup water! The shadow was then boiled until the soup was strong enough to serve as normal, hospital chicken soup!

A REBEL VALENTINE

To trample on "our dear Old Flag",
You rashly did attempt;
The Valentine most meant for you,
Is a Neck-tie made of hemp.

● 𝑖 ● 𝑖 ● 𝑖 ● 𝑖 ●

Every elected official is plagued by self-proclaimed "staunch supporters" who demand a job because of their self-sacrificial efforts for the election of the official. President Lincoln was no exception and post offices seemed to be one of the most sought-after jobs. Here is a satirical account of the matter, just as the war erupted.

POLITICAL PATRONAGE MUST BE OLD AS WAR

In view of the impending conflict, it is the duty of every American citizen, who has nothing else to do, to take up his abode in the capital of this agonized Republic, and give the Cabinet the sanction of his presence. Some base child of treason may intimate that Washington is not quite large enough to hold every American citizen; but I'm satisfied that, if all the Democrats could have one good washing, they would shrink so that you might put the whole blessed party into an ordinary custom house. Some of the Republicans are pretty large chaps for their size, but Jeff Davis thinks they can be "taken in" easily enough to make them contract like sponges out of water.

The city is full of Western chaps, at present, who look as if they had not got beyond gruel diet yet. Every soul of them knew old Abe when he was a child, and one old boy can even remember going for a doctor when his mother was born.

I met one of them the other day (he is after the Moose-hic-magunticook post-office), and his anecdotes of the President's boyhood brought tears to my eyes, and several tumblers to my lips. He says, that when Abe was an infant of sixteen, he split so many rails that his whole county looked like a wholesale lumber-yard for a week; and that when he took to flat-boating, he was so tall and straight, that a fellow once took him for a smoke-stack on a steamboat, and didn't find out his mistake until he tried to kindle a fire under him. Once, while Abe was practising as a lawyer, he defended a man for stealing a horse, and was so eloquent in proving that his client was an honest victim of false suspicion, that the deeply affected victim made him a present of the horse as soon as he was acquitted.

I tell you what, my boy, if Abe pays a post-office for every story of his childhood that's told, the mail department of this glorious nation will be so large that a letter smaller than a two-story house would get lost in it. —*Orpheus C. Kerr.*

● 🏃 ● 🏃 ● 🏃 ● 🏃 ●

During the Civil War, an Irishman in the Union's service, having come by surprise on a small party of soldiers who were foraging, seized their arms which they had laid aside. He then presented his musket, and with threats drove them before him into the Union camp, where the singularity of the exploit occasioned some wonder. He was brought, with his prisoners, before General Grant who asked him how he had taken them.

"By god, General," said he, "I surrounded them."

● 🏃 ● 🏃 ● 🏃 ● 🏃

One day Chauncey Depew met a Union soldier who had been wounded in the face. Depew asked him in which battle he had been injured.

"In the last battle of Bull Run, sir," he replied.

"But how could you get hit in the face at Bull Run?"

"Well, sir," said the man, "after I had run a mile or two I got careless and looked back."

One day, President Lincoln was asked how many men the Confederates had in the field. Lincoln astonished them by saying, "Twelve hundred thousand, according to the best authority. No doubt of it. You see, all of our generals, when they get whipped, say the enemy outnumbers them from three or five to one, and I must believe them. We have four hundred thousand men in the field, and three times four make twelve. Don't you see it?"

TO THE SURGEON.

Ho! Ho! old saw bones, here you come,
Yes, when the rebels whack us,
You are always ready with your traps,
To mangle, saw, and hack us.

At the outset of the war there was an acute shortage of surgeons. Many were young, unskilled, and only partially trained.

Some had no preparation other than a quick course in military surgery. Others relied on pamphlets which were hastily prepared to act as a guide. There were strict rules concerning amputations, for example, which this valentine refers to. "Amputate with as little delay as possible," advised one handbook on surgery.

A veteran told the story of a private in the Civil War, who during the first battle of Bull Run found a post hole into which he lowered himself, so that only his eyes were above the level of the ground. An officer seeing this cowardly act ran to the spot, and with a threatening gesture of his sword, shouted, "Get out of that hole!"

But the soldier did not budge. On the contrary, he put his thumb to his nose and waggled his fingers incultingly.

"Not a chance!" he retorted. "Get in your own hole. This one's mine!"

Near the end of the Civil War, when the Confederate forces were falling back on Richmond, an old slave, who was asked by his mistress for some *encouraging* news, replied:

"Well, Missy, due to de pitch of de land where dey's afightin' dem Yankees is a retreatin' forward while we is advancin' backwards."

Draft dodgers, like death and taxes, have always been present whenever there is a war. The Civil War was no exception and here, satirizing all the excuses, complaints, plaintive begging that went into draft dodging during that trying war, is PETROLEUM V. NASBY, one of the greatest satirists this country has ever produced. He was a strong Union man and his technique was to write as if he were a barely literate Southerner with all the bigotry, debauchery and illiteracy that northern propaganda tried to impute to the South during that bitter war between the states.

WHY HE SHOULD NOT BE DRAFTED

I see in the papers last nite that the government hez institooted a draft, and that in a few weeks sum hunders uv thousands uv peeseable citizens will be drafted to the tented field. I know not wat uthers may do, but ez fer me, I can't go.

Upon a rigid eggsaminashun uv my fizzlekle man, I find it wood be wus ner madnis fer me 2 undertake a campane, to-wit:

1. I'm bald-headid, and hev been obliged to ware a wig these 22 yeres.
2. I hev dandruff in wat scanty hair still hangs around my venerable temples.
3. I hev a chronic katarr.
4. I hev lost the use uv wun eye entirely, and hev cronic inflammashen in the other.
5. My teeth is all unsound, my palit aint eggsactly rite, and I hev hed bronkeetis 31 yeres last Joon. At present I hev a kuff, the paroxisms uv which is friteful 2 behold.
6. I'm holler-chestid, am short-winded, and hev allus hed panes in my back and side.
7. I am afflicted with kronic diarrear and kostivness.
8. I am rupchered in 9 places, and am entirely enveloped with trusses.
9. I hev verrykose vanes, hev a white swellin on wun leg and a fever sore on the uther—also wun leg is shorter tother, though I handle it so expert that nobody never noticed it.
10. I hev korns and bunyons on both feet wich wood prevent me from marchin.

I dont suppose that my political opinions, which are agin the prossekooshn uv this unconstooshnel war, wood hev any wate with a draftin orfiser, but the above reasons why I cant go will, I maik no doubt, be suffishent.

Petroleum V. Nasby
August 6, 1862

● 𝑓 ● 𝑓 ● 𝑓 ● 𝑓 ●

Two young slaves managed to escape from the plantation during the height of the Civil War. Trudging along a dusty side road they came upon a regiment of Union troops. They were received with glad cries of welcome from other former slaves who had made their way to freedom and were now fighting the Confederacy.

"We might ez well jine up too," said the older of the two escapees. "I think I'll jine de calavary."

"Not me!" said the other. "I ain't jinin' no calavary. "I's gwine intuh de infantary."

"You gwine tuh do lots uv walkin'," the older youth reminded his companion. "In de calavary you gits tuh ride a hoss."

"Man, you ain't thinkin' rightly," retorted the other. "When dem bullets start a-flyin', I ain't gwine have time ter pull no dang hoss 'long wid me!"

● 🛡 ● 🛡 ● 🛡 ● 🛡 ●

A regiment of Union soldiers was making a long dusty march across the dusty fields of Tennessee. It was a hot, blistering day and the men, longing for water and rest, were impatient to reach the next town.

A boy rode past.

"Say, boy" called out one of the regulars, "how far is it to the next town?"

"Oh, a matter of two miles or so, I reckon," called back the lad. Another long hour dragged by, and another lad was encountered.

"How far to the next town?" the men asked him eagerly.

"Two miles."

A weary half-hour longer of marching, and then a third Southerner.

"Hey! How far's the next town?"

"Not far," was the encouraging answer. "Only about two miles."

"Well," sighed an optimistic sergeant, "thank God we are holdin' our own!"

PICKETING – AN AFFECTING WAR INCIDENT

While on my lonely beat, about an hour ago, a light tread attracted my attention, and, on looking up, I beheld one of Secesh's pickets standing before me.

"Stranger," says he, "you remind me of my grandmother, who expired before I was born; but this unnatural war has made us enemies, and I must shoot you. Give me a chaw terbacker."

He was a young man, in the prime of life, and descended from the first families of Virginia. That is to say, his mother was a virgin. At least that's what I understand by the first families of Virginia.

I looked at him, and says I, "Let's compromise, my brother."

"Never!" says he. "The South is fighting for her liberty, her firesides, and the pursuit of happiness, and I desire most respectfully to welcome you with bloody hands to a hospitable grave."

"Stand off ten paces," says I, "and let's see whose name shall come before the coroner first."

He took his place, and we fired simultaneously. I heard a ball go whistling by a barn about a quarter of a mile on my right. When the smoke cleared away I saw the Secesh picket approach me with an awful expression of woe on his otherwise dirty countenance.

"Soldier," says he, "was there any thing in my head before you fired?"

"Nothing," says I, "save a few harmless insects."

"I speak not of them," says he. "Was there any thing *inside* of my head?"

"Nothing!" says I.

"Well," says he, "just listen now." He shook his head mournfully and I heard something rattle in it.

"What's that?" I exclaimed.

"That," said he, "is your bullet, which has penetrated my skull, and is rolling around in my brain. I'll die happy, with an empty stomach, but there is one thing I should like to see before I perish for my country. Have you a quarter about you?"

Too much affected to speak, I drew the coin from my pocket and handed it to him. The dying man clutched it convulsively and stared at it feverishly.

"This," said he, "is the first quarter I have seen since the fall of Sumter and had I wounded you, I should have been totally unable to have given you any quarter. Ah, how beautiful it is! How bright! How exquisite and good for four drinks! But I have not time to say all I feel"

The expiring soldier laid down his gun, hung his cap and overcoat on a branch of a tree, and blew his nose. He then died.

And there I stood, on that lonely beat, looking down upon that fallen type of manhood, and thinking how singular it was he had forgotten to give me back my quarter. The sight and the thought so affected me that I was obliged to turn my back on the corpse and walk a little way from it. When I returned to the spot the body was gone! Had it gone to heaven? Perhaps so. Perhaps so, but I haven't seen my quarter since.

– Anonymous

● 🪖 ● 🪖 ● 🪖 ● 🪖 ●

Consecrated Milk – A form of condensed milk used in the Union Army. A pun on *concentrated milk*.

Descrated Vegetables – A pun on dessicated vegetables of all kinds, shredded and formed into flats or cubes to be used in stews and soups. Sometimes referred to as baled hay.

Old Colonel Beauregard was a devil with the ladies, still charming the daylights out of them at seventy-seven. In fact, on his seventy-seventh birthday he adopted the practice of cutting a deep notch on his cane to mark each new conquest. That's what killed him on his seventy-eighth birthday: he made the mistake of leaning on his cane.

● ⚊ ● ⚊ ● ⚊ ● ⚊ ●

Headquarters In The Saddle – This meant that the general officer concerned had his head in the saddle (where his butt ought to be!).

General Bragg's Bodyguard – The soldiers' way of entitling and describing lice . . . and General Bragg!

To Lay Pipe – To use influence to get a personal favor or advantage from someone in authority.

Army Banjo – A shovel!

● ⚊ ● ⚊ ● ⚊ ● ⚊ ●

A Confederate soldier who was from the woods surrounding Mena, Arkansas, told this story about his grandfather who had fought in the Mexican War. Someone asked the grandfather, then a young soldier, how he liked army life.

"Well, I'll tell ya this," he answered. "The drinkin' is plumb fine, along with the card-playin'. And them Mexican fillies ain't bad atall. But them battles . . . I want to tell ya . . . them battles is mighty dangerous."

● ⚊ ● ⚊ ● ⚊ ● ⚊ ●

The Southern colonel at Saratoga Springs, soon after the Civil War, told the Negro waiter at his table in the hotel: "You kin bring me a Kentucky breakfast."

"An' what is that, Sir?" the waiter inquired.

The colonel explained, "Bring me a great big steak, an Irish terrier and a quart of bourbon whiskey."

"But why do you order an Irish terrier?" asked the puzzled waiter.

"To eat the steak, suh!" snapped the colonel.

● ⚊ ● ⚊ ● ⚊ ● ⚊ ●

Sergeant Murphy had a squad of recruits on the rifle range. He tried them on the 500-yard range, but none of them could hit the target. Then he tried them on the 300-, 200-, and 100-yard ranges, but with no better success. When they had all missed on the shortest range, he scratched his head and regarded them perplexedly. Suddenly he straightened up,.

"Squad, attintion!" he commanded. "Fix bayonetts! Char-r-ge!"

• ⚔ • ⚔ • ⚔ • ⚔ •

ARKANSAS AND THE CIVIL WAR

During the Civil War the soldiers at Helena, Arkansas, used to amuse the inhabitants by telling them yarns, of which the following is a sample:

Some time ago Jeff Davis got tired of the war, and invited President Lincoln to meet him on neutral ground to discuss terms of peace. They met accordingly and after a talk concluded to settle the war by dividing the territory and stopping the fighting. The North took the Northern states, the South took the Gulf and seaboard Southern states. Lincoln took Texas and Missouri, and Davis took Kentucky and Tennessee. All were parceled off except Arkansas.

On that they split. Lincoln didn't want it, Jeff wouldn't have it. Because neither would consent to take it, the war has been going on ever since.

• ⚔ • ⚔ • ⚔ • ⚔ •

To Bring A Brick Along – To return to camp under the influence of "The Ardent", or to be drunk as a skunk!

Hellfire Stew – A stew comprised of anything the cook could get his hands on!

• ⚔ • ⚔ • ⚔ • ⚔ •

Zebulon Baird Vance was a North Carolinian who served as governor, senator, and was a leading lawyer of his state. He was a fine soldier in the Civil War, much admired for his humor as well as his keen legal mind. The following story is told of his captivity:

Zeb Vance turned the tables on the Yankees when he went to Massachusetts to deliver a lecture. The Bay Staters, knowing his droll manner and practical jokes, baited him by hanging Robert E. Lee's picture in the men's outhouse. When Vance returned from it he disappointed them by remaining silent. Finally, they were compelled to query him.

"Senator, did you see General Lee's picture hanging in the privy?" someone asked.

"Yes," Vance replied indifferently.

"Well, what did you think of it?" they prodded.

"I thought it was very appropriate," he responded. "That is a good place for General Lee's picture. If ever a man lived who could scare the dung out of the Yankees, that man was Robert E. Lee!"

● 𝑖 ● 𝑖 ● 𝑖 ● 𝑖 ●

This same Zeb Vance, when a U.S. senator, was visiting a ship in Chesapeake Bay with other men and women. Zeb stepped aside to allow one of the ladies preference in mounting the ladder. As the lady climbed, Zeb happened to glance up just as she glanced down.

"Senator Vance!" she scolded. "I can see that you are no gentleman!"

"Begging your pardon, Madam," Zeb replied, "but I can see that you too, are not!"

● 𝑖 ● 𝑖 ● 𝑖 ● 𝑖 ●

Barracks 10 – The guardhouse. *Also named the stockade, company Q, the bull pen.*

Barrel Overcoat – Punishment used while in the field for minor offenses. The guilty soldier was forced to don a barrel with a hole cut in the top to fit his head through, and two holes - one on each side - for his arms. Obviously, an uneasy way to sit, sleep or commit acts of nature!

Company Q Or Battery Q – The guardhouse.

War Hotel – The lovely place they send prisoners for delightful safekeeping! It was said, "the gentleman in charge (of the prison) will be pleased to entertain you, free of cost."

Bullring – A military court, especially when the charge may result in execution.

To Guard The Flagpole – This meant that the soldier was confined to barracks or to camp (to guard the flagpole!) for a minor offense.

Bobtail Discharge – Severance from service for inexcusable screw-ups.

● 𝑖 ● 𝑖 ● 𝑖 ● 𝑖 ●

Lice, known as cooties, graybacks, *Pediculous Corporis* or just any profane term that comes to mind, have been an irksome companion to soldiers in every war. Baths, disinfectants, insecticides were few and far between in our Civil War. Thus, the louse had a great feast. And, as always, the Civil War soldier made the misery of his scratching somewhat more bearable by telling stories about the louse . . . or writing songs and poems about the pest.

Here is a poem recited by Chaplain John Hogarth Lozier at
the National Camp Fire of the Grand Army of the Republic back in
1886.

> Ah! Comrades, what wonder you seem appalled?
> What queer sensations creep o'er us.
> At thought of that insect, technically called,
> *"Pediculous Corporis!"*
> Now, if my meaning you fail to see
> In this ancient Roman name,
> Just call it a *Blouse* and skip the ".B,"

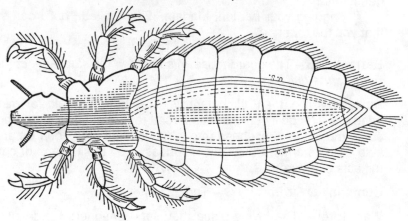

"Pediculous Corporis"

> And you've caught it just the same!
> Yet no soldier here will drop e'en a tear
> For his "gray" old "companions" of yore;
> Tho' admitting the fact that they "stuck to your back"
> Through all the grim fortunes of war!
>
> And none of this "sectional hostility,"
> His generous nature e'er knew;
> The friend of the traitorous rebel was he.
> As of Loyalty's legions in Blue.
> When he and his family came to our camp,
> Full many a big tree and thicket,
> Hid even you chaps who wore feathers and straps.

"In force, under arms."

Thus prejudice patriotism o'erpowers;
  For no one among us denies
There was more "soldiers blood" in their veins than
      in ours,
  In proportion, of course, to their *size!*

And who were more watchful and active than they,
  Amid all war's dreadful alarms?
You never attacked them by night or by day,
  But you found them "in force, under *arms!*"
You never betrayed them by guile or surprise,
  And nothing their ardor could smother;
If you caused them to "git" from a certain "arm'd pit,"
  You soon found them safe in the other!

"Private duty on *pick it.*"

Of course your big officers would not confess
    To these "naked facts" when you'd "tree" 'em,
But would boldly declare they had only been there
    To drill for the army *lice-see-'em!*–(Lyceum).
If "practice makes perfect" we all will admit,
    That going so often to "train" ment,
That, "stripped for the strife," they would *sacrifice life,*
    To make a "crack" entertainment.

And now, unlamented by "Reb" or by "Yank,"
    The grayback in solitude sleepeth;
But the chases we gave him o'er breast work and flank,
    Each veteran's fond memory keepeth;
In "foraging off" of the country he beat
    "Old Billy" the marcher and "bummer";
And none of us doubt that he *did* "fight it out"
    Like Grant, though it *took him all summer!*

It is probably best that I "give you a rest,"
    Though it be not the "rest" of my rhyme.
With so "lively" a theme, it would naturally seem
    That you don't want *too much* at a time.
I'm glad if my rhymes of our soldiering times
    Shall add to your measure of joys;
For my *subject* I know, in those days long ago,
    Has "tickled" the most of you "Boys!"

"Parade's Dismissed."

White Oak Chips – The hardest of native woods is the white oak. Soldiers called their ubiquitous hardtack, their bread, "White oak chips." 'Nuff said?

Gigadier Breneral – A rather disrespectful referenoc to a brigadier general.

Hlsh And Hash – About the same as hellfire stew . . . chow comprised of anything available at the time.

Furniture – Eating equipment for the soldier.

The Ghost Walks – Payday.

Slow Deer – A Confederate farmer's hog, fair game for hungry soldiers.

Black Book – A "notebook" known, today, as *the shit list.*

Salt Horse – Corned beef. Sometimes called *old bull.*

HOW I PASSED THE DOCTOR –
AN INCIDENT DURING THE DRAFT

The other day Chief Engineer Dean, of the Fire Department, called at the office where I make shoes for a living, and handed me a big white envelope, notifying me that I was drafted and must report myself for examination, at Lawrence, on the 18th of August.

Now I consider it the duty of every citizen to give his life, if need be, for the defence of his country, so on the morning of the eventful 18th, I put on a clean shirt and my Sunday clothes, and started for Lawrence, to see if I could get exempted.

Lawrence is situated on the Merrimac river, and its principal productions are mud, dust and factory girls. The city proper, at least that part that I saw, consisted of a long, narrow entry, up one flight of stairs, adorned overhead with a frescoing of gas meters, carpeted with worn out tobacco quids, and furnished with one chair, two settees, and many huge, square packing cases, marked "Q. M. D." Scattered around this palatial entrance-hall were some forty or fifty conscripts, looking very much as if they expected to be exempted by reason of old age, before the young man with a ferocious moustache should notify them of their turn. Most of them, however, were doomed to disappointment, for while they counted the hours of delay, the door would suddenly open, and the tall young man would single out a man and march him through the open doorway, to be seen no more.

By-and-by–that is, after several hours waiting–my turn came.

"John Smith!" shouted the door-keeper.

"That's me," says I, and with a cheer from the crowd, I entered a large square room where two persons sat writing at a table, and a third, evidently a surgeon, was examining a man in the last stages of nudity.

One of the writers at the table, a young man with curly hair and blue eyes, nodded to me, and dipping his pen in the ink, commenced–

"John Smith, what's your name?"

"John Smith," says I.

"Where were you born?"

"Podunk, Maine."

"What did your great-grand-mother die of?"

"Darned if I know," says I.

"Call it hapentap," says he; "and your grand-father too?"

"I don't care what you call it," says I, for I was a little riled by his nonsensical questions.

"Did you ever have boils?" says he

"Not a boil."

"Or fits?"

"Nary fit."

"Or delerium tremens?"

"No sir-ee!"

"Or rickets?"

"I'll ricket you," says I, for I thought he meant something else.

"Did you ever have the measles?" says he.

Here I took off my coat.

"Or the itch?"

"Yes sir, I–that ere fist (and I shoved a very large brown one within three inches of his nose) has been itching, for the last ten minutes, to knock your pesky head off, you little, mean, low-lived, contemptible whelp, you."

"My dear sir," said the mild-spoken gentlemanly surgeon, laying his hand on my arm, "calm yourself, I pray. Don't let your angry passions rise, but take off your clothes, so I can see what you are made of."

So I suppressed my anger, and withdrawing to a corner, I hung my clothes up on the floor, and presented myself for examination, clad only with the covering nature had given me, except about a square inch of court-plaster on my right shin, where I had fallen over a chair, the night before, feeling for a match.

"Young man," said the surgeon, looking me straight in the eye, "you have got the myopia."

"Yes, sir," said I, "and a good one, too–a little Bininger, with a drop of Stoughton, makes an excellent eye-opener, of a morning."

"And there seems to be an amaurotic tendency of the right eye, accompanied with opthalmia."

"Show!" says I.

"And that white spot in the left eye betokens a cataract."

"I guess you mean in the ear," says I, " 'cause I went in swimming this morning, and got an all-fired big bubble in my left ear," and here I jumped up and down two or three times on my left foot, but to no purpose. As soon as I stopped he mounted a chair and commenced feeling the top of my head.

"Was your family ever troubled with epilepsy?" says he.

"Only the two boys," says I; "when they catch them, my wife always goes at them with a fine tooth comb, the first thing."

Jumping off the chair he hit me a lick in the ribs that nearly knocked me over, and before I had time to remonstrate, his arms were round my neck and his head pressed against my bosom the same way that Sophia Ann does, when she wants me to buy her some new bonnets and things.

"Just what I thought," says he; "tuberculosis and hemoptysis, combined with a defect in the scapular membrane and incipient phthysis!"

"Heavens!" says I, "what's that?"

"And cardiac disease."

"No?" said I.

"And Pendardites!"

"Thunder!" said I.

"Stop talking! Now count after me – one!"

"One!" said I, dead with fright.

"Asthma! Two."

"Two," I yelled.

"Exotis of the right febular! Three."

"Three!" I gasped.

"Coxalgia! Four."

"Murder!" said I. "Four."

"Confirmed duodenum of the right ventricle! Five."

"Oh, doctor, ain't you most through? I feel faint!"

"Through? No! Not half through. Why, my friend, Pandora's box was nothing to your chest. You have sphynixiana, and gloriosis, and conchoilogia, and persiflage, and–"

Here my knees trembled so I leaned against the table for support.

"And permanent luxation of the anterior lobe of the right phalanx."

My only answer was a deprecatory gesture.

"And scrofulous diathesis and omnipodites."

I sank to the floor in utter despair.

"Elutriation!" he yelled, for he saw I was going fast–"and maxillarium and–"

From Portrait Monthly of the New York Illustrated News, Vol. 1, No. 5, November, 1863, p. 71, cols. 2-3.

● 𝍈 ● 𝍈 ● 𝍈 ● 𝍈 ●

And last but far from least, Hiz honor, the cause of it all, the **Company Bean Boiler** – The much-maligned company cook.

● 𝍈 ● 𝍈 ● 𝍈 ● 𝍈 ●

One of the most popular speakers at Confederate reunions was Sandy Martin, a great orator and storyteller. When Sandy finished with the main body of his speech, he always ended his talks with the following story.

"Our brave boys whupped old Sherman out of Mississippi, Alabama, and Georgia into South Carolina. By the time they got to South Carolina they was mad and on the run. They was getting close to the center of things. And you know the way it is with a Yankee. Shoot at him and he gets all the madder. Well, he and his boys bummed their way to the Pee Dee River. And this is what happened.

"They crossed the Pee Dee by the light of burnin' ginhouses. *And that ain't all they done.*

"They blowed up the courthouse and burnt down the churches in Wadesboro. *And that ain't all they done.*

"They called Colonel Jim Bennett out on his piazzy and shot him dead. *And that ain't all they done.*

"They drove the mules and the horses and the cows and

calves and hogs to the swamps and shooed the guinea hens and the pea-fowls and the geese over the tall timber. *And that ain't all they done.*

"They throwed dead mules into widow-women's wells and split open feather-beds and scattered them over the houseyard. *And that ain't all they done.*

"They stabled their horses in Miziz Judge Marshall's parlor and fed 'em in Miss Minnie Minervy's peeanner box. *And that ain't all they done.*

"They caught Little Billy Barrett with a busted old rifle gun and hung him to the oak tree by the Four-Mile board. *And that ain't all they done.*

"Ladies and gentlemen, *that ain't all they done.* You know *that ain't all they done.* That wasn't the worst they done.

"Ladies and gentlemen, here I pause to expectorate, spit, and squirt forth ambeer on their tracks and in the direction of where they lie buried in dishonor.]

That wasn't all they done.

They sneaked up to Jim Swink's house, tolled out Ring and Jerry, and shot the two best damned coon dogs in Anson County."

● 𝍖 ● 𝍖 ● 𝍖 ● 𝍖 ●

Wormy Hardtack

While before Petersburg, doing siege work in the summer of 1864, our men had wormy "hardtack," or ship's biscuit, served out to them for a time. It was a severe trial, and it taxed the temper of the men. Breaking open the biscuit, and finding live worms in them, they would throw the pieces in the trenches where they were doing duty day by day, although the orders were to keep the trenches clean, for sanitary reasons.

A brigade officer of the day, seeing some of these scraps along our front, called out sharply to our men: "Throw that hardtack out of the trenches." Then, as the men promptly gathered it up as directed, he added: "Don't you know that you've no business to throw hardtack in the trenches? Haven't you been told that often enough?" Out from the injured soldier heart there came the reasonable explanation: "We've thrown it out two or three times, sir, but it crawls back."

– H. Clay Trumbull

Ha, ha! don't you think you're brave?
No officer e're looked *bolder*,
    But, all who march with you,
Think the asses head should be upon your shoulder.

HUMOR OF

WORLD WAR I

There are two schools of thought as to which contributes more to victory . . . weapons or morale. One forceful school holds: "Grab 'em by the balls and their hearts and minds will follow!" In other words the fight, the battle, the weapons are decisive.

The other school of thought holds that the state of mind of the rulers, the political heads as well as the officers and men – that this comes first and is decisive. This view insists that "victory and defeat turn on mental impressions and only indirectly on physical blows."[1].

What the Encyclopedia Britannica terms "mental impressions" we term "morale". And morale is boosted and held high by the degree of humor the fighting man uses to lessen the anguish of war and win it.

As in all our wars, the humor that the doughboy found during World War I, made the wounds, deaths and fears bearable. Doughboy jokes, cartoons, funny stories, letters, wacky characters all gave him support and helped keep high the morale of officers and men in the face of terrible new weapons: submarines, dreadnoughts, machine guns, poison gas and the airplane.

The following pages contain only a bit, a smidgin of the superb humor that distinguished our fighting man, the Doughboy, in World War I. But these examples of his humor illustrate a decisive quality in the American soldier that contributed greatly to his victory over the enemy. Laughter may have been America's secret, winning weapon.

1. Encyclopedia Britannica. Vol. 23. P. 775. 1964.

In not only the Civil War but World War I, body lice, the ubiquitous "cootie," was an endless problem. Then, of course, they did not have the effective chemical destroyers of insects. Curiously, the problem was not confined to overseas duty. From 12 to 20 per cent of troops arriving in France were already afflicted with the "crawling catastrophe."

Not only in World War I and the Civil War but in all our wars the soldier eased his problem by joking about it. Some examples of the use of his literary "art" in the cause of humor, a practice that made life a tad more bearable, will be found throughout this section. In prose and poetry, these are examples of his self-developed and administered "medicine." As one GI put it, "Now I know why Napoleon kept his hand shoved between his coat lapels!" and elsewhere, one might add, because one definition of the louse was . . . "mechanized dandruff"!

THE COOTIES

The cooties are a busy crew,
They have to keep me busy, too.
They ramble up and down my back,
And use my neck for a racetrack.

They bite me on the arms and chest,
And in my shirt they make a nest.
They dig their trenches strong and stout,
And it takes many baths to drive them out.

I hunt all through my underwear,
And from my mouth there comes a prayer!
Oh, how I wish they would only cease,
And once more let me sleep in peace.

Fighting Germans is what I crave,
But fighting cooties makes me rave,
I'll save them till I find a Boche,
And plant them in his shirt b'gosh!

Stars & Stripes – Sergeant John J. Curtin, Infantry

● ✵ ● ✵ ● ✵ ● ✵ ●

Cootie, Cootie – The body louse. Probably borrowed from the British since it comes from the Malay *Kuti.* As they said, "cooties ain't cuties."

HOW TO
KEEP YOUR
NEW YEARS RESOLUTIONS

MAKE OUT A GOODLY NUMBER OF RESOLUTIONS
YOU ABSOLUTELY INTEND TO KEEP AND HAVE
THEM FRAMED. BEND THE FRAME NEATLY IN FIVE
SEPARATE PARTS. EVEN BREAKING THE GLASS IF
NECESSARY, AND HIDE IN THE BOTTOM OF YOUR
BARRACKS BAG OR ONE OF THE TOP SERGEANTS
TRUNKS. BY DOING THIS YOU CAN EASILY KEEP
YOUR RESOLUTIONS FOR ANY INDEFINITE PERIOD
WITHOUT DISCOMFORT TO YOURSELF.

WHEN EVENING COOTIES CRAWL

This parody on "When Evening Shadows Fall" was written by William S. Blass and widely sung in the engineer train to which he belonged.

When evening shadows fall,
The cooties bother most of all.
Some day I hope to smile,
For I'll miss you all the while;
Some day you'll die, you pest,
Then I in peace can rest;
Seems to me I feel you crawling
When evening shadows fall.

THE ARMY BUGS
Tune: "Sweet Bye and Bye"

Soldiers sing of their beans and canteens,
   Of the coffee in old army cup,
Why not mention the small friends we've seen
   Always trying to chew armies up?

Chorus
Those firm friends, tireless friends,
   Hardly ever neglecting their hugs,
Their regard never ends –
   How they loved us, those old army bugs.

Galloping Dandruff – Crab lice.

Military Police – A poem illustrates the regard in which this unit was held:

   Oh, the MPs, the MPs,
   With sidearms up and down.
   The MPs, the MPs
   Who take your pass to town.
   The MPs, the MPs
   They work and never play.
   And I wouldn't be a damn MP
   For a million bucks a day.

From the above poem, it is easy to see what the initials might stand for in GI slanguage . . . *Miserable Pricks!*

● 🪖 ● 🪖 ● 🪖 ● 🪖 ●

Gas Barrage – Foolish bragging and talk. Hot air!

   In winter I get up at night
   And have to scratch by candlelight;
   In summer quite the other way,
   I have to scratch the livelong day.

   A soldier boy should never swear,
   When coots are in his underwear,
   Or underneath his helmet label –
   At least, so far as he is able.

   The trench is so full of a number of coots,
   I'm actually growing quite fond of the brutes.

● 🪖 ● 🪖 ● 🪖 ● 🪖 ●

Carrier pigeons are arousing the interest of the Yanks. A private suggests that the pigeon be crossed with parrots in order that the birds may deliver their message orally instead of by "flimsy" (light paper).

                              Stars and Stripes – May 24, 1918

Der kaiser had a caisson and
Its guns were mounted well,
It went to scare der Yanks one day,
And got shot all to hell.

● 🪖 ● 🪖 ● 🪖 ● 🪖 ●

The Order of the Shovel – Death and burial.

The difference between American and French auto driving is this: In America, when your tire blows up, you say, "Good heavens, there goes our tire!" and in France you say, "Hooray! That was only the tire!"

● 🪖 ● 🪖 ● 🪖 ● 🪖 ●

VIVACIOUS VERSES
No. 1

Dear Madge:

While at home was no zest
In my heart for the dainty called spinach,
But now I have learned to digest
It innich by innich by innich.

But since I have eaten in France –
One must eat you know, in a pinich –
I find there's a touch of romance,
As well as of garlic and spinach.

And, oh, they are on to their biz,
And that, little girl, is a cinch
Though I don't know just what it is
That they do to a fistful of spinach.

So, dear, while I'm wintering here
And you're playing tennis in Greenwich –
I'll try, when it's over, to steer
You a cook who can Frenchify spinach.
If I cannot find one, I fear
That never again can we clinich,
Because, though I'll do without beer,
I can't live a week without spinach.

● 🪖 ● 🪖 ● 🪖 ● 🪖 ●

THEY SOMETIMES R.
"And now, brother," asked the visiting parson to the Y.M.C.A.

official a former preacher; "tell me; are these lads aware of the presence of God?"

"Well, I don't know, brother; but they do seem – particularly the muleskinners – to talk out loud to God a good deal!"

Stars and Stripes. May 17, 1918

● 🪖 ● 🪖 ● 🪖 ● 🪖 ●

A soldier, returned to the U.S., had one need in mind. He rushed to the drugstore and asked the clerk for a glass of plain soda, without flavor. [In those days drugstore and soda fountain were almost synonymous].

"Yes," replied the clerk. "But without which flavor do you want it?"

"I'll take it without strawberry, please."

The clerk looked among his syrup bottles. "Sorry," he said, "We ain't got it. But, I can give it to you without vanilla."

Stars and Stripes – May 30, 1919

● 🪖 ● 🪖 ● 🪖 ● 🪖 ●

Zezette: "The *armee* Americaine must have *beaucoup* mechanics in it."

Paulette: "Pourquoi, ma petite?"

Zezette: "Because the General Pershing sent so many to the *Toul* section."

● 🪖 ● 🪖 ● 🪖 ● 🪖 ●

PFC – The term means Private First Class but, since it is the lowest grade of promotion, it is known also as Pretty Fucking Cheap!

● 🪖 ● 🪖 ● 🪖 ● 🪖 ●

An instructor in American history often invited people who had been a significant part of that history to lecture to her class. So, when she reached the period of World War I, she asked a Swedish friend to discuss his experience flying for the British in that war.

"Vell," he addressed the class, "der vas da time I vas flying our Schpads offer Chermany ven, all to a sodden, zeez two Fuckers come at me. All to voncet, I qvick do a loop but dem tam Fuckers nevair leaf my tail. So I did anodder loop und shtill dem tamn Fuckers dey shtay on my tail . . . ."

"Excuse me, Sir," the teacher interrupted him, "but the class needs to know that the speaker is referring to a class of airplane the Germans called Fokkers – F-o-k-k-e-r-s."

"Ya, dat's so," said the speaker. "But in dis case dem two Fuckers vas flying Messerschmidts."

Short Arm – The penis. Short arm inspection means that male soldiers will be examined to determine the extent of venereal disease.

Short Arm Practice – Sexual intercourse.

THE COY AND PLAYFUL COOTIE

With a manner quite invidious
And an attitude insidious
He will plant himself upon a mortal's frame,
And with gimlet, pike and auger,
And the cant-hook of a logger,
He will do his best to viscerate and malm.
Since the days of ancient Rome,
The human body's been his home,
A sort of perennial sacred niche;
And he chuckles with great pleasure
As you dance the cootie measure
To the gleeful time of his eternal itch.

He dotes on Yank and French,
And the English in the trench,
He cares not for a permanent location;
But when he finds a human,
All his friends and he start roomin',
And establish a splendid habitation.
And when it seems that coals of fire
And that flaming darts aspire
To seek an inlet to your very heart,
Stop your scratchin' just to reason
That this is the cootie season,
And your body's now a busy cootie mart.

Stars and Stripes – May 31, 1918

They send us pocket Bibles
    To make us lads behave,
They send us bright trench mirrors,
    To help us when we shave;
Powders for our face and feet,
    Cold creams and camphor ice,
But never any poison for
    The hungry army lice.

They send us Wrigley's doublemint,
  It's really very nice,
They send us little sewing kits,
  With which we sew and splice;
Wristwatches and bright wristlets,
  And ukes on which to strum,
But never any poison
  For the hungry army crumb.

Oh yes, dear friends, we've got them,
  And we've got them mighty bad,
The pesky things keep biting,
  Till they almost drive us mad;
They're after us continually,
  Morning, noon and night,
And every time they grab a chunk,
  We know old "Sherm" was right.

Corporal "Jerry" Jerome
Stars and Stripes, Headquarters Co. – 26 April 1918

● 👤 ● 👤 ● 👤 ● 👤 ●

The Big Five – A sharp and snappy salute.

Black Death – GI coffee!

Blanket Drill – Bunk duty or sleep. Also called "Bunk fatigue."

Cow – Could be either the disliked Commanding Officer's wife . . . or a milk pitcher!

Sea Gull – A prostitute who served marines and sailors, moving with them from port to port.

Foxhole – A pit large enough to hold two men. Sometimes it was named, *hasty pit.* The name was flexible as, for example, the time a nurse ducked into a foxhole for safety and emerged to call it a "wolfhole."

● 👤 ● 👤 ● 👤 ● 👤 ●

One of the horrors of war – When your platoon is taken out for a nice little breather, at double time, by a lieutenant who used to run on a cross-country team.

● 👤 ● 👤 ● 👤 ● 👤 ●

The Armed Forces sing and prate and boast about infantry-men, flyers, engineers and field artillerymen but who extols the cooks? Never! So . . . here's a paean of praise for them:

We never were made to be seen on parade
  When sweethearts and such line the streets.
When the band starts to blare, look
    for us – we ain't there,
  we're mussing around with the eats.
It's fun to step out to the echoing shout,
  Of a crowd that forgets how you're fed.
While we're soiling our duds hacking
    eyes out of spuds –
You know what Napoleon said.

When the mess sergeant's gay, you can
    bet hell's to pay
  for the boys who are standing in line;
When the boys get a square, then the
    sergeant is there
  with your death warrant ready to sign.
If you're long on the grub, then you're damned for a
dub.
  If you're short you're a miser instead,
But however you feel, you must get the next meal,
  You know what Napoleon said.

You think it's a cinch when it comes to the clinch,
  For the man who is grinding the meat;
In the heat of the flight, why, the cook's out of sight
  With plenty of room to retreat.
But the plump of a shell in the kitchen is hell,
  When the roof scatters over your head.
And you crawl on your knees to pick
    up the K.P.'s –
You know what Napoleon said.

If the war ever ends, we'll go back to our friends –
  In the Army we've nary a one –
We'll list to the prattle of this or that battle,
  And then when the story is done,
We'll say when they ask, "Now what
    was your task,
  And what is the glory you shed?"
"You see how they thrive – well, we
    kept 'em alive?"
You know what Napoleon said.

And what does all the poetry, the paean of praise get them? This!

Belly-Robber – Mess sergeant (naturally!).

Egg – A brand new soldier who arrived in France for duty with the Army Expeditionary Force.

Fag – A cigarette.

A famous American general tells the story of a Junior Officer to whom was assigned a brand new recruit for duty as his orderly.

"Soldier, your duty will be to clean my clothes, my shoes, buttons, belt, and the like. You'll shave me, see to my horse which you have got to groom thoroughly, and clean the equestrian equipment. After that, you repair to your tent and move on to help serve breakfast. After breakfast, you will lend a hand cleaning up. You will go on parade from eight o'clock until noon . . . . "

"Excuse me, sir," replied the new man, scratching his head in a puzzled manner, "But ain't there nobody else in this man's army 'cept me?"

Twenty pledges would I sign
And forego all shades of wine.
Just to get a chance to draw,
Choc'late sody through a straw.

"Why didn't you enlist, George?"
"I had trouble with my feet."
"Flat or cold?"

SIX REASONS WHY HENRY IS AT THE FRONT
Carrie
Louise
Dorothy
Mildred
Josephine
Mary

First camp cook: "The captain was in here today and raised hell with me. Says he, 'Cook, this soup tastes like dishwater.' "

Second cook: "An' what did you say?"

First camp cook: "What could I say? It *was* dishwater."

Officer: "Pat, the government will pay you five dollars for every German you kill."

Pat (looking "over the top" and seeing about 50,000 Germans coming toward him): "Sure and begorry, thin our fortunes are made."

• 🙂 • 🙂 • 🙂 • 🙂 •

A gang of Southern rookies passed a gang of black convicts who were working on the county road just outside Camp Johnson. One of the rookies called out:

"Sam, how'd you like to swap jobs?"

Without hesitation Sam replied, "No, sah, you all don't swap no jobs with me. Ah knows how long ah's in fo'."

• 🙂 • 🙂 • 🙂 • 🙂 •

Officer: "And why did you assault the sentry in this brutal way?"

Mike: "Well, der guy sez he challenges me, so I bust him one on the jaw."

• 🙂 • 🙂 • 🙂 • 🙂

CAMOUFLAGE

Hidden in the picture above is the 31st division marching to the trenches in France. To the right is a dinner table under the trees, set with wines and all the delicacies of the season, around which privates are taking their seats at mess. But so well has the artist camouflaged these important military maneuvers – to prevent the enemy from discovering the position of our forces – that the whole presents the appearance of nothing out of the ordinary.

ONE WAY OUT

"You claim no exemption,"
"How'd you guess it?"
"I've seen your wife."

Come-Along – An apt name for the device to move reluctant prisoners. It was composed of barbed wire and formed a collar and leash that was most effective!

Burt (as Bill comes down the muddy trench): "Bill, take your dirty feet out of the only clean water we've got to sleep in."

Peter Cheater – A sanitary napkin.

Army officer giving commands: "Shoulder Arms. You too."
"Forward March. You too."
"To the Rear March. You too."
Other Officer: "Fine, but I don't get the idea of that 'you too.' "
"Well, I'll tell you. I know this gang. They're a hard lot. Every time I ask them to do something, I know that, under their breath, they're going to tell me to go to h--l and I want to invite them to go first."

Crowbar Hotel – The guardhouse.

A very baffled looking private of the A.E.F. approached his sergeant one morning while his company was in rest quarters at a tiny French hamlet several hundred miles behind the front lines.

"Sarge," said the private, "I am in a jam with a French lady down the road. I just bought some eggs from her and I think I got gypped when she made change for me. I have been trying to explain what I meant, but she keeps jabbering at me in French, and I don't know what the hell she is talking about. Do you know how to speak French?"

"Yep," said the sergeant.

"Well, then," said the private, "if it ain't too much trouble, come and help straighten this out for me."

The sergeant lumbered to his feet and walked with him to the woman's farm.

"Madame," he began impressively, "parlez vous Francais?"

"Oui, oui," said the French woman.

"Okay," said the sergeant. "Then, fer chrissake, give my buddy his right change!"

● ☗ ● ☗ ● ☗ ● ☗ ●

Rookie (studying famous 1917 war poster of Uncle Sam pointing his finger with the caption, "Where do you fit?"): "Cain't rightly say," the rookie replies, "but mah paw fit in the Civil War."

● ☗ ● ☗ ● ☗ ● ☗ ●

Sam Jones was enjoying a brief furlough in Paris where he announced that he was a "pilot" in the cavalry. When asked "How can that be?", he explained, "I pile it here and I pile it there."

● ☗ ● ☗ ● ☗ ● ☗ ●

Queen Mary, while visiting wounded men in an English hospital, saw an American boy.

"And where did you get your wound," she asked him kindly.

"Wipers," he said.

"Eep!" she corrected.

"Wipers."

"You're wrong, dear boy. Eep!"

"Wipers."

"No! No! No! Eep!"

Then the Yank said, "Your Highness, you really ought to take something for those hiccoughs."

● ☗ ● ☗ ● ☗ ● ☗ ●

"I want you to know I'm a West Pointer!" the second lieutenant shouted.

The doughboy raised his eyebrows and remarked, "Sir, you look more like an Irish Setter to me."

● ☗ ● ☗ ● ☗ ● ☗ ●

During World War I, the Army had a great deal of trouble convincing soldiers that the $10,000 life insurance policy offered them was not only a great bargain but a necessary investment to protect their families. The officer in charge of one unit called his top sergeant to his office and asked him to speak to the men and convince them to accept the insurance. The sergeant agreed to try. His talk to the outfit went about like this:

"Now all you men know me. We've eaten together, fought the enemy together, even got drunk together. So trust me. Now this here U.S. government of ours has to pay ten thousand bucks every time one of you gets killed in battle . . . if you have this insurance. But it don't cost the U.S. government a penny if you don't have insurance and you get killed. Now I want you to stop and consider a moment . . . which soldier is going to be sent to the front to get killed? The one Uncle Sam has to pay ten thousand bucks to his family, if he gets knocked off, or the one that don't cost Uncle Sam a nickel . . . if he gets killed? You got it! So step right up here and sign up for the deal to make sure you finish this war alive!"

● 🎖 ● 🎖 ● 🎖 ● 🎖 ●

Blooey – All screwed up! Inadequate officers were sent to Blois, (Blooey!), France, to get them out of the way! Hence, the term, meaning all messed up, which many will recall from earlier days.

SOL – Shit out of luck! Without hope.

AEF –The true meaning was American Expeditionary Force, but the GI had other definitions like After England Failed, or, American Expeditionary Farce, or, Ass-End First.

● 🎖 ● 🎖 ● 🎖 ● 🎖 ●

HAD NO OUIJA BOARD

In Russia, after the war, an American officer kept a bunch of cockneys busy at cutting down trees, a new experience for them.

They were beavering away, gnawing at the tree with their inexpertly used axes, when the officer asked, "Corporal, in which direction are you going to fell that tree?"

" 'Ow the 'ell do I know?" asked the corporal. "Do I look like a bloody prophet?"

● 🎖 ● 🎖 ● 🎖 ● 🎖 ●

ROOKIE: "I sure do need a pair of shoes, Sergeant."

SERGEANT: "Are your shoes worn out?"

ROOKIE: "Worn out! Man, the bottom of them shoes is so thin, I can step on a dime and tell whether it's heads or tails."

● 🎖 ● 🎖 ● 🎖 ● 🎖 ●

In a regimental team-shooting contest, one squad's record was hurt by the last marksman, who had performed badly.

"Great heavens!" wailed the sergeant. "Two outers and a magpie after nine shots. How many cartridges have you got left?"

"One, Sergeant," replied the poor shooter.

"Well, go behind the bush and shoot yourself," snarled the sergeant.

The man retired, and a moment later a shot rang out from behind the bush. The horrified sergeant rushed to the spot.

"Good lord!" he screamed. "What did you do to yourself?"

"It's all right," grinned the soldier as he rose from the shrub. "I missed again."

• 🪖 • 🪖 • 🪖 • 🪖 •

PIANISSIMO

The sergeant sang out at a company parade: "All those who enjoy music, step two paces forward!"

With visions of soft jobs in the regimental band, half a dozen men stepped forward.

"Now, then," yelled the sergeant, "you six guys get cracking and carry that grand piano from the basement up to the officers' quarters on the tenth floor!"

• 🪖 • 🪖 • 🪖 • 🪖 •

Goldfish – Typical GI slang for canned salmon. A song illustrates GI distaste for it:

> I've et so much goldfish,
> I've growed me a tail.
> And if I eat more,
> I'll grow fins like a whale!

Son-Of-A-Bitch Stew – Water, hardtack and bacon cooked together.

Coushay Avec – When you wanted to sleep with a French girl, such was the invitation you might have used. And if you truly wanted her, were consumed with urgent horizontal wishes, you used the entire phrase: *Voulez-vous coucher avec moi?*

• 🪖 • 🪖 • 🪖 • 🪖 •

A trainload of newly drafted men reached their cantonment in the afternoon. By the time they had passed through the recruiting station and the hands of the doctors, it was midnight. Twenty of them were awakened at four o'clock the following morning to help the cooks prepare breakfast.

As one sleepy man got to his feet, he said, "Golly, it don't take long to spend a night in this army."

• 🪖 • 🪖 • 🪖 • 🪖 •

The rookie watched the forty-mile-an-hour wind blowing sand into the "chow" on the camp cook's stove.

"Why don't you put the lid on that pot?" he asked.

"Shut up" answered Cookie. "You're not here to make suggestions but to serve your country."

"Sure, I'm willing to serve it, but not to eat it."

Dead Soldier – An empty booze bottle.

● 𝑖 ● 𝑖 ● 𝑖 ● 𝑖 ●

Sentry: "Halt! Who goes there?"
Rookie: "Friend."
Sentry: "Advance, friend, and be recognized."
Rookie: "Heck fire, you don't know me. I only got here yester-
day!"

● 𝑖 ● 𝑖 ● 𝑖 ● 𝑖 ●

A group of enlisted soldiers were waiting to be "shot" when
one of them remarked, "In a way, this compulsory vaccination
makes us genuine draftees."
"How so?"
"We are forced to bare arms!"

● 𝑖 ● 𝑖 ● 𝑖 ● 𝑖 ●

Dandy Jack – An officer overly zealous about his appearance
who needed to look spiffy, or properly "dooded-up".

● 𝑖 ● 𝑖 ● 𝑖 ● 𝑖 ●

Mike and Pat belonged to the same regiment and were
inseparable friends until Mike got a commission. Mike was quite
puffed up over the promotion and totally ignored his old pal. Pat's
Irish finally got the best of him and, approaching the new lieutenant with his most military salute, he said, "Lootinant, phwat
would happen if a private should call the lieutenant a bastard to
the lieutenant's face?"
Mike answered that the offender would be arrested and
thrown into the guardhouse.
"And what would happen if that same private only *thought*
that about the lieutenant?"
Mike didn't see that anything could be done in that case.
"Well," said Pat, "Oi'll jist let it drop at that."

● 𝑖 ● 𝑖 ● 𝑖 ● 𝑖 ●

A pretty girl was visiting among the wounded in the hospital.
"My dear boy, how many Germans did you kill before they
wounded you?"
"Exactly twenty, ma'am."
"And what did you kill them with, bullets or bayonet?"
"Neither, ma'am. I used my bare fist."
Impulsively the girl grabbed his hand and kissed it twenty times.
After she had gone a bunkie said, "You dern fool, why didn't
you tell her you bit them to death?"

Old Soldier's Home – The latrine.

GI Songs, Some Variations on the "Darktown Strutter's Ball"

VERSION USED BY BATTERY C, 21ST F.A., FIFTH DIVISION

Chorus

I'll be down to get you in an ambulance, Captain,
I'll be there with a helping hand,
When the boys cross No Man's Land.
Sure I'll be there but I won't be fighting,
When the Germans throw the gas and shell;
We won't retreat, but we'll advance like hell,
Now I think I'm smelling gas,
As the shells are falling fast,
'Way down there where they play that shell-hole rag.

AIR SERVICE VERSION (KELLY FIELD)

Chorus

I'll be down to meet you with my pick and shovel,
We'll wander down to the old gravel pit,
And it will take some grit to be there
When the sergeant starts in callin'.
And then we'll get our mess kits, Sonny,
And fall in right at the head of the line;
When we've mixed them beans and stews,
Why, we'll sing the Quarantine Blues,
Tomorrow night at the mess-hall Cabaret.

VERSION OF UNKNOWN ORIGIN

Chorus

When the war is over and I get back home,
You can bet your life I'll never roam.
I'll have a captain driving my limousine,
Lieutenant colonel buying my gasoline.
I'll have a major in the garden with a rake and hoe,
My old top-sergeant a-pressing my clothes,
An M.P. at my door,
First and second looey scrubbing my floor,
When the war is over and I get back home again.

• 🪖 • 🪖 • 🪖 • 🪖 •

OH, HOW I HATE TO GO INTO THE MESS HALL

Parody on "Oh! How I hate to get up in the Morning"

Oh, how I hate to go into the mess hall!
Oh, how I long for the foods at home!
For it isn't hard to guess

Why they call the meals a mess –
You've got to eat beans, you've got to eat beans,
You've got to eat beans in the Army.
Some day I'll murder the cook in the kitchen;
Some day I'll throw him into the lake,.
And when the bloomin' war is through
I'll say: "To h--- with beans and stew!"
And spend the rest of my pay on steak.

● 👤 ● 👤 ● 👤 ● 👤 ●

The Kaiser and his chief minister were at dinner.

"Your Majesty, who started this war?"

"Why, we've proved it was England, France and Belgium, to say nothing of Russia.

"Yes, I know," said the chief minister, "but whom do you account truly responsible?"

"Well," said the Kaiser, "America is the culprit." You remember when Roosevelt came back from Africa, I showed him all around one day. We reviewed the army together. When we got back to the palace, Teddy clapped me on the back and said, 'Kaiser Bill, you can lick the world!' Like a fool, I believed him."

● 👤 ● 👤 ● 👤 ● 👤 ●

Flute – A sodomite, a homosexual male.

● 👤 ● 👤 ● 👤 ● 👤 ●

At a roll call in a Russian-American regiment, the officer sneezed and four soldier answered "Here."

● 👤 ● 👤 ● 👤 ● 👤 ●

Kaiser: "I will now review der Fifth Army Corps."

Major; "Your Highness, since the gallant victory of the Fifth, yesterday, over the hated American Marines, der Fifth Army Corps aindt!"

● 👤 ● 👤 ● 👤 ● 👤 ●

"How's your son getting along in the Army?"

"Fine. He got a medal for something or other but he writes such a lousy hand that I can't tell whether it was for bugling, burgling or just plain bungling."

● 👤 ● 👤 ● 👤 ● 👤 ●

Pimple On A Buck Private's Ass – A phrase used to evaluate a fellow officer, such as "He couldn't make pimple on a buck private's ass!"

● 👤 ● 👤 ● 👤 ● 👤 ●

"Do you think we'll ever make it back?" asked the recruit during fierce combat.

"I dunno about you," said his buddy, now badly scared, "but if that first shot don't hit me, all the rest are gonna fall short."

• ⚔ • ⚔ • ⚔ • ⚔ •

"How come the draft board rejected you?"

"Bad teeth."

"I thought they needed you to fight the Germans, not to bite them to death."

• ⚔ • ⚔ • ⚔ • ⚔ •

The sergeant had worked hard to teach a rookie the Manual of Arms. Finally he said, "Private, you should be in the Air Corps."

"Why do you say that?"

"Because you ain't no good down here on earth.'

• ⚔ • ⚔ • ⚔ • ⚔ •

A guest ordered his dinner at a fashionable hotel. "Noodle soup, veal cutlet with tomato sauce and a cream puff.,"

The waiter, who had been a soldier, shouted toward the kitchen, "Bowl of submarines, camouflage the calf, and a custard grenade."

• ⚔ • ⚔ • ⚔ • ⚔ •

Duck – A corruption of *deduct* used to describe what the army took from a doughboy's paycheck. The story is told about a black GI who, when asked if he had any money, replied that he hadn't any because the ducks got it all. "De big man up there he 'ducks fo' dis and he 'ducks fo' dat till they ain't nothin left . . . . De ducks got it all."

• ⚔ • ⚔ • ⚔ • ⚔ •

Captain: "How did you get to be so able in the use of the bayonet?"

Private: "Reaching for vittles at my boarding house."

• ⚔ • ⚔ • ⚔ • ⚔ •

Pat and Mike who were on a 48-hour pass, went to bed very drunk the first night. They repeated that routine the next night. The next morning, they dressed hurriedly to catch the train back to camp.

Mike went down the dark passageway of the hotel, feeling with his foot for the top step of the stairway. The elevator door was open and he stepped down and fell ten stories.

Soon Pat came along and reached the open elevator door. He yelled down to Mike: "Hey, Mike! Is this the stairway?"

"That it is," Mike yelled back, "but be damned careful of that first step, it's a steep son-of-a-bitch!"

Hotel D'barbweyer – The stockade!

• 🪖 • 🪖 • 🪖 • 🪖 •

The storm had swept some of the deck fittings overboard and things looked so dubious the commander decided to send up a distress signal. Just as the first rocket shot up into the inky blackness of night, the new sailor spoke up, "Captain, I don't want to cast a damper on any man's high spirits, but this seems like a helluva time to be setting off fireworks."

• 🪖 • 🪖 • 🪖 • 🪖 •

First Boot: "I heard that the drill sergeant called you a block-head."

Second boot: "No. He didn't make it that strong."

First Boot: "What did he actually say?"

Second boot: "Put on yur hat, here comes a woodpecker."

• 🪖 • 🪖 • 🪖 • 🪖 •

Sergeant O'Toole had a squad of recruits on the rifle range.

He tried them on the 500-yard range, but none of them could hit the target. Then he tried them on the 300-yard, the 200-yard and the 100-yard ranges, in turn, but with no better success. When they had all missed the shortest range he looked around in despair. Then he straightened up.

"Squad, attention!" he commanded. "Fix bayonets! Char-r-ge!"

• 🪖 • 🪖 • 🪖 • 🪖 •

Following inspection, the commanding officer of a black regiment was making a speech to his men in which he warned them that, while courtesy is necessary at times, one should always use tact in one's relations with other people.

Afterward, two of the soldiers were discussing the difference between courtesy and tact.

"Well," said one, "Ah can't 'splain the difference but Ah knows. 'Fo de wah Ah was a plumber and one day a lady calls me on de phone and sez, "Hurry right down heah, the baft-tub done sprung a leak,' and down Ah rushes. Ah bust right in de front do' and up the back stairs into the baft-room. and, boy, there was a lady in the tub. And Ah jest speaks right up, 'Good mawnin'. Sir!' Now that there 'Good mawnin' was courtesy, but the 'sir' was tact."

• 🪖 • 🪖 • 🪖 • 🪖 •

Iodine Spillers – Personnel of the Medical Corp. Also, pill rollers.

KYPIYP – Keep Your Pecker In Your Pants. Advice given young soldiers who, in a flurry of need, might be tempted to place it elsewhere with attendant danger of disease . . .

● ⚐ ● ⚐ ● ⚐ ● ⚐ ●

A New York policeman met a brother "copper" whose features looked as if they had suffered from a rather violent rearrangement. "Hello, guy! Whatever happened to you? Been in a fight with a drunk and disorderly?"

"No."

"Well, what the hell happened to you?"

"So, I'll tell you. You know the lady with the fair hair who lives in the last house on my beat?"

"Yes, I know," said the first man, "the one whose husband is at sea in the Navy."

"Well," replied the other, "he ain't."

● ⚐ ● ⚐ ● ⚐ ● ⚐ ●

The soldier was a small, stoop-shouldered and utterly weary private in a black company working on the docks at Brest. He was homesick and mighty miserable, so he went to his sergeant, right after the armistice was signed, and said, "Sarge, I'se mighty tired and jest pinin' away to git back to Alabama. I done toted dem boxes from de ships to de railroad cars 'til my shoulders is done wore out to de bone. I enlisted fo' de duration of diseyer waw and now dat waw am ovuh. So I wants to git out an' go home. Kin ya fix dat fo' me?"

The black sergeant looked the private soldier over from head to toe, in absolute contempt. Then he replied, "Man, yo' don't know nothin'! Yo' is plain iggerant, dumber'n a mule! Don't ya know dat even if'n diseyer waw am ovuh, de duration am jes started! So git y'sef back t'work!"

● ⚐ ● ⚐ ● ⚐ ● ⚐ ●

A draft of Missouri mules had just arrived at the corral, and a black buck private made the common but sad mistake of approaching too near to the business end of one of them. His comrades caught him on the rebound, placed him on a stretcher and started him for the hospital.

On the way the invalid regained consciousness, gazed at the blue sky overhead, experienced the swaying motion as he was being carried along, and shakily lowered his hands over the sides, only to feel space. "Mah gawsh!" he groaned, "Ah ain't even hit de ground yit!"

● ⚐ ● ⚐ ● ⚐ ● ⚐ ●

I Hope To Shit In Your Mess Kit – A form of assurance, a promise, as, "I hope to shit in your mess kit, if it ain't true!"

SOS – Same old shit. "I asked for a weekend pass but they refused, giving me the SOS."

● 🪖 ● 🪖 ● 🪖 ● 🪖 ●

There was a captain in our Army who had made himself thoroughly disliked by his company. One night, on his way back to camp, he fell into a pond. One of his own men saw him fall in but hesitated before going to the officer's rescue. However, his humane feelings got the better of his natural dislike of the captain. He fished the officer out of the pond.

When the captain had recovered his breath a bit, he said, "Jones, you have saved my life. How can I reward you?"

"Oh, that's all right, Captain," said Private Jones.

"But I'd like to do something to show my gratitude."

"Well, if you really want to do something for me, do me a favor and say nothing about it to the company. If the other men heard about it, they'd bust my ass!"

● 🪖 ● 🪖 ● 🪖 ● 🪖 ●

In the Great War, a company of soldiers found themselves under heavy fire and dove into a shell hole.

The captain commanding said, "Boys, I'm afraid we're in a heluva spot. Fight like the devil until you're out of ammunition, and then run. I'm a little lame, so I'll start now."

● 🪖 ● 🪖 ● 🪖 ● 🪖 ●

Grubcrabber – A GI who constantly gripes about the mess, his chow.

Guardhouse Lawyer – A soldier who is always ready with advice on army regulations and how to get around them! As a result, followers end up in the guardhouse and, quite often, so does the *guardhouse lawyer*! But that doesn't stop him, for even there he offers his (in)expert advice.

● 🪖 ● 🪖 ● 🪖 ● 🪖 ●

A black son of Alabama was busily engaged in getting rid of cooties. When asked by a sergeant what he was doing, he replied, "I'se a-huntin' fo' dem 'rithmetic bugs."

"Why do you call them arithmetic bugs?'

" 'Cause dey add to ma misery, dey subtracts from ma pleasure, dey divides ma attention, and dey multiply like de dickens."

Hardtack – Those hard crackers made of unleavened, unsalted flour extensively baked for long life. Also called wormcastles, teeth dullers and sheet-iron crackers!

In the war a corporal drilled an awkward squad. When he ordered "About face!" he watched the men's foot to see that the order was obeyed smartly. He lost his temper when one pair of shoes failed to turn.

"Hey, you!" he yelled at the owner of the shoes. "Why didn't you about face?"

"I did," answered the soldier.

"But you didn't turn your feet."

"I did turn 'em," said the unhappy soldier. "But the pair of shoes they issued me are so damn big that I turned inside 'em."

● 🪖 ● 🪖 ● 🪖 ● 🪖 ●

MY, HOW SHE HAS CHANGED!

The late General Nelson A. Miles, who fought in the Civil and Spanish wars, was a soldier of the old school, and he believed that a proper uniform had a good deal to do with the fighting qualities of a soldier.

When very old, he addressed a bunch of recruits, all togged out in nice, brand new W.W.I uniforms. "That is the way I like to see soldiers neatly dressed and smart looking. I expect you to do credit to your uniforms and your flag. I expect each of you to act like a general officer."

"But then who'll do the fighting, General?" asked one of the men.

THERE ARE SHIPS
Parody on "Smiles"

There are ships that carry rations,
There are ships that carry mail.
There are ships that carry ammunition —
There are ships that merely carry sail.
There are ships that carry President Wilson —
There are mighty giants of the foam;
But I'd trade them all for just a rowboat,
If that rowboat would carry me home.

A drill instructor was dressing down a new recruit. "Now, Murphy, you'll spoil the line with those feet of yours! Draw them back instantly man, and get them in line!"

Murphy's dignity was hurt. "Please, sergint, they ain't mine," he replied. "They're BIG Tom O'Brien's in the rear rank!"

• 𝚡 • 𝚡 • 𝚡 • 𝚡 •

A soldier went to his colonel and asked for leave to go home to help his wife with her spring cleaning.

"I don't like to refuse you," said the colonel, 'but I've just received a letter from your wife, saying that you are no use around the house."

The soldier saluted and turned to go. At the door, he stopped, turned and remarked, "Colonel, there are two persons in this regiment who handle the truth loosely, and I'm one of them. I'm not married."

• 𝚡 • 𝚡 • 𝚡 • 𝚡 •

An old soldier, on leaving the Army, wrote to his colonel as follows:

"Sir, After what I've suffered, you can tell the Army to go piss . . . er . . . to go to blazes."

He received a reply in the usual official manner:

"Sir, Any suggestion or inquiries as to movements of troops must be entered on army form 112XYP, a copy of which I am enclosing."

• 𝚡 • 𝚡 • 𝚡 • 𝚡 •

Soldiers call only once
  On Sally Maggy Bump –
When they suggest a drink
  She leads them to the pump.

• 𝚡 • 𝚡 • 𝚡 • 𝚡 •

"Sarge, was your dame pleased when she put on her new bathing suit?"

"Man, was she! You should have seen her beam."

• 𝚡 • 𝚡 • 𝚡 • 𝚡 •

Cunt Cap – The garrison cap, used from World War I until today. It took this name from its fancied resemblance to the anatomical item it was thought to resemble.

To Ride The Sick Book – The goof-off who is always playing sick, going on sickcall to avoid duty.

Red Disturbance – Whiskey.

Said a certain young man we all nough
  "I wonder what makes us rock sough
I know its real tough
    That the water is rough"
Then he stood at the rail and said "Ough."

THE SOLDIER'S PHILOSOPHY

One of two things is certain: Either you're mobilized, or you're not mobilized

If you're not mobilized, there is no need to worry; if you are mobilized, one of two things is certain: Either you're behind the lines, or you're at the front.

If you're behind the lines, there is no need to worry; if you're at the front, one of two things is certain: Either you're resting in a safe place, or you're exposed to danger.

If you're resting in a safe place, there is no need to worry; if you're exposed to danger, one of two things is certain: Either you're wounded, or you're not wounded.

If you're not wounded, there is no need to worry; if you are wounded, one of two things is certain: Either you're wounded seriously or you're wounded slightly.

If you're wounded slightly, there is no need to worry; if you're wounded seriously, one of two things is certain: Either you recover or you die.

If you recover, there is no need to worry; if you die, you can't worry.

● 🛉 ● 🛉 ● 🛉 ● 🛉 ●

Goof Burner – The slang name for marijuana was *goof*, hence a goof burner was a smoker of marijuana, or as we say now, *pot-smoker*. *Goof*, back in World War I, meant an inept soldier, a *sad Sack* or, the more general term *fuck-up*!!

● 🛉 ● 🛉 ● 🛉 ● 🛉 ●

I never saw a purple cow,
I never hope to see one.
But from the color of our milk
I know that there must be one.

● 🛉 ● 🛉 ● 🛉 ● 🛉 ●

Sailor (In the brig) – What time is it?

Guard – What do you want to know for, you ain't goin' no place?

● 🛉 ● 🛉 ● 🛉 ● 🛉 ●

Footslogger – An infantryman.

● 🛉 ● 🛉 ● 🛉 ● 🛉 ●

A chipper lieutenant named Leigh
Found himself in a ship out at sea.
"Though I'm feeling quite well

This tub's rocking like – well
And the land will look good to meigh."

● 👤 ● 👤 ● 👤 ● 👤 ●

Flopper Stopper – A brassiere.

● 👤 ● 👤 ● 👤 ● 👤 ●

There was a young soldier named Lee
"I'm happy" he shouted with glee.
"I should worry or grieve.
With M.P. on my sleeve
I can punch anybody I see."

● 👤 ● 👤 ● 👤 ● 👤 ●

A (Kentucky) mountaineer fighting overseas in the First World War kept getting nagging letters from his wife back home. He was too busy fighting to write letters, even to his wife. At last, stung to action by his wife's scolding missives, he sat down and wrote her:

Dear Nancy: I been a-gittin yore naggin letters all along. Now I want to tell ye, I'm dam tired of them. For the first time in my life I'm a-fightin in a big war, and I want to enjoy it in peace as long as it lasts.

Yours, etc.

● 👤 ● 👤 ● 👤 ● 👤 ●

A hillbilly walked down the street near the draft board. A neighbor said, "You had better stay away – you are liable to get drafted." The boy, who actually had not even heard of the war, was unable to understand. The neighbor explained the situation. The hillbilly said, "Well, I always figure I have got two chances: I might get drafted and I might not. And even if I'm drafted, I still have two chances: I might pass and I might not. And if I pass, I still have two chances: I might go across and I might not. And even if I go across, I still have two chances: I might get shot and I might not. And even if I die, I still have got two chances!"

● 👤 ● 👤 ● 👤 ● 👤 ●

A bishop and an admiral died and presented themselves for entry through the Pearly Gates. St. Peter sized them up, pulled the admiral inside and closed the gate in the bishop's face. A long time elapsed, during which the bishop heard great activity inside – trumpets blowing, angels' voices singing and all other indications of a big party.

After a long time, the gate opened again and the bishop saw

the end of the admiral's reception – velvet carpets over the gold paving, flowers scattered everywhere, and a rain of rose petals in the air. There were many garlands on the admiral, who was being escorted by a large bevy of the most beautiful angels. While the bishop watched, they rolled up the carpet, brushed all the flowers away and made preparations for a common garden reception. The bishop got sore and wanted to know why so much preferment was shown for the admiral and so little for himself.

"We are all the time bringing bishops through the Pearly Gates," was the reply, "but this is the first time within anyone's recollection that we have had an admiral!"

● 🎖 ● 🎖 ● 🎖 ● 🎖 ●

Mud Crusher – The same as a mud thumper . . . an infantryman.

● 🎖 ● 🎖 ● 🎖 ● 🎖 ●

"The Yankees on the Marne"

Oh, the English and the Irish, and the 'owlin Scotties, too,
    The Canucks and Austryluns and the 'airy French Poilu –
The only thing that bothered us a year before we know,
    Was 'ow in 'ell the Yanks 'ud look and wot in 'ell they'd do.

They 'adn't 'ad no tryenein' they didn't know the gyme,
    They 'adn't never marched it much – their shootin' was the syme;
An' the only thing that bothered us that day in lawst July,
    Was "ow in 'ell the line 'd 'old if they should run aw'y.

They leggy, nowey new 'une, just come across the sea –
    We couldn' 'elp but wonder 'ow in 'ell their guts 'ud be.
An' the only thing that bothered us in all our staggerin' ranks
    Was wot in 'ell 'ud 'appen w'en the 'uns 'ad 'it the Yanks.
My word! It 'appened sudden w'en the drive 'ad first begun;
    We seed the Yanks a-runnin' – Gaw blimy! 'ow they run!
But the only thing that bothered us that seed the chase begin
    Was 'ow in 'ell to stop 'em 'fore they got into Berlin!
They didn't 'ave no tactics but the bloody manuel,
    They 'adn't learned no horders but "Ooray!" an' "Give 'em 'ell!"
But the only thing that bothered us about them leggy lads
    Was 'ow in 'ell to get the chow to feed their "Kamerads!"

So we're standin' all together in a stiffish firin' line.
    If anyone should awsk you, you can say we're doin' fine.
But the only thing that bothers us – an' that don't bother much –
    Is 'ow in 'ell to get the dirt to bury all the Dutch.
Gaw's-trewth! t's rotten fightin' that all our troops 'as seen,

The 'Un's a dirty player, becos 'e's alwus been;
But the only thing that bothers us in 'andin' 'im our thanks
Is 'ow in 'ell we'd done it if weren't fer the Yanks.

Oh, the English and Irish, and the 'owlin' Scotties, too,
The Canucks and Austryluns and the 'airy French Poilu –
The only thing that bothered us don't bother us no more;
It's why in 'ell we didn't know the Yankee boys before!

Emeron Hough of the Vigilantes

● 𝑓 ● 𝑓 ● 𝑓 ● 𝑓 ●

A DOUGH BOY DICTIONARY

Spiral Puttees – Part of a scheme to increase the size of fatigue squads by making a larger number of men late to reveille.

Underwear – The favorite ration of the goat, sheep-tick and a superb hide-a-way for fleas!

Mess Kit – A collapsible contrivance designed to convey beans from the mess line to the table.

Mess Tools – A collection of implements, designed to convey beans from the mess kit to the human's mouth.

Buttons – The modern counterpart of the sword of Damocles – "You hold them – but by a single hair."

Muffler – Something you wear by the dear ones at home, that you would like beyond anything to wish on the bugler's mouth!

Mule – A hardy and thick-skinned quadruped which must be approached with the same caution and trepidation with which one approaches a dead bomb.

Socks – Foot coverings composed of a substance represented to the government or the Red Cross as being wool, and possessed of the same capacity for contracting holes as is a machine gun target at fifty yards.

Trench – A hole in the ground without ending or beginning, entirely filled with water and very frequently the object of the enemy's attention.

Trenches (plural) – The things which the people back home imagine we are in all the time.

Dugout – The most satisfactory life insurance policy sold in the less healthy portions of France.

Machine Gun – An arrangement alleged to do the work of fifteen men but requiring the work of thirty men to keep it in operating condition.

Court Martial – A scheme to separate you from your money or your liberty.

Insurance Premium – Something that puts about one-sixth of your pay where you will never be able to get it.

SOME CHANGE
"Comment ca va" – How do you do?"
You see we've changed our styles.
We weight ourselves in *"livres"* now,
And "metre" off our miles.
For bread we say, "Give me a 'pain',"
And add "Si voulez vous."
We used to call our money Bill,
But now it's Frank and Sue.

Stars and Stripes – O.D. Miller Q.M.C.

● 𝑖 ● 𝑖 ● 𝑖 ● 𝑖 ●

Hash is a staple dish in the American home but not in the army. Therefore, when a mess sergeant repeated the hash diet several days, he was asked, "How do they make thiseyer hash?"

"They don't make hash; it jus' 'cumulates." Yank. February 15, 1918.

● 𝑖 ● 𝑖 ● 𝑖 ● 𝑖 ●

Private Pat: "Make, what the hell kind of fish be them ye're eatin?"

Corporal Mike: "Them's sardines."

Pat: "Sardines is ut? An where do they grow?"

Mike: "Pat! Sich ignorance! Thim grow in the Atlantic, Pacific, Injun, Arctic – in all thim oceans. An the big fish, thim whales an thim halibuts and sharks – they live off'n eatin' thim sardeens."

Pat: "Them does, does they? . . Thin tell me this, Mike, how in hell do they git the damn box open?"

● 𝑖 ● 𝑖 ● 𝑖 ● 𝑖 ●

The old general was out walking when he was stopped by a beggar.

"Don't refuse a trifle, sir," said the beggar, "I'm an old soldier."

"An old soldier!" replied the general, "well, I'll test you. Shun! Eyes right! Eyes front! Stand at ease!" He stopped, then asked, "What comes next?"

"Present alms," replied the beggar hopefully.

Pvt. Broke: "How ya doin' fer money?"

Pvt. Broker: "Well, the wealth of this country is estimated to be $988,000,000,000, and the last nine figures represent what I have now."

● 👤 ● 👤 ● 👤 ● 👤 ●

"He says it's the only way he can sleep."

● 👤 ● 👤 ● 👤 ● 👤 ●

Recruit (in orderly room): "See here, my name"s Wrightt and you've spelled it wrong twice. Two wrongs don't make a right."

Clerk: "That's right."

Recruit: "But it's wrong."

Clerk: "If it's wrong it can't be right."

Recruit: "You don't understand. My name is Wrightt."

Clerk: "How do you write it, Wright?"

Recruit: "But that's not right."

Clerk: "Then you don't write it Wright?"

Recruit: "Right."

Top Dick: "If you two jailbird prospects don't stop the argument, I'll use my right, right where it'll settle the matter."

The army post was evacuating and one soldier was detailed to make an inventory of the commanding officer's office. The big gun left the GI to his own resources. They found an inventory later on, that read thus:

Desk, mahogany – one; chairs, mahogany – three; rugs, brown – one; decanters, whiskey, full – three; decanters, whisky, full – none; three desks and, if you don't believe me, count them, fibe hundrerthiosand ophelanys, green, blue, purple; one pink bisom. . . large blue sopysts; revolving door mt, oneone whheeee phwaaaa.

● 👤 ● 👤 ● 👤 ● 👤 ●

Lady: "How were you hurt, Young Man?"
Soldier: "By a shell, ma'am."
Lady: "'Did it explode?"
Soldier: "No. It crept right up and bit me."

● 👤 ● 👤 ● 👤 ● 👤 ●

"For the last time," shouted the sergeant, "What is fortification?"

The recruits stood fast to a man. No one answered.

Striding up to one man the N.C.O. bawled out, "Tell me what fortification is!"

The answer slowed up the works: "two twentifications, Sergeant."

● 👤 ● 👤 ● 👤 ● 👤 ●

Soldier: "But, dear, let's try companionate marriage. We'll live together and if we find we've made a mistake, we can separate."
She: "Yes, dumplin', but what will we do with our mistake?"

● 👤 ● 👤 ● 👤 ● 👤 ●

A black soldier in the stevedore corps met a friend who was covered with bandages.

"War'd you get all dat blighty, man?" he demanded.

"Ah done got saluted by an army mule!"

Boilermakers – Boilermaking is/was a very noisy trade and so it was quite natural to give that title to. . .what else?. . . the Army bands.

● 👤 ● 👤 ● 👤 ● 👤 ●

My parents told me not to smoke.
    I don't.
Nor listen to a naughty joke.
    I don't.
They made it clear I mustn't wink
At pretty girls or even think
        About intoxicating drink.

I don't.
Wild youth chase women, wine and song.
I don't.
I kiss not girls, not even one.
I do not know how it is done.
You wouldn't think I had much fun.
I don't.

Rumbler Advance. Overhaul Park T-1

• 👤 • 👤 • 👤 • 👤 •

Profane – A special form of exhortation spoken by sergeants, mule-skinners and, occasionally, an imaginative officer. A typical sentence might begin, "You dirty-assed, goddam, shit-faced son-of-a-bitch of a blue-balled, cock-suckin' Guatemalan shit." Such language, it is said, could propel troops through uncut barbed-wire.

• 👤 • 👤 • 👤 • 👤 •

1st Stenographer: "Say, Mac, what does O.I.C. stand for?"
2nd Stenographer: "Officer in Charge, you bone head!"
1st Stenographer: "Oh, I see."

• 👤 • 👤 • 👤 • 👤 •

A COOTIE CURE

If the sufferers from cooties will rub their clothes full of salt and allow it to remain there about two days, they will be surprised at the results, if the clothes are then laid beside a basin of water or a creek.

The cooties will leave the clothes to get a drink and the soldier can then grab his olive drabs and run.

Upon returning and finding the clothes gone, nine out of ten cooties will die of mortification and the tenth will die of lonesomeness.

• 👤 • 👤 • 👤 • 👤 •

I know just what a shell can do
    if you are on the spot!
I know when shrapnel whistles through
    it doesn't help a lot;
But on the land or on the sea,
    or in a raiding pinch,
If they'd abolish reveille,
    this war would be a cinch.

Stars and Stripes – Aug. 1, 1918

We were to be issued new underwear and one boy asked the chaplain if it would be winter underwear and warm. The chaplain replied he thought it would, since it was to be fleas-lined!

Stars and Stripes – Nov. 8, 1918

● ⚔ ● ⚔ ● ⚔ ● ⚔ ●

One boy, a painter, had been appointed battalion artist. We had had trouble getting rations, so the chaplain sent for the artist to draw them!

Stars and Stripes – L. Wolff, F.S.B.

● ⚔ ● ⚔ ● ⚔ ● ⚔ ●

If you are unable to find a Army dentist with enough equipment to dispose of your dental difficulties, brush your teeth violently with iodine every morning for three days and then have them all pulled out.

Stars and Stripes – Jan. 31, 1919

● ⚔ ● ⚔ ● ⚔ ● ⚔ ●

A good post – A post that you just left or the one you hope to be transferred to.

● ⚔ ● ⚔ ● ⚔ ● ⚔ ●

Customer: "Three suits of underwear, please."
Clerk: "What size, sir?"
Customer: "Oh, any size will do. I used to be in the Army."

● ⚔ ● ⚔ ● ⚔ ● ⚔ ●

Bugle oil – The item that new, gullible recruits were sent after, along with, perhaps, a tent wrench or, just maybe, four feet of skirmish line!

● ⚔ ● ⚔ ● ⚔ ● ⚔ ●

KUSSING THE KAISER

Tune: "Here We Go Round the Mulberry Bush"

If you want to "Kuss the Kaiser,"
(Fuss the Kaiser, Muss the Kaiser)
If you want to Kuss the Kaiser Out
In many a different key—
"Bless him out" poetically,
Phonetically, hypothetically,
Then seal him up hermetically
And sink him in the sea.

"K-K-K-KATY" AND PARODIES

This "stammering song" was a great favorite with the troops and had numerous parodies. It was composed by Geoffrey OHara.

K-K-K-KATY

K-K-K-Katy, beautiful Katy,
You're the only g-g-g-girl that I adore,
When the m-m-m-moon shines over the cow-shed
I'll be waiting at the k-k-k-kitchen door.

PARODIES

K-K-K-K-P
Dirty old K.P.,
That's the only army job that I abhor,
When the m-moon shines over the guardhouse,
I'll be mopping up the k-k-k-kitchen floor.

C-c-c-cootie,
Horrible cootie,
You're the only b-b-bug that I abhor,
When the m-moon shines over the bunk-house,
I will scratch my b-b-b-back until it's sore.

AIN'T IT AWFUL?

To the editor of the **Stars and Stripes**:

Speaking of mud, if you ever saw this camp you would grow web feet and most likely squawk like a mud hen and try to dive through the floor when you attempted to speak. Mud! You don't know what mud is.

There is real mud here. There is so much that the buildings float around from one place to another. Last night the colonel's headquarters floated around so much it changed places with the Q.M. supply house and this morning the quartermaster issued out all the colonel's clothes before he finally made the discovery. The colonel came down to his office in a rowboat about 9 A.M. and ate a lot of moth balls that were sitting on the Q.M.'s desk, mistaking them for a box of candy he had placed on his desk the night before. A hurry up call was sent in for the doctor and the orderly rowed to 22 different locations before he finally located the infirmary, which had floated round back of the camp. The doctor had a terrible time finding the infirmary and when he treated the Colonel with what he thought was C.C. pills he discovered that it was horse medicine.

There is so much mud here that our top sergeant rows out to a telephone pole in front of our barracks and stands on the top of the pole while he calls the roll. As fast as he calls off the names we go to the door and answer present. When this formality is concluded the top turns round on the pole, salutes the captain, who sits on a raft 30 yards away, and reports all present or accounted for. The captain returns the salute and then goes paddling off hunting for his billet, which always changes its locations every time he leaves it.

As to drill, we do that, too, only we do it in boats. We were having a squad drill yesterday with two rows of four boats each when the major dropped his paddle and ran slam into the top's boat. The major sure did bawl the top out.

Last night our mess sergeant rowed out to the gate so he could go up town after some eggs for blue mud pies. When he came back to the gate, his boat was gone. He shouted to us but we didn't hear him, so he ate the eggs and swam back towards the mess shack.

If you care to send a reporter down, wire ahead of time and we will arrange to meet him with a launch at the main gate.

Henry V. Porter, Pvt. 1st C.
Stars and Stripes – Feb. 14, 1918

• 🪖 • 🪖 • 🪖 • 🪖 •

"Whadaya mean writing your girl that you were C.O. yesterday? Weren't you on K.P.?"

"Same thing! C.O. Means 'cuisine operator', doesn't it?"

VOLUNTEER VIC'S BIG IDEA

BY LEMEN IN THE
ST. LOUIS POST-DISPATCH

THE FLIES OF FRANCE

We tried 'em out on sulphur, but they seemed to like the
    smoke
And they buzzed around and brought back millions more;
We mixed 'em up some sugar and some formalde-hyde au
    lait,
But they fattened up – marked "lunch room" on our door.

We got some Red Cross netting, didn't have to pay a cent,
And tacked it over every hole and crack;
Two pulled apart the threads and let the rest come sailing
    through
We're still looking for the hole to chase them back.

They're affectionate and friendly, they like to chase around
In your stable, billet, kitchen, office, mess;
They know no union hours – if you think they'll let you sleep,
You're sort of S.O.L. – you miss your guess.

When you crawl into your bunk and pull your blankets round
    your head,
And say your "Now I lay me down to sleep,"
You think you feel a cootie walking post along your spine –
It's a fly that just came in to take a peep.

They make dugouts in your sugar, perish nobly in your meat,
Every meal you drink your coffee a la mouche;
When you open up the jam pot, they come buzzing tout de
    suite,
And you wish you had an anti-fly cartouche . . .

Some day when we go sailing home – way off in the bye and
    bye,
Where war is just a something to forget,
We'll all remember France for her ever-present fly –
"Doggone the luck, they're pestering me yet!"

● ✻ ● ✻ ● ✻ ● ✻ ●

THE ELUSIVE COOTIE

His teeth are sharp and he's quick on his feet,
His office is just where your shirt and pants meet;
From the top of your head to the tip of your toes,
The tiny, elusive wanderer goes.

You can duck a bullet, dodge a shell,
Race a shrapnel sent from hell,
But the wise Old Doc, is sure to find
Your speed won't leave the cooties behind.

● ✻ ● ✻ ● ✻ ● ✻ ●

I love corned beef – I never knew
How sweet the stuff COULD taste in stew!
I love it baked and called MEAT PIE,
I love it camouflaged in HASH –
A hundred bucks I'd give in CASH
To have a BARREL of such chow
A standing here before me now.
I say "YUM YUM" when "soupie" blows
I sniff and raise aloft my nose;
CORNED WILLIE! Ha! Oh, boy, that's FINE!
Can hardly keep my place in LINE.
I kick my heels and wildly yell;
"Old Sherman said that "WAR IS HELL."
But GLADLY would I bear the heat
If corned beef, I could get to eat!
I love it HOT, I love it COLD,
CORNED WILLIE never WILL grow old.

I love it – now PAUSE – listen, friend;
When to this war there comes an end,

And PEACE upon this earth shall reign,
I'll hop a boat for HOME again.
Then to a restaurant I'LL speed –
No dainty MANNERS will I need –
But to the waiter I will cry;
"Bring me, well, make it corned beef PIE!
And corned beef COLD – I'll take that too.
And – now don't think I'm a crazy man,
But could you bring a corned beef CAN."
and – WAIT! – I'm not through ORDERING yet –
I want a SIRLOIN STEAK you BET,
With hashed brown SPUDS, now LISTEN friend,
I've got the CASH – you may depend –
Right HERE it is – Let's see, I'll try –
Oh, better a piece of hot MINCE PIE.
And ALL that stuff that's printed here;
My appetite is HUGE I fear."

Then, when he's filled my festive board
With all these eats I'll thank the Lord,
(For that's the PROPER thing to do).
And then I'll take the CORNED BEEF STEW,
The corned beef PIE and corned beef COLD
And RAM the whole WORKS into it,
And say, "NOW damn you, THERE you sit!
You've haunted every dream I've had –
You don't know what shame IS. Egad!
Now SIT there, Bo – see how you FEEL –
And watch me eat a REG'LAR MEAL!"

● 👮 ● 👮 ● 👮 ● 👮 ●

SOMEWHERE IN FRANCE

Why is it that from yonder tower,
    The colonel's lamp is burning still,
Though it's past the midnight hour,
    And all's serene o'er vale and hills.

'Tis not the wisdom of the sages
    Nor army lore his mind enchants;
An earthlier task his mind engages;
    He's sewing buttons on his pants.

                    Stars and Stripes. May 2, 1918

Things we hear but never see:
A satisfied private.
A mess sergeant with a friend.
A soldier retiring on his income.
A general stopping his car to compliment a soldier on
his military bearing.
Spiral puttees that will not come down.
A worse war than this one.

Stars and Stripes – May 2, 1918

● 𝑓 ● 𝑓 ● 𝑓 ● 𝑓 ●

Weather Forecast: Mebbe it will and mebbe it won't. Most likely it will.

● 𝑓 ● 𝑓 ● 𝑓 ● 𝑓 ●

Timid Sentry: "Halt! Who goes there?
(O.D. keeps on going.)
Sentry: "Halt! Who went then?"

Stars and Stripes. Frapper, GA 11th Marines

● 𝑓 ● 𝑓 ● 𝑓 ● 𝑓 ●

"The Kaiser is so low he would have to make an altitude flight in an airplane to reach hell."

Stars and Stripes. Billy Sunday

● 𝑓 ● 𝑓 ● 𝑓 ● 𝑓 ●

Pvt. Christiansen: "Should you spell "Army" with a capital?"
Pvt. Tweed: "No. There is no capital in army. Only labor."

● 𝑓 ● 𝑓 ● 𝑓 ● 𝑓 ●

As to the origin of the term "doughboy", one soldier reported that it was given to soldiers in the Philippines in 1898 who, when marching in the hot humid weather, mixed sweat with dust until their skin resembled dough. Hence . . . doughboy.

Another soldier, "an old one," refuted the argument by stating that the origin of the term came about because doughboys are the "flour" of the Army.

Still another GI said that the old army uniform buttons created the term. These buttons were rounded, light colored and gave the appearance of a rising loaf of unbaked bread.

● 𝑓 ● 𝑓 ● 𝑓 ● 𝑓 ●

I ain't much worried 'bout them Boche,
An' worry less about them Turks,
An' the Austrians ain't a-doin' much,
A-judgin by their works.

I 'low from readin' papers,
　Seein' what them rulers say,
That they're gettin' tired of fightin'
　An' we'll all have peace someday.

An' I ain't a-feelin' sorry,
　Cause I've lost a blame-good pal;
An' my heart ain't had no crackin'
　Jus' because of some durn gal.

An' the ole high cost of livin'
　Never troubles me no more;
An' I ain't had no crackin'
　'Bout some job at the close of the war.

But there is one pesky question,
　That is always puzzlin' me,
An' they ain't no use in tryin' –
　I cain't make it leave me be –

An' the doggone cause o' trouble
　That is bringin' all this wail
Don't take very long in statin' –
　Where the hell is all our mail!
Stars and Stripes. Cpl. Vance C. Chriss. Engrs.

Voice from the mess line: "Now I know why they call it the standing army,."

Rook: What's that stuff?
Cook: Eat some and find out.
Rook: I did. That's why I asked.
Steering Wheel (Hq, M.T.C.)

"No, Mabel, A.E.F. doesn't mean After Every Female. And S.O.S. doesn't mean Souse on Souse.

• 𝆺 • 𝆺 • 𝆺 • 𝆺 •

Here are some interesting, often poetic, naval terms explained by LOGAN E. RUGGLES, (chief printer, U.S. Navy) 1918. Edwin D. Appleton, N.Y., publisher.

STRAIGHT KICK – For a man to be discharged undesirably by the commanding officer of a vessel. No formality, just set him on the beach, In some cases the men are tried by summary court martial, and in some they are not.

POGGY BAIT – The sailorman's pet name for candy and sweets. The ship's canteen or store carries a goodly store of candies, cakes and canned fruits. In port, the canteen very often sells milk, pies, cakes and ice cream.

DOWN FOR A CHANCE – To be placed on the report; to have a report made against a man. He is down for a chance and has to go before the captain and receive his punishment or if he can put it over, the captain excuses him.

DREAM SACK – The hammock is universally known as the dream sack. The hammock is the only bed a sailor has (sometimes cots are issued) and he hangs one end – the clews – to a hook and the other end – clews and foot lashing – to another hook. Every man has a designated hook and always can be found at the same place. The hammock consists of a mattress cover, mattress and two blankets; more blankets can be had if the man so desires, but usually one or two is sufficient. The hammock is lashed up in the morning with seven half hitches and is stowed in a designated place.

PIE WAGON – To be confined in the ship's brig is to be "in the pie wagon." All prisoners are kept in the wagon and there is no pie served out, instead it is usually bread and water.

DITTY BOX – A small box issued to every man on board ship. In it he keeps his tobacco, soap, comb and brushes, stationery and other articles such as needles and thread. It is similar to a trunk and has a small tray in which pencils and pens may be kept. A ditty box is 14 inches long and about ten inches wide. Often it is called "ditty house," by the gobs.

GOT THE WRINKLES OUT – Some man who came into the service when he was hungry and who has had the sensation of hunger removed is the man who "got the wrinkles out." If he would scorn the chow some loyal sailor would remark: "Yes, you are one of those geeks that come in the outfit hungry; now you have the wrinkles out, and you are kicking. Say, you were so hungry when you hit this packet your stomach thought your throat was cut."

GOING DOWN HILL – Any man who has two years' service to his credit is going down hill. In present day slang, he is over the top and is on his way to the bottom.

SKINNING PARLOR – The barber shop of a warship. All of the large naval vessels have a well equipped barber shop and several good barbers working all the time. Men must keep their hair and face "skinned" at all times.

MAIL BUOY – There hain't no such animal. The mail buoy is a myth. It does not exist, although many men have stood out on the forecastle many hours trying to locate the mail buoy in mid-ocean. A new recruit generally is picked out by the older fellows to stand by to get the mail sack from the buoy when they pass it. He is equipped with a long boat hook to pull in the mail. It is a hammock ladder gag.

PRUNE PICKER – A native of California. So called because of the abundant prune crops.

PUTTING IN HIS OAR – When an argument is in progress and some fellow butts in one of those will always remark, "Well, stupid, who asked you to put in your oar!"

JACKASS RIG – For a man to be out of uniform, to be wearing a pair of white pants and a blue jumper. Any man improperly dressed, especially with two different colors of clothing, is in a jackass rig.

JAKE – the navy man's way of saying a thing is good. If it is a jake with him it is all right. "I had a jake time," is commonly heard.

JAWBONE – To stand a fellow off for articles ashore. To get clothes or eats on credit with a promise to pay "when the eagle walks." To get credit was to get jawbone.

JAWHAWKER – Some new country boy who is continually star gazing at objects when he should be paying attention to his duty.

JACK – A name very often given to sailors by laymen, but which receives very unfavorable comment among them. As has been said, Gob is the pet name for sailors and they take it in preference to that of Jack, Jack Tar; and if you want to get an old-time sailor-man good and goaty, call him a Jackie. The Union Jack is spoken of as the jack by quartermasters and signalmen, as are many things naval which have lengthy names and need a little trimming down.

JANE – The best girl is the Jane, widder, skirt, calico, the old lady, weezel, broad, judy, dame, tomatoe, was doll, jelly bean, fair one, or wench. There is no vulgar thought in using the above mentioned words and they are characteristic of the present-day sailormen.

JACK-OF-THE-DUST – The jack-of-the-dust is a man in charge of the commissary stores and storerooms; keeps the keys to the issuing room and serves out the rations for the day's consumption. He is generally a ship's cook or had some experience in the galley.

JACK LOCKER – A place to keep money; a locker in which a man may keep his change. His pocket, if there is any jack in it, is often known as the jack locker. "Are you going ashore?" a man might ask another, and the answer would be: "There is no jack in the jack locker," meaning in short that he was broke.

SHAKES A MEAN LIP – A man who has a mean or bum line of chatter is always said to shake a mean lip. This person is always telling some imaginative yarn or spinning stories of which he knows absolutely nothing.

MONEY – The sailormen of the navy probably coin more words for money than any other body of men. Almost every pay day there seems to be a new name for money: Sheckles, iron men, washers, clackers, jack, cart wheels, simoleons, kopex, mazuma, palm grease, evil metal, oro, jingles, liberty bait, gilt, sou, armor plate, holy stones, joy berries and many others.

HOLYSTONE – A stone about the size of a brick used to scour the decks of a warship. Sand is thrown upon the deck, soapy water is sprinkled around and then the holystone is pushed back and forth over the sand by the aid of a long stick – broom handle – and it cleans the deck and makes it snow white when dry. It is also called a holy-brick, or the rock of ages.

DONKEY'S BREAKFAST – In the old navy all mattresses were made of straw and when a man would go to get his hammock when it was time to turn in he would say, "Now for some horizontal exercise on the donkey's breakfast." The mattresses in the navy to-day are made of the finest hair or kapock cotton.

HORIZONTAL EXERCISE – Applies to a man sleeping or lying down. When a sailor is caulking-off on the deck he is taking his horizontal exercise.

BREAD – Is called "punk"; sugar, "sand"; salt is "sea dust"; butter is "axle grease"; coffee is always "Java"; milk is "lachie" (Spanish); eggs are "gas bombs" and "depth bombs"; tapioca is "snake eyes"; sausages are "repeaters" (because they try to come back); chicken croquettes are "fowl balls"; chicken is "seagull"; salmon is "submarine shark."

BUNK LIZARD – That fellow who is always sleeping; never able to get out of his bunk or hammock.

SMOKE STACK – One who imagines he is stewed, gowed up, drunk, when in reality he is putting on. Some fellow who has wiped his hands on the bartender's towel might think "he has a smoke stack jag on."

PELICAN – The man of the ship's company who can eat more than any other six men on the ship. He frequently says he doesn't get enough to eat, but, whoee, how he can scoff.

GOWED UP – When a man is gowed up he has had too much liquor or other intoxicating drink. It is a purely sailor slang word and I have never heard where it originated, neither have I ever heard it outside of a circle of navymen.

FAKER'S PALACE – The ship's sick bay. The hospital of a vessel is sometimes referred to as the faker's palace. If there is a hard day's work ahead some of the lazy men might try to evade it by going to the sick bay and "faking the list."

DRAW MORE WATER – When a man has been advanced in rating, he draws more money and naturally has a greater scope of authority; hence he draws more water.

● 𝑥 ● 𝑥 ● 𝑥 ● 𝑥 ●

The "Dere Mabel" and "Dere Bill" collection of letters that "Bill" wrote to "Mabel" (and the reverse), were the most popular humorous stories of World War I. Printing after printing was made until by the 15th printing, 550,000 copies had been sold.

Edward Streeter wrote the "Dere Bill" stories and Bill Breck illustrated them. Both men were in the 27th Division (New York).

Florence E. Summers wrote the Mabel letters to Bill and the illustrations were done by Natalie Stokes.

The tone, humor, ideas of these stories seemed to catch the imagination and titillate the funny bone of the American people during those tough war years of 1917 and 1918.

Mon Cherry Mable:

Thats the way the French begin there love letters. Its perfectly proper. I would have rote you sooner but me an my fountin pens been froze for a week. Washington will never know how lucky he was that he got assigned to valley Forge instead of here. It got us out of drill for a couple of days. Thats somethin. I guess Id rather freeze than drill. Its awful when they make you do both though.

Two of my men has gone home on furlos. Me bein corperal I took all there blankets. The men didnt like it but I got a squad of men to look out for an my first duty is to keep fit. duty first. Thats me all over. I got so many blankets now that I got to put a book mark in the place I get in at night or Id never find it again.

We spent most of our time tryin to find somethin to burn up in the Sibly stoves. A sibly stove, Mable, is a piece of stove pipe built like the leg of a sailurs trowsers. Old man Sibly must have had a fine mind to think it out all by hisself. They say he got a patent on it. I guess that must have been a slack winter in Washington. the government gives us our wood but I guess that the man who decided how much it was goin to give us had an office in the Sandwitch Islands. I says the other day that if theyd dip our allowance in fusfrus wed at least have matches, eh Mable? Im the same old Bill, Mable. Crackin jokes an keepin everybody laffin when things is blackest.

I was scoutin round for wood today an burned up those military hair brushes your mother gave me when we came away. I told her theyd come in might handy some day.

" BUILT LIKE THE LEG OF A SAILURS TROWSERS "

They say a fello tried to take a shouer the other day. Before he could get out it froze round him. Like that fello in the Bible who turned into a pillo of salt. They had to break the whole thing offen the pipe with him inside it an stand it in front of the stove. When it melted he finished his shouer an said he felt fine. thats how hard were gettin, Mable.

I bought a book on Minor Tackticks the other day. Thats not about underaged tacks that live on ticks as you might suppose, Mable. Its the cience of movin bodies of men from one place to another. I thought it might tell of some way of getting the squad out of bed in the morning but it doesnt. All the important stuff like that is camooflages sos the Germans wont get into it.

Camooflage is not a new kind of cheese Mable. Its a military term. Camooflage is French for cauliflower which is a disguised cabbage. It is the same thing as putting powder on your face instead of washin it. You deceive Germans with it. For instance you paint a horse black and white stripes an a German comes along. He thinks its a picket fence an goes right by. Or you paint yourself like a tree an the Germans come an drink beer round you an tell military sekruts.

Well I guess its time to say Mery Xmas now Mable. I guess it wont be a very Mery Xmas withut me there, eh? Cheer up cause Im goin to think of you whenever I get time all day long. Im pretty busy nowdays. I got to watch the men work. It keeps a fello on the jump all the time. I like it though, Mable. Thats me all over. Isnt it?

Dont send me nothin for Christmas, Mable. I bought somethin for you but Im not going to tell you cause its a surprize. All that I can say is that it cost me four eighty seven ($4.87) which is more than I could afford. An its worth a lot more. But you know how I am with money. A spend drift. So dont send me anything please although I need an electric flash light, some cigarets, candy an one of them sox that you wear on your head. Ill spend my last sent on anyone I like but I dont want to be under no obligations. Independent. thats me all over.

You might read this part to your mother. I dont want nothin from her ether.

Rite soon an plain Mable, cause I dont get much chance to study.

Yours till the south is warm,
Bill.

Your mothers present cost me three seventy seven ($3.77).

Dere Bill,

Your all the time writin me askin me what I think you done now? Well, Im writin you askin you what you think I done now? The way I happened to think of it was this. Since so many of the fellos joined the home guard an got uniforms, the girls have got so flirty I cant afford to go with them like I sued to. Why, Maggie Sams has to be the kind that frizzes her hair out on the side like baked potatoes an looks in the barber shop and reads Bevo signs. So of course I had to quit goin with her an the rest is just as bad. The way Nellie does for a married woman is scandalous. So not bein able to go with them any more I get more time to think of things concernin you an me after the war. So what you think I done now? Ive started a war chest

I aint goin to call it a hope chest cause Nellie would be sure to say I ought to call it a hopeless chest, never missin the chance to say something hateful. I reckon if youve got seven dollars ($7) saved up toward them green shutters for our white house, I orter begin to think about some curtins to go behind them, so I went down town the other day an got some swell goods to make them out of, payin twenty-five cents (25¢) a yard for it. Its got yellow cupids on it, holdin lavender flowers in there hands. Thcres purple ribbon ticd to their wIngs that flyin an flutterin while theyre scatterin the flowers. They ought to brighten the dining room up some. Ive took flower sacks an hemmed us enough dish rags to last till old man Gabriel blows the last time. Im tryin to work the practical in with the ornamental. Maybe Ill get along faster on it next week, as pa's got a liver attack an ma's got the flue.

I reckon youve heard about the epidemick. Somebody sneezes without their handkerchief up an it spreads. thats what Dr. Luford says. he says the only good thing about it is that when a patient dies theres plenty more gettin sick. The doctors is the only ones that dont have to worry. Your mothers been wearin a flue mask sos she wont get it, an it improves her looks mightily.

I got a date tonight – reckon I dont have to tell you its with Roy. Were goin to prayer meetin. He always asks me for a date prayer meetin night, cause he knows pa says I got to go an it wont cost him nothin. I sure do miss you, Bill. I aint seen the inside of a picture show since my ticket to the Happyhour punched out. The man that preaches tonight has got a B.V.D. or somethin tacked on to the hind part of his name. I guess he didnt study out of one of them little Bibles like your mother gave you to carry in your pocket when you went to war. I bet he knows the big one plum through.I got them white carnations you sent me for Thanksgivin, but there must a been some mistake. The card says "Rest in Peace." I guess the florist got things mixed with the epidemick.

> Hoping you are the same,
> *Mable*

P.S. – Ma says keep your feet dry. Anybody can get it.

"BILL"

HUMOR OF

WORLD WAR II

World War II is now thought of as "the good war." The nation was truly united and solidly behind the President, the Congress and the Military throughout the hectic period of organization for war. And it was even more cohesive throughout the agonized prosecution of that war.

The over-riding factor cementing our unity was the clear recognition that the enemy was committed to world conquest motivated by a belief in the "genetic" right of one national group to rule absolutely over all groups outside that "genetically endowed" group. This was in direct opposition to every value, every ideal that the founding fathers cherished as irrevocable—the concept of the Declaration of Independence that "all men are created equal" and that they are endowed with the inalienable right to "life, liberty and the pursuit of happiness".

And so we went to war, unified as never before—or after.

The humor of the GI, in World War II, reflects his assurance, his buoyancy that he was fighting a decent, a righteous and moral war. It is an upbeat, bright, sharp and altogether delightful humor.

SHIPPING LIST

Scene; dawn. Location; military secret. Temperature; colder than a polar bear's pajamas.

A rasp-voiced Sergeant bellows lustily; "Answer 'here' when you name's called and take the mush outa yer mouth."

"Abrams, Ardovino, Brown, Blanding, Cosgrove, Dansino, De Soto, Davis, Epstein, Englehardt, Franchetti, Foley, Goulden, Gozocki, Hulse, Hunt, Ingoldsby, Inverarity, Jacobs, Jensen, Johnson, Kaidinoff, Kopp, Lopez, La France, Lazarro, Lyons, MacWhirter, McVey, Moe, Morse, Naas, Nielsen, Otto, Pedersen, Popolopus, Quan, Quigley, Radinsky, Rasmussen, Roe, Safarik, Samson, Sondergaared, Terwilliger, Twitt, Tyler, Ung, Urban, Van Zandt, Von Holt, Walters, West, Wolf, Xydias, Yee, Yong, Yonge, Young, Zabriskie, Zarro, Zolopoff."

Here's what you've been waiting for.
Ireland. England. Singapore.
You're on your way . . . and War is War.

When you're going, you do not know.
When you gotta go, you gotta go.
So, take it easy. Heigh-de-ho!

Where you're going, you can not tell.
It may be tough and it may be swell.
But you're going there. So what t'Hell!

You were sitting pretty . . . then quick as scat,
Orders came from the Big Brass Hat.
(*Life* is a whale of a lot like that)

It may be *thus* . . . it may be *so*.
Africa? Yes? Australia? No?
Iceland? MAYBE IT'S TOKIO.
Let's GO!

Don Blanding. PILOT BAILS OUT.
Dodd Meade & Co. N.Y. 1943

On patrol off the Philippines, the officer of the deck on the destroyer asked the starboard lookout what action he would take if a man fell overboard.

"Sir, I would yell, 'Man overboard!'"

Then the officer asked what he would do if an officer fell overboard.

For a time the sailor was silent, then he brightened and asked, "Which officer, sir?"

In a Marine office in the Pentagon there is a sign, remarkable for its keen observation of the situation in that building: "If you can keep your head when all about you are losing theirs, maybe you just don't understand the situation."

An Air Force officer, new to his base, went to the base library to write some letters. The librarian was a beautiful young member of Women in the Air Force, and the officer made repeated trips to her desk to ask for stationery, pen, envelopes, white-out and the like. In this way he was able to look her over from propeller to tail. When he went up for stamps, the pretty librarian handed him three!

"You're a mind reader," he said.

"Hardly," she said sardonically, "because, if I were, you'd be court-martialed."

"How was your date?" one girl asked her friend. "Wel-l-l, let me put it this way. He just got out of the Navy . . . you know . . . sort of a post-naval drip."

A veteran who had served four years with the military police was telling another veteran of his experiences. "After all," said the former MP, "we suffered more casualties than any other branch of the service."

"Of course you did!" sniffed the other veteran. "And why shouldn't you, with enemies on both sides."

They tell this story of that innovative genius, Admiral Rickover, father of the nuclear submarine. It seems that at New York's Belmont Park, a horse named after the Admiral won the sixth race.

Admiral Rickover commented, "That's a first. No other admiral in all history has ever had a whole horse named after him."

After the chaplain preached a most dramatic sermon on the Ten Commandments, one soldier was left in a most serious mood of self-examination.

"There's one redeeming feature," he said. "I've never made a graven image."

Capon Colonel – A specialist in civilian life, commissioned to do special army duty, as in preserving art captured or damaged in combat. The capon is a castrated rooster.

Cement City – A cemetery.

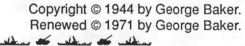

It is the annual custom that commanding officers make "efficiency" reports about officers in their command. Here are some examples:

This officer can express a sentence in three paragraphs at any time.

This officer is quiet, reserved, most careful, industrious and neat, but I refuse to have this officer as a member of my command.

Presented with any change in policy or procedure, this officer will offer the unlikely, hypothetical situation in which the change suggested cannot work.

Is always open to suggestion, most agreeable to it, but then never follows same.

He never makes the same mistakes twice, but this officer seems to have made them all once.

A group of GIs were receiving their many shots before going overseas. One of them asked for a glass of water and the administering officer asked if he felt like fainting.

"Nope," the GI replied. "I just want to see if I'm watertight."

An American pilot shot down over Europe awakened, after a long period of unconsciousness, in an English hospital. He blinked, looked around him and asked, "Where am I?"

"You're in the hospital," answered the nurse. "In jolly old England," she added in her cockney accent.

"Oh my! Did they send me here to die?"

"No, laddie, not a bit of it. You came here yesterdie . . . "

A young Air Force officer was chosen to bowl with a group of high-ranking officers. He was so nervous that he drank the Brigadier General's beer, smoked his cigarettes and mistakenly used the General's bowling ball.

"It's a good thing, Lieutenant," the General growled, "that you don't know where I live!"

LAMENT

I went for a Wac
With great velocity.
So sad: that lack
Of reciprocity.

– Tom Stack Y1c
Puptent Poets. Stars and Stripes

On his first day of retirement, a former master sergeant was asked, "How do you feel now that you've been retired?"

"Great! Just great because, when I joined the Army, I had

twenty dollars in my jeans. Today I have seventeen bucks. Now I ask you, where else can a man stay for over twenty years for only three dollars."

Private Al Myers, a furniture salesman all his life, told the following about his war years in the infantry.

"After one big action I went on leave," Myers said, "and I took it in Paris. Boy, was I eager for some action. Well, I wandered the streets looking for a playmate when I saw this mighty pretty girl sitting on a park bench. I didn't speak French and she didn't speak English, so I drew a picture of a taxi and she nodded 'yes'.

"We drove around a bit, then I drew a picture of two sets of dinnerware and she nodded again.

"So we had dinner. After that I drew a picture of the two of us dancing and she nodded. so we went to a swell French nightclub where, about midnight, I took her aside and we went to get our coats to take her home.

"I'd had enough, but she pulled me back into a chair and drew a big double bed! Well, I couldn't believe it. I hadn't hinted or anything and yet, somehow, that little ol' French gal knew that I was in the furniture business."

Weep for the fate of Sergeant Thin,
A man of desperate courage was he,
More he rejoiced in the battle's din,
Than in all the mess hall revelry;
But he died at last of no ugly gash –
He choked on the hair of his own mustache.
                                        – Henry Glassoford Bell

Among Marines, the Texans had the greatest pride and self-assurance that they could win the war much quicker if only Texas Marines were used. At any rate, a group of them was playing cards when the door burst open and another marine rushed in shouting, "A landing party of Japs just hit the beach."

"I'll go," said one Texas Marine, rising, stretching, yawning. "I'm dummy."

Anchor Clanker – A sailor.

Applesauce enema – To chew a man out. To "stick it to him" or up him in a gentle way so as to make him a better soldier without resentment.

Armored Diesel – A shot of whiskey, sugar and lemon juice.

The WACS and the WAVES were essential factors in the fighting and the winning of World War II. They had their Sad Sacks, too, and they called her Ginny the ninny.

"There's a song about her: Ginny the ninny of the first platoon."
Max Barsis. THEY'RE ALL YOURS UNCLE SAM.
Stephen Daye. 1943

The base psychiatrist, new at the job, received his first patient at the Army reception center and began questioning the draftee . . "Your name?"

"Sidney Mishigas."

"Age?"

"Twenty."

"And how do you feel about being drafted?"

"Wonderful! Doc, I could hardly wait to get in, to put on a uniform, eat in the same dining room with hundreds of other guys and get this great Army food. Then hit the sack early and get up at five o'clock and go again to the mess hall and get more of that superb food. Wow! It's the most exciting, fun, simply wonderful thing in the world!"

The psychiatrist was amazed and puzzled. "You must be crazy!" He disbelieved his own ears and looked wonderingly at the new soldier. "Man! You must be nuts!"

"Please, Doc. Write it down, just the way you said it!"

OBSERVATION

The things in life we deem most delectable
Are all too often "unrespectable."

– S-Sgt. Gary Wilcox
Puptent Poets. The Stars and Stripes

It was a hot battle in the Pacific during which an American pilot landed his plane on an aircraft carrier. He climbed out of the plane, began pulling his jacket off, and told about the flights he had had that day.

"Well, you won't believe it, skipper, but I had me one helluva day. Sank a Jap tanker, shot down four Jap planes and got off a good solid hit on a battleship. Yep! One helluva day."

Just as he got his jacket over his head, he heard a voice behind him say, "Velly, velly good, Mr. Yank. But you make one velly bad mistake."

A sailor hurt his foot and had to go to the naval hospital to have an x-ray. When the job was done he was told to sit in the reception room and wait for the report.

Shortly afterwards, a lady with a small child came in and sat down. An orderly gave the sailor a large pill, then took the mother and child back to the physician.

The sailor walked to the drinking fountain, swallowed the pill and returned to his seat. A bit later the orderly appeared with a large pan of water.

"Okay, sailor," he said, "just put that large pill I gave you into this pan and we'll soak that foot of yours."

During operations in the Far East, our officer of the deck glanced up and noticed that the No. 2 periscope of our submarine was in a dangerous raised position. He yelled down the conning tower, "Hey, Quartermaster, get crackin' and . . . and . . . and house the scope!"

"Just fine, thank you, Sir, just fine," was the reply.

A recently inducted sailor lost his weapon while on the rifle range. He was told that he'd have to pay for it. "What!" he screamed! "Suppose I was driving a 2 1/2 ton truck and some jerk stole it. Would you make me pay for that, too?"

"Yep! Sure would," was the reply.

"I'll be damned," said the new sailor. "Well, anyway, now I know why the captain always goes down with his ship."

A WAVE was home on leave and recounting her experiences. "They told me," she related, "that I should say 'Yes, sir!' all day and 'No, sir!' all night."

An Italian emigrated to the United States, served the necessary time here and, finally, became a citizen. He practiced his craft of tailoring until drafted into the Army where he was assigned to a camp where the accounts were in a fretful mess. He was put on special duty, freed of all training assignments and told to get to work. After a month, his commanding officer discovered he had done no work on the messed up books. The angry officer demanded to know why.

"I'm sorry, sir, but I didn't know how. I'd 've made things worse."

"Then why in hell did you list yourself as a C.P.A.?"

"Because that's my work, the way I earn a living – Cleaning, Pressing and Alterations."

"Take off yer hat when ya mention sex here.
It's a reverint subject."
Bill Mauldin. THE BRASS RING.
W.W. Norton. N.Y. 1971

A farm boy, only recently inducted into the service, was the butt of many practical jokes. But he was smarter than the boys knew. At any rate, one night when he was on guard duty, the men planned to play a joke on him. They got an officer to help them play the game, then had the officer approach the gate where the country lad was on guard duty.

As the officer approached, the guard called out, "Halt. Who goes there?" according to regulations.

"General Christ," answered the officer.

"Oh, yeah," responded the country kid. "In that case advance and give the Sermon on the Mount."

"The Army ain't changed a danged bit in spite of what the papers been asayin' about it," said a soldier recently relieved from service. "The Army ain't changed a bit. You still do just like they orders you to do and when they say 'eyes right!' by God, them officers expect to hear 'em click!"

A GI was given extra duty for reporting late to roll call. His punishment: to move a truckload of potatoes, by hand, from the unloading dock to the mess hall. Immediately he complained of a bad back and reported on sick call. The kind M.D. took pity on him and wrote a note excusing him from carrying anything heavier than a few pounds.

Elated, the GI rushed to his sergeant who read the note, looked skeptically at the soldier and said, "OK. You win. So you'll move the stack two potatoes at a time . . . one in each hand . . . until the whole damned stack is relocated."

Two old friends at home on leave met at a base recreation center. After greetings, the one said, "Y'know, at our base it's just like home. We pray before every meal."

"Not at ours. Nope. We got a good mess sergeant."

The sergeant was fed up with the recruit who never seemed to follow drill instructions. To punish him he said, "See that red light out yonder. Now, soldier, you run to that light and back and maybe you'll follow instructions better after that."

So the soldier took off. Three weeks passed before he returned and reported to the sergeant. The soldier's eyes were red, his clothing filthy dirty, and he was unshaven and exhausted.

"Where the hell have you been, soldier," the sergeant demanded.

"Well, you sent me to run to that red light and back. The only trouble was . . . it wasn't no traffic light, it was a truck and I ran after it all the way to Milwaukee before I realized what it was."

A towheaded country boy reported to the recruiting sergeant and prepared to answer questions. "What are you called," the sergeant asked.

"Byminishils," the kid replied.

The sergeant looked, "What was that? Say that again."

"Byminishils."

"You mean to tell me that's your name?"

"No, it shore ain't. You didn't ax me name. You axed whut I'm called. And I don tol' ya . . . I'm called by my 'nitials."

A lieutenant was explaining the latest devices in chemical warfare to his commanding general. "General, sir, this is mighty powerful stuff. One teaspoonful of it can wipe a billion people off the face of the earth . . . OOOPS!"

The army chaplain was giving the soldiers a heart-to-heart talk to encourage them. "You shouldn't worry," he advised them. "The worst thing that can happen is that you get killed. But then your home will be in heaven, men, a wonderful home in heaven."

"Maybe so, Chaplain," one of the men remarked. "But I ain't been homesick. Not . . . one . . . bit."

An infantry battalion was at maneuvers in the field, doing camouflage exercises. The officers were delighted that the camouflage was so effective. Then suddenly, a soldier camouflaged as a tree yelled wildly and tore off his disguise of bark branches and leaves.

His officer ran to him and ordered the soldier to report to the commanding officer's tent. Once there, the C.O. said, "had you acted like that you might have got the entire battalion killed."

"I'm sure sorry, sir," the soldier replied.

"You should be! But tell me this . . . what the devil caused this irresponsible conduct. What!"

"Well, Sir," the soldier said contritely, "there I was, a picture of immobility and disguise. Then a danged woodpecker started pecking away at my arm. That didn't bother me. Soon a dog came along, sniffed me all over and then pissed all over my leg. I could stand all that. I managed to stay immobile until some squirrels came along, ran up my pants leg and started prying around my groin. and even that didn't move me, not until one of them said, 'Let's take the one for chow now and save the other for winter!' "

"It was an awful winter in France. To keep his infantry men from freezing, the officer in charge of the company decided to quarter his troops in the nearby village.

The first place he decided on was a grocery store. The owner had a large family but was decent enough to take on one soldier.

"Wonderful!" exclaimed the officer. "I'll leave Private Cox with you. He's the shortest man we got and will take up the least room."

At the next village, the officer stopped his company in front of what was an obvious brothel. He knocked on the door.

When the madam appeared the officer explained that his men needed war beds for the night. "If you could accommodate my soldiers, I'd sure be grateful, ma'am."

Worried for fear the Americans would overwhelm her girls, the madam asked, "How many you got?"

"Thirty," he replied, "without Cox."

"In that case," the madam said, sighing with relief, "Come right in."

A recent theory about the superiority of our communications in World War II dealt with the whys and wherefores. One theory advanced was that American scientists crossed a carrier pigeon with a woodpecker, and this produced a messenger-bird that not only delivered messages but knocked on the door!

Rabbi Israel Walters tells of when he served as an army chaplain during World War II. Part of his job entailed working with soldiers in Ward Eight, the "psycho ward."

"One evening, upon leaving the hospital, I walked to my car and noticed that one of the tires was flat. I jacked up the car, pulled the tire and put the nuts in the hubcap. But I tripped on the hubcap and the nuts rolled out, over to, and then through an iron grill above the sewer. I didn't know what to do about the loss when suddenly I heard one of the men from Ward Eight.

"Chaplain, sir," he called through the chain link fence, "why don't you take one nut off each of the other three wheels and use them on the fourth? That should do you until you drive to a service station."

"Great idea, soldier," I exclaimed. "How come you thought of that?"

"Well, sir, you see it's this away. I may be crazy but I ain't stupid."

DIARY OF A NURSE

I dreamed I'd see this country,
If I ever had the luck;
But in my wildest fancies,
It was never made by truck.

Nurse Nightingale before us
Carried candles through the mist;
The modern maid of Mercy
Totes a helmet in her fist.

Nostalgic waves encompass me
Though I'm still patriotic;
Tonight, my dear, I long to see
A land that ain't exotic . . .

–Lt. Rose C. Craig,
Puptent Poets. Stars and Stripes

Once upon a time there was a wild and woolly drill sergeant who got mad as all get out when one of his recruits had slept beyond reveille. The sergeant called the squad to attention and bellowed, "Private Jones, step wha-hun step forward."

Private Jones stepped.

"All right, Mister Beauty Sleep Jones. From now on you will *rise* and *shine* at five ayem. Ya understand that? and, by God, y'll be there if I got to feed ya a pound of *yeast* and a bucket of shoe polish every dadblamed night."

One of the young fellows reported at the draft center for his preinduction physical. He carried huge bundles, endless pages of medical records, doctor's certificates, statements from nurses in various schools.

The induction officer leafed through the material and then asked, "Tell me, young man, just how did you get to the center here? By ambulance?"

During a course of study on explosives at Lowry Air Force Base, Colorado, the students were learning the tough job of removing fuses from live bombs and other explosives. They had been at the job for many trying, nerve-wracking days when one soldier, a particularly nasty and obnoxious one, asked the

sergeant, "Isn't there an easier way to learn all this?"
"Yep. There is . . . for you . . . the trial and error method."

One hot July day at Fort Bliss, Texas, the infantry was going through the last phase of training, which entailed a long march through the desert with full field pack. The sun grew hotter and the packs heavier. Finally, the Sergeant announced a five-minute break. One GI turned to his buddy and said, "I figure this pack weighs not less than a ton. A full ton, man."

His buddy glanced at him, shrugged and said, "What did you forget?"

You may think that the Army does not consider civilian expertise when assigning new recruits to their units. Just consider the new soldier who had been a funeral director and embalmer in civilian life. The Army classification office did a fine job of considering the past experience of this soldier. They assigned him to the Fort Bragg dead letter office.

At a Marine training base, the drill instructor was a true, hard-nosed non-commissioned officer. He strutted back and forth before the new troops standing at rigid attention before him. "Now you men get this and don't forget it!" he growled. "My name is Sergeant Stone and I'm one helluva lot harder than my name. If any of you has any idea of crossing me, you'd goddam well better bow out now or you'll regret every last minute of the three months you'll spend here."

Then he marched up the line of rigid troops, asking the name of each man. When he reached the smallest lad in the line, there was only silence. "C'mon, private, speak up. Or do you want trouble! What's your name? Tell me! What's . . . your . . . name?'

The poor guy murmured, "Stonebreaker, sir."

HAPPY SOLDIERS

It's easy to pick California soldiers,
They are not in the least downhearted;
They're smiling because they're right at home,
Now that the autumn rains have started.

— Cpl. Harry P. Volk
Puptent Poets. The Stars and Stripes

Sad Sack

"Sad Sack" is an Army term,
Signifying you're a germ.
Though "jerk" conveys a mental lack
There's nothing sadder than a "Sack."

— Pvt. Frank Robichaud

THE GOLDBRICK

Stripe-Assed Ape – A mythical critter that moved at unbelievable speed; as, "we took off quick as a herd of stripe-assed apes."

Two GIs, buddies in combat and wounded, were at a base hospital for treatment. They'd been in the South Pacific for almost two years and hadn't seen a girl in most of that time. What a joy it was when they were greeted by a pretty army nurse. They looked her over from top to bottom, then bottom to top.

"Well," the nurse remarked, "is everything just as you remembered it?"

The captain of the ship looked over his crew and began to lecture them. "In this man's navy, we don't say, this isn't *my* ship . . . this isn't *your* ship. We say it's *our* ship. Got that?"

From the crew lined up for the lecture there floated a voice: "Good. Let *us* sell it."

A GI was giving his report of an accident to the MP station. "There I was, driving along, minding my own business when all at once a drunk came down the road and bang! He smashed right into me."

"And how did you know he was drunk?" he was asked.

"He had to be, Sir. Why the bastard was adrivin' a tree!"

POSTSCRIPT

Two things I'll miss this winter
As I shiver in my sack,
Are your cold feet implanted
In the middle of my back.

— S-Sgt. Gray Wilcox Jr.
Puptent Poets. Stars and Stripes

The wife of a submarine commander gave birth to a baby girl while her husband was on duty in the Pacific. She sent him a cable: "Ahoy, skipper. Brand new craft launched at seven bells. Tonnage is seven pounds and there's no periscope. All shipshape. That is all. We hope. Love, Nancy."

Mothers with sons away at war were often angered at the sight of other young men in comfortable jobs and security at home. One, driving through the country one day, noticed a young man milking a cow. She stopped the car and went up the the busy milker and demanded, "Young man, why aren't you at the front like my son?"

"They ain't no milk at that end, ma'am."

An Alabama country boy was driving hell-bent for election to the rear as a fierce battle went on behind him. It was night and as he careened along he saw a soldier in the road trying to flag him down. He screeched to a halt to give the GI a lift, but was terrified to see that the man was a brigadier general.

"Why are you speeding to the rear, soldier?" the officer demanded.

"Suh, mah officer done tol' me thet ah waz too valooble a man to be wasted back theah, so he tol' me to go to the reah."

"That doesn't sound right, soldier. Do you know who I am?"

"No suh."

"I am General Rogers! In command here."

"Well I be dognabbed," the soldier said. "Ah nevuh woulda figgered Ah could git so far back so fast in so shoat a time."

WAR SUMMARY

Hostilities
Aren't subtleties.

That's all chum,
That's the po-um.

— Lt. David E. Eiener.
Puptent Poets. Stars and Stripes

Up Your Ass With Bugs And Gas – The poetic cognomen of the Nuclear, Biological and Chemical Warfare Experts.

WAC Quarters – Wackery, wackshack, hen pen, chicken house.

Zigzag – Sexual intercourse.

COME STA?

Felice is happy, *triste* is sad,
Buono is good and *cattivo* is bad;
Male is ill, *bene* is well,
Morto is dead and *war* is hell!

— Pvt. Clyde Hermann

Perhaps the most famous cartoon of World War II

Bill Mauldin THE BRASS RING
W.W. Norton, N.Y. 1971

A newcomer to a remote island in the South Pacific found the days passing slowly. But he never realized just how slow time passed there until he casually asked the time of a veteran out there.

"July," was the reply.

Private Edger was a constant and always successful gambler. He would bet on anything! But his gambling was having a demoralizing influence on his unit. The captain could not cure him and sent him to the battalion C.O. After that interview, with reprimands and instructions from the battalion commander, the latter sent for the captain and told him, "I think I've cured Private Edger of his gambling habit . . . I've shown him he CAN lose a bet. I asked him why he couldn't stop betting and he said, 'Sir, it's compulsive, a habit I can't ever seem to lose. Like now. I'll bet you fifty bucks that you have a mole on your right shoulder.' I knew I didn't have one there so I took off my shirt and proved it to him. He grinned sheepishly and paid me fifty bucks. I think now he won't try to gamble ever again!"

"Sir, I think you're wrong. My guess is that he will gamble again."

"How can you be so sure?"

"Because Private Edger bet me one hundred bucks that he'd have the shirt off your back within fifteen minutes after he met with you."

At West Point, they tell the story of one cadet in a class of engineering drawing. He kept embellishing his work with all sorts of – what he thought of as – artistic creations. For example, after drawing a picture of a bridge over a stream, he put on the bridge two quite artfully drawn children. The instructor curtly demanded that he remove the children from the bridge. He did so but . . . .

The next time the instructor examined the cadet's drawing he found that the children had, indeed, been removed but only to the river bank. "Now listen!" the instructor yelled, "you get rid of those children Now!"

On his next time around to inspect the cadet's drawing he discovered that the children had been done away with. In their place were two tiny tombstones.

After a long, grueling day, the tough drill sergeant remarked to the worn-our recruit, "I reckon that you'll make a special trip to my grave when I die. You probably hate me so damned much."

"No, sir! Not me, Sergeant, 'cause when I get out of here I ain't never gonna stand in line again!"

Cannon Rocker – An artilleryman.

Rear Guard Rangers – Same as canteen commandoes. GIs stationed in the rear, yet posing as tough, front line troops.

"I don't care HOW Washington crossed the Delaware!
Sit down!"
Dave Breger. DAVE BREGER IN BRITAIN.
Pilot Press, London, 1944

AWAKENING

The purple night has flown into the West,
And in the East young Phoebus starts anew
His journey, and the pearls of evening dew
Begin to vanish from the Earth's green breast;
In country ways the cock crows far and wide,
As from their sleep return the hosts of day,
Nocturnal creatures cease their work of play,
The chilly owl seeks his lair to hide'
Where darkness slept will come the shine
Of light on metal, and the voice of men,
To laugh and boast of petty deeds again,
Or start to seek more laughter and more wine
And rousing all, the Sergeant's thundrous shout:
"All right, youse lousy bums, I said 'Fall out.' "
— T-5 Harold P. Williams
Puptent Poets. The Stars and Stripes

A truly tough sergeant said to a new recruit, "Just what in hell were you, man, before you got drafted?"

"Happy, sir, mighty happy!"

The troops were entertained on one special occasion by an all-girl chorus. After the concert, the leader approached the C.O. of the base and asked if they might have dinner on the base.

"Sure," said the C.O. "Would you girls enjoy to mess with the officers or the enlisted men, this evening?"

"Either would be just fine, Sir, but we'd like to eat first."

They tell the story of one very innocent draftee who, on his first day, was given a comb. The next day the army barber sheared off his hair. A few days later he was given a toothbrush and the next day the dentist pulled four teeth. Later he was given a jockstrap and was never seen on that base again.

There are four rules concerning duty in an officers' mess hall. All recruits would do well to memorize and always put to good use these rules.

1. If it moves, salute it.
2. If it doesn't move, sweep it up.
3. If it's too big to sweep it up, pick it up.
4. If it's too big to pick up, paint it.

Here's one to remember: If you think old soldiers just fade away, try getting into your old Army uniform.

The supply sergeant asked the recruit how his new uniform fit.

The recruit replied, "Just fine. But one thing . . . them trousers are jist a smidgen tight around the armpits!"

The mess officer had received many complaints about the bread served in the enlisted men's mess. "Listen," he finally snapped at the soldiers, "you guys don't know when you're well-off. Why, if Napoleon had had such good bread as that, he'd have been pleased as punch!"

"Yes sir!" rejoined one soldier. "But it was fresh then."

SNAFU – A WWII phrase that appears to be immortal: Situation normal . . . all fucked up!

To Snap Shit – To be told to get on with it, as, "Snap shit, soldier! We ain't got all day."

⚓ ✠ ⚓ ✠ ⚓ ✠ ⚓

An officer about to go on active duty received a wire from the medical board. "Regret to inform you that tests show you have contracted tuberculosis and have serious heart trouble."

This notice was followed a day later with another telegram. "Please disregard our last wire. We confused your record with another."

The pleased officer wired to them, "Sorry, but I got your correction too late. I committed suicide two hours ago."

⚓ ✠ ⚓ ✠ ⚓ ✠ ⚓

At Wright Field, Private Edwardo Sokolnik gave his newborn son a middle name: Furlough.

⚓ ✠ ⚓ ✠ ⚓ ✠ ⚓

A marine stationed far in the Pacific, received a note from his fiancee asking him to return her picture because she was going to marry a 4-F civilian. He was so depressed that his buddies all tried to help him.

They collected all the pin up girls, snapshots and photographs they could lay their hands on. They piled the pictures into a huge crate and shipped them to the fickle female.

when the gal opened the crate, she found a note that read: "Do find the photo of you and return the others to me. Sorry, it sure is embarrassing, but I can't recall which one is yours."

⚓ ✠ ⚓ ✠ ⚓ ✠ ⚓

An army corporal in the field artillery asked for an immediate furlough, because his wife was going to have a baby. Permission was given and when all the furlough papers were ready, the officer-in-charge asked exactly when the baby was due.

"Approximately nine months after I get home, sir," was the reply.

⚓ ✠ ⚓ ✠ ⚓ ✠ ⚓

Fart Sack – Bedroll or bed where a GI sleeps.

Fire In The Hole – Venereal disease – in a woman. Or, simply, V.D.

Flub The Dub – Foul up, louse up the deal, blunder.

Take a Flying Fuck At A Rolling Doughnut – Go to hell! Go dry up! Go piss up a rope!

Fort – Permanent installation that GIs disrespectfully join to similar-sounding name, as Fort Swill (Fort Sill, Oklahoma), Fort Uterus (Fort Eustis, Virginia), Fort Lost-in-the-Woods (Fort Leonard Wood, Missouri).

NIGHT CAPPED

A GI who camped near bologna
Sent home to his wife a kimogna
she wrote him next week
And called him a sneak —
For it reeked with Eau de Cologna.

— S-Sgt. James I. Goodrich.
Puptent Poets. Stars and Stripes

A cavalry officer from Texas arrived at the pearly gates and found things to be just as had been reported. A receiving angel took charge of him and asked him if there was anything he wanted.

"Yep, shore is. Y'know, I always liked choir music. So if y'all would be so kind, I'd like to have ten thousand sopranos. Could you arrange that?"

"No problem. You got them. Anything else?"

"Give me ten thousand alto voices to go along with them sopranos."

"Right. You got 'em, too. Anything else?"

"Wal-l-l, as you know, now I'll need ten thousand tenors. And that'll be enough for right now."

"You mean to not ask for the bass singers? Won't you need ten thousand for your choir?"

"Nope. I'll sing bass."

A young chaplain and his senior in the service were having a friendly argument over denominational matters.

"Let's not argue anymore, Captain Brown. We shouldn't argue over such matters. After all is said and done, aren't we both busy in the Lord's work?"

"We certainly are, Major Smith. That's for sure!" said the junior chaplain, completely won over.

"Well, then, let's both do our work to the best of our talents and ability. You do it in your way and I'll do it in His."

FINALE

As can be told by any fule
During the joyous season of yule
You bring in the log, open the bottle,
There's no telling happen what"ll.

— T-5 Hal Travis
Puptent Poets. Stars and Stripes.

In formation for drill, the sergeant marched up to Private Jenkins and demanded to know why he had not shaved.

"Why, you mean to say I ain't shaved?" Jenkins said.

"You sure as hell ain't, man, and I want to know why!"

"Well, the only thing I can figure is that while I was shaving this morning, alongside about a dozen other guys, all using the same long mirror, well, damn it, I must have shaved somebody else."

"The story is out that you were court-martialed in the Army. Is that a fact?"

"Yes. I'd only been in the service a few months when I got that deadly alphabet habit."

"Alphabet habit? I don't understand."

"Well, you see, it was like this. I went A.W.O.L."

"Yeah. And what was the sentence when you got back?"

"Same old alphabet deal . . . J.A.I.L."

"Did you serve in the Army in World War II?"

"Yep! Sure did. Four years."

"Get a commission?"

"Nope. Just the regular salary."

"I hear you got kicked out of the Army. Any truth to it?"

"It's true. I got bounced out for taking a furlong."

"Furlong? You mean furlough, don't you?"

"No. Like I said, it was a furlong. I went too fur and stayed too long."

The Goldbrick

The Goldbrick really hates to work
And every detail tries to shirk
But here's the joke, and listen well,
In ducking jobs, he works like hell!

                    Puptent Poets. The Stars and Stripes

Then there was a certain call girl who was picked up just outside Kelly Field, Texas. Why? Well, the report said she was contributing to the delinquency of a major.

All army doctors hold the rank of first lieutenant . . . or better . . . except for one physician who is a private first class. He made the mistake of giving the commanding officer of the base a thermometer and telling him what he could do with it.

Two GIs were bragging about their service outfits back in the good old days. "Why, man, my outfit was so well-trained," the one old soldier said, "that when those guys presented arms you could hear the snap, pop and click and nothing else."

"That's not so much," said the other man. "Why, when my outfit presented arms the sound of their slap, pop and jingle was deafening."

"What was that jingle?" asked the first GI.

"Just the sound of our medals," replied the other man.

The country boy was being given his first physical examination. He passed everything. All that remained was the urine test.

"I want you to pee in one of those little bottles on that shelf over there at the side of the room."

"Would you repeat that, sir," the young man said.

"Just urinate in one of those small bottles over there on the shelf at the side of the room," repeated the physician.

"Sir, you can't really mean that . . . I got to do it all the way from here?"

Advice to GIs who enter latrines:
a. GIs with short rifles had best stand within firing range.
b. Ballplayers with short bats please stand close to the plate.
c. Pilots who have short engine mounts would be well advised to taxi up close.

At a battalion reunion, one of the officers was bragging about the skill of his men. "Our boys demolished eight bridges, destroyed three ammunition dumps and completely demolished a key military installation. Then we were sent overseas."

It seems that a high ranking general officer of the U.S. Marine Corps was invited to go hunting on the estate of a very important English nobleman, a duke. After the hunt he reported that he had bagged an animal unlike any he had ever seen before.

"Why, it had the biggest shoulders I've ever seen, a helluva long nose, droopy ears and an enormous rear."

"Good gad, Sir, you've just shot the Duchess!" exclaimed the Duke.

A high ranking officer, terribly disliked by everyone, returned to the ship much the worse for booze. He staggered to the gangplank, swerved half the way and suddenly lurched over the side.

The crew was tickled pink. Then a boatswain yelled, "You gobs! Don't just stand there and do nothing. Somebody throw him an anchor."

An older man was trying to enlist in the Army. He was asked if there were any peculiarities the Army ought to know about.

"Well," the ambitious middle-ager said, "I'm the father of twelve kids and, yes, I am a confirmed nudist and proud of it."

"Nudist? Nudist?" the sergeant sneered. "Hell, man, you just never had time to dress."

On sick call, a recruit heard two old timers discuss the medical officer in charge.

"That old boy don't kid around none," said one veteran. "Fellow came in here the other day saying he had ptomaine poisoning. So the Doc, he up and cuts off his toe."

"I heard about that." said the other soldier. "And did you hear about the guy with erysipelas? The Doc cut off his ears."

Upon hearing this, the recruit seemed to have turned green. "I got to get out of here," he moaned, "I've got asthma!"

For many years and until the end of World war II, it was generally believed that black soldiers did not make good combat troops. This unfair canard was finally, belatedly dispelled and gave rise to many stories that combine the prejudice with the reasons for the end of it.

A white officer who had doubts about the combat ability of the black unit he commanded, got an order to storm an entrenched German position. He put the unit into the line and sent the blacks on the attack. The attack was successful and, after it was over, the officer-in-charge interrogated a German prisoner.

"Your men seemed not to fight very hard," the officer said. "Otherwise we'd never have taken you."

"But we did," responded the German officer. "We fought like hell. Harder than my men have ever had to fight."

"What happened to your automatic weapons?"

"Nothing. We used them all the time. And hard."

"And you used poison gas, too. Damn you."

"Had to and that didn't stop them. But it did have a remarkable effect on your soldiers. It turned them black and made their hair kinky."

A black sentry on duty heard someone approach.

"Halt! Who goes there," he sang out.

"Colonel Peters," a voice answered

"Advance and be recognized, sir."

Colonel Peters walked up to the sentry, snatched his rifle from his hands and stepped back. He looked contemptuously at the black sentry and sneered, "A hell of a soldier you are! Just look at you. Helpless!"

"Colonel," responded the sentry. "Anybody so much as lifts that rifle to shoot'll find it ain't even loaded. But this here .38 pacifier I got in my shirt . . . see it now? Well, I'll tell ya this much . . . it AM sure as hell loaded."

A WAAC unit had recently arrived in the theater of operations. The commanding officer of the base advised the head of the unit that she restrict her girls after duty hours. "Or else there'll be trouble."

"Not with my wonderful girls," said the WAAC leader. "Those girls of mine are plenty savvy. They got it all and it's up here," she said, tapping her head.

"Listen to me" demanded the officer. "I don't give a damn where your girls have it. My men will find it! Restrict them."

"I need a couple guys what don't owe me no money
fer a little routine patrol."

Bill Mauldin. UP FRONT
Henry Holt & Co. 1945

"Now read those letters on that chart," demanded the draft board physician.

"Wel-l-l, y'know, I can't see any chart," the draftee said happily.

"You got it just right. There isn't any chart and you are 1-A!"

On leave I didn't lose one bit of time
when with my date, sweet Nancy.
She surely was a lovely lass,
and surely caught my fancy,
But soon my red hot ardor cooled,
and only regret lingers.
She had a wooden leg, y'know, and I got splinters in my fingers.

A chaplain and five officers were on leave, seated on the train and discussing this and that. When hungry, they rose to enter the dining car and the chaplain took the aisle seat in the dining car. The train lurched suddenly causing the waiter to spill a bowl of hot soup on the chaplain.

"I sure would appreciate it, fellows," the chaplain ground out between gritted teeth, "if one of you would grit your teeth and yell a few words appropriate to this occasion."

RESPECTFULLY SUGGESTED

A happier way, it's one of my tenets,
Of answering all of our gripes,
Is to cut apart some second lieutenants.
And pass them around – as stripes.

– T-5 John Radosta.
Puptent Poets. Stars and Stripes

Private Edwards displayed very erratic behavior almost every day. His sergeant took the lad to the base hospital and reported: "Private Edwards spends most of the day picking up odds and ends of papers around the base . . . ."

He paused and nodded to the doctor to observe the soldier going through the waste basket examining each piece of paper. "See that? He does that kind of thing all day long, sir."

The medical officer called the sergeant over and whispered a few words to him, after which the sergeant left to get the soldier's discharge papers.

"Sure sorry, Private Edwards," the physician said later, "but you'll be better off with this" he said, handing him his discharge papers.

"At last!" yelled Private Edwards. "Finally, I've found it!"

The men were in line for inspection. The captain walked in review, checking them before the base commander arrived to make a closer inspection. He stopped before one soldier. "Where's your bayonet, soldier?"

"Darn. Left it at the barracks, sir."

"Get it! Now!" ordered the captain.

"Yes sir!" responded the soldier and he ran to his barracks and returned with bayonet in place.

"Good," said the captain. "But where's your helmet?"

"Darn it, sir, I must have set it down and, in my hurry, forgot to get it."

"Get it now. And be quick about it."

The soldier returned with his helmet. "That's better," said the C.O. "Can't you remember anything, soldier? What goes with you? What did you do in civilian life?"

"I was a plumber, sir," replied the GI.

I've gone to six or seven schools
And learned an awful lot.
I'm an expert in almost everything,
I'm a Johnny-on-the-Spot.
But there's one thing I do not know,
It really bothers me:
What else is there for me to do
To make a P. F. C.?

Pvt. Phil Krutchik. Stars and Stripes

The draftees had been in the Army for scarcely a week and were having a difficult time mastering the manual of arms. They were exceedingly awkward and the sergeant in charge was losing patience. Suddenly he noticed one soldier just standing in line, doing nothing, his rifle at his side.

"Soldier, what in hell are you doing, just standing there and not moving?"

"Sir, I'm just kind of standing by waiting till you decide just which shoulder you want this rifle to rest on."

"Does anybody here know how to do shorthand?" asked the sergeant. Four men stepped forward.

"Good. Mighty fine. Now if you men will get your ass over to the mess hall, they'll be pleased. They're shorthanded."

A wounded soldier lay on his hospital bed. His head was deeply bound in bandages, his eyes and ears were covered. Only his nose and mouth were exposed.

"You poor fellow," moaned a sweet old lady, "how sad. Did they hit you in the head?"

"No, madam, they did not. They hit me in the leg, but the darned bandage keeps slipping up."

There is a rumor going the rounds that PFC means, "Praying For Corporal."

The elderly mother of a new Marine was visiting him when she met a young officer.

"What's your job here, captain?" she asked.

"I'm a naval doctor," he answered.

"Well, I do declare," murmured the elderly lady. "They have specialists for just about everything these days, don't they."

"Bet ya never saw a medal like this one I got on. It's very special," said the soldier to his girl.

"Right. I never have seen one like it," she replied. "What did you do to get it?" she asked breathlessly.

"I saved my entire outfit," he replied.

"How wonderful. How'd you do it?"

"Shot the mess sergeant."

"And that durned bullet went right through here," said the GI, pointing to his chest.

"But it must have gone right through your heart," she gasped.

"You could say that," said the GI.

"I don't understand. Then how come you're not dead?"

"Well, y'see, when it happened my heart was in my mouth."

It's an odd thing but whenever the subject of parachutes not opening at the jump comes up, everybody laughs like crazy. Consider this one:

The paratrooper asked his sergeant what to do if his parachute failed to open after jumping.

The sergeant replied, "That's easy. Just take the chute back to the supply room and get yourself another one."

It must have been the same paratrooper who, later asked what would happen if the *second* chute did not open.

"You use your emergency chute," replied the sergeant.

"OK," nodded the paratrooper. "But what happens when I land?"

"There'll be a truck waiting to pick you up."

And so, after weeks of training, the trooper got on the plane and, on command, jumped. He pulled the rip-cord but nothing happened. He remembered instructions and pulled the emergency chute's rip-cord. Still nothing happened. Then recalling instructions, he said to himself, "by god, I'll just bet that blamed truck won't be there, either."

Circular File – A waste basket.

Cocksucker Bread – French bread. The same notion-association calls French toast, what else, *cocksucker toast*.

Creamed Foreskins – Creamed chip beef on toast.

Cue Ball – Bald head.

An Alabama soldier really yearned for his girl. After basic training, he tried every trick he knew to get a pass to visit her. But he was refused at every attempt. Finally, in desperation, he swiped some civilian clothes, put them on and tried to bluff his way past the guard at the gate.

But the guard was experienced. He knew a flim-flam try when he saw it, and refused the soldier.

Nothing said could sway that guard until, finally, the soldier pulled a long knife from his belt and said, "Soldier, Ah knows you is doin' yore duty and Ah respects you for it. You're adoin' yore duty as ya sees it. But me, Ah got me a Mama in heaven, my Papa's in hell, and the sweetest li'l old gal in the world is jes' ten minutes from heah in town. An Ah says this to ya, soldier! Ah aims to see one of dem befo' mawnin'."

They tell the story of a GI who had had too many drinks. He staggered his way back to the base but ran into a tree. And again. And again, that same tree. Ten times he ran into that same tree. "Oh Lord," he moaned, "save me from this fuckin forest."

But this soldier was no more befuddled than the sailor, drunk as a lord and staggering his way back to his ship. He, too, ran into a tree. But this tree was protected by an iron tree-guard. Cautiously, he felt his way around it twice. Then one more time.

Then he slumped to the ground saying, "Oh me, oh my! Locked in again."

It was winter but the U.S.O. troupe still managed to perform with wonderful dancers. This one battalion had marched back from the lines for a little rest and recreation. They eagerly awaited the performance of the lightly clad girls.

The commanding officer felt sorry for the girls so he asked, "Are there mackintoshes among you men that I could borrow to keep these young ladies warm?"

"No," was the reply from one of the assembled men. "But we sure as hell have some Smiths and Browns and Joneses willing to try to replace them."

"Captain," reported the first scout," I want to report that in those woods ahead of us there are six German soldiers."

"O.K., Corporal. I want you to get your ass over there and bring those heinies out. Now!"

"I'll do it, Captain, but if you see a bunch of men running out of those woods, for Pete's sake don't shoot the first one."

"Don't shoot," cried the Panzer Division soldier. "Please, please! I haf got ein vife und dree childer."

"Too hell with that crap!" shouted the GI. "But I will remember your widow and three orphans!"

(This macabre story has been told in every war Americans have fought.)

Two soldiers had promised one another that if either was wounded, the other would carry him to the aid station. Well, this one soldier was hit in the leg and asked his friend to take him to the aid station. His buddy put the wounded man on his shoulder and started off. En route a shell took off the head of his buddy, but the walking soldier was unaware of it. He passed an officer.

"Where are you taking that man, soldier?" the officer asked.

"To the aid station. He's got a bad bullet wound in his leg."

"His leg? You're nuts. His head is shot off."

The soldier set down his burden and surveyed his headless friend. "Damn him." said the GI, "He always was a liar."

PEEP HOLE SIGHTS
IF YOU SEE THE FOLLOWING:

"Sign the Pledge"

"Call the C.O."

"Take An Aspirin"

"Hold Your Fire"

"SQUEEZE TRIGGER – DON'T MISS!"

THE WAR MAKES MEN, AND OTHER ASSORTED PRODUCTS

When war is through, they notify us,
The Army means to un-GI us,
For, after all this rough campaigning,
We'll need civilian basic training.

I never thought they'd undermined me
So bad that now they have to find me!
I have to be repatriated
Before I'm re-United Stated!

        – Pfc. Henry B. Mackey
    Puptent Poets. The Stars and Stripes

"I don't mind the shell with my number on it. That's not what's bothering me!" one soldier said to his buddy. "Nope, that one doesn't bother me at all. It's the one that has written on it, 'To Whom It May Concern!' that worries me."

The American sailor was proud of his tattoos. For a friend, he removed his shirt to show the wonderful tattooed art on his chest.

"Beautiful," exclaimed his friend. "You have the American flag tattooed on your chest to lead you."

The sailor turned around.

"Wow! Uncle Sam on your back. Swell! You got the flag on your chest to lead you and Uncle Sam to back you up. Who could ask for anything more?"

"There is one thing more," replied the sailor. "You ought to take a look at what I'm doing to Hitler."

Probably no food has ever had so much fun poked at it as spam. But the best definition of it is: "Ham that has flunked its physical."

ORDER

"At eight AM we're pulling out,"
The general sternly said,
So the colonel sent the order down,
"At five we leave our bed."
Well, the captain took no chances,
Because captains never do,
And so he told the topkick,
"Have the men get up at two."
At midnight the sergeant woke us,
And here we sadly sit,
Because it now is noontime,
And we haven't pulled out yet.

— T-5 Carl D. Westerberg
Puptent Poets. Stars and Stripes

Important supplies were delivered by Private Brown fully 12 hours late and the receiving officer was furious. "Private Brown," gritted the officer, "you'd better have an airtight excuse. So . . . what happened?"

"Sir. It's a short story. Y'see, I picked up this chaplain along the way. He needed a lift. And from the moment I had him aboard, those blamed mules I was drivin' couldn't understand a single one of my commands."

Armored Frigidaire — A tank (in winter!).

Ball-Bearing WAC — Same as titless WAC, or A GI doing women's work.

Balls Up — Absolute, utterly unmitigated confusion.

Did you hear about the draftee in the Army who wrote home to his parents that he'd grown another foot? His mother knitted him a third sock.

And that same draftee, kinda dumb, was told to put on a fresh pair of socks each day. After a couple of weeks had passed, the sergeant called for a company inspection. When he sighted our boy, he about busted a gut.

"Where are your boots, soldier?" he yelled.

"I couldn't get the blamed things on over fourteen pair of socks, Sergeant."

A SPECIAL INSIGHT INTO THE WAY THINGS
GET DONE IN THE ARMY

The Colonel calls the Major
    When something must be done.
The Major calls the Captain
    And starts him on the run.
The Captain then gets busy
    And strives to make things suit
By shifting all the baggage
    On a "shavetail" Second Lieut.
The said Lieutenant ponders
    And strokes a beardless jaw,
Then calls the trusty Sergeant
    And to him lays down the law.
The Sergeant calls the Corporal
    And explains how things must be,
And the Corporal calls the Private –
    And that, my friends, is ME.

Two sailors were talking about the eminent end of the war.

"Where do you expect to work when the war ends," one sailor asked the other.

"I'll tell you what I'm going to do," his buddy replied. "I'm going to hoist an oar on my shoulder and start walking west. And the first person that asks, 'What in the world is that thing you're carrying on your shoulder,' why, that's where I'm going to stay for the rest of my life."

A company of black troops was under fire for the first time. The bombardment got heavier and heavier until one of the soldiers, a minister in civilian life, dropped to his knees and prayed.

"Deah Lord, please do be sendin' down your son to he'p us 'fore we is all blowed to kingdom come. Oh Lawd, please send your Son ...

"Don't you be doin' dat, Lawd," a comrade interrupted. "Don't be sendin' your Son! Y'all come y'self, Lawd. Dis sho ain't no job for a boy."

A corporal was getting a shave and the post barber asked, "Haven't I shaved you before?"

The corporal replied, "No, I got that scar from a wound at Pearl Harbor."

Colonel Berry and his wife returned to the base he commanded. They had been on leave. He was challenged by the sentry who refused to let them enter the base.

"See here, soldier," exclaimed the irate wife, "We're the Berrys."

"I don't care if you are the cat's pajamas, you can't get on this army post without the password."

It was tall tale time at the PX. One soldier related his experience that afternoon at the base hospital. "I bent over to take the shot, just as they ordered me to do, and Doc stuck that needle in my left rump. Well, boys, the needle was so long it put out the cigarette I was smoking."

But that tale was only the beginning! Another GI told of his experience on Guadalcanal. "Hey, guys, you won't believe it but this is the gospel truth. One of those Guadalcanal mosquitoes kind of soared down on our air field, the bomber strip to be exact, and before we could stop them, two guys had put ninety gallons of gas in the pesky critter. Thought it was a P-40!"

"Speaking of gas," said another one of the boys whose reputation for telling windies was very good, indeed, "My brother back home read an advertisement for a 'gasoline saver'. What with the shortage of gas, and all, he figured a real saving since the advertisement claimed a sixty percent saving of gasoline. A few days later, he read another gas saver advertisement that guaranteed a savings of seventy percent. So my brother equipped his car with both devices and . . . it's hard to believe with both devices installed, he saved 130%. His car actually began to manufacture gas! Naturally, he got a presidential citation for furthering the war effort."

The sergeant was a known brawler back home in Texas. Every saturday night he'd go to town, get liquored up and have himself a fight. But now the shells were bursting all around him.

He said to his buddy who shared his fox hole, "Johnny, if and when I get back home, the onliest thing I'll ever be arrested for is singing too loud in church."

The tough sergeant was instructing a batch of new recruits, "When that bugle sounds tomorrow mornin', men, I want to see two big clouds of dust come aboilin' out of those tents. And, when those clouds settle, and things clear up, why, I expect to see two rows of absolutely immovable statues!"

Illegitimis Non Carborundum – "Don't let the bastards wear you down."

Jody Jodie – a mythical American noted for his sexual conquests and his avoidance of military duty!

> Two-mouth Mary, known for sin,
> One mouth's for Jody, the other's for gin!

The bugler in our outfit sure liked to sleep in of a morning. But he had to blow reveille every morning to get the troops out of their bunks. He hated only that part of his job, so he figured and figured and finally devised a way to get out of it. He worked out his exact position with slide rule, compass and even more sophisticated tools. He discovered an exact position facing the Rocky Mountains in which to face the sound reveille. The echo of his bugle would return exactly twenty-four hours later.

Our bugler sure enjoyed sleeping in, absolutely sure that the echo of his call made twenty-four hours earlier would rouse the men. But still he worried. So, when he heard that a camp about sixty miles away needed a bugler, he volunteered to go down and teach the new man. Our boy went to work with slide rule and topographical maps and taught the new bugler the exact pitch to sound on his bugle and the exact position to assume facing the Rocky Mountains when he sounded off.

And do you know that exactly twenty-four hours after the rookie bugler blew his reveille sixty miles away, that echo, bouncing back from the mountains, sounded in our bugler's camp? That old boy not only got to sleep late but didn't even have to blow reveille.

On maneuvers in Alabama last year, most of the motor transportation was lost. But we still had to move supplies. So we hired a mule named Annie, from a nearby farmer.

She was a heckuva fine mule and got the job done. but one morning we found her dead in the field. Couldn't revive her, no matter what we did. So we skinned her and gave the skin to the farmer.

The next year we returned to the area and made a sympathy call on the farmer.

"Boys, you done made a mistake last year," he told us. "Annie wasn't dead last year only sleeping. I forgot to tell y'all that when Annie sleeps, nothin' won't git her awake. Nothin'! So-o-o, later, after you give me her hide, she come awalkin' home. I'd just done butchered some sheep so I hung their hides on Annie and fastened 'em real tight with blackberry thorns.

"By golly, boys, it worked real fine. Annie was mighty happy. And we was, too, because I sheared 172 pounds of wool off of her and my missus picked 44 quarts of blackberries."

Then there's the story of the artillery man who left the service but missed it so much that he looked for a similar job. All he could find was work as a human cannonball. He got along just fine, took *two shots* every day and was going GREAT GUNS. Then, all at once, he got FIRED! Sad, right? Not so. The boss had to hire him back because he couldn't find another man of our soldier's CALIBER!

NOT IN BROOKLYN

I'm glad that I'm American,
I'm glad that I am free
I wish I were a pup
And Hitler were a tree!

– T-5 E.W. Botten]
Puptent Poets. The Stars and Stripes.

An ex-GI named John B. Thomas told this superb true story to the editor of **Argosy** magazine.

"Back in the late forties, I was stationed in the Pacific and an old islander taught me a new way to catch fish. It's a priceless skill and I hope your readers will use it wisely.

"First, you place your hand in a stream, palm up, and wait until a fish - bass, trout or what have you - swims across your hand. Carefully, you manipulate your fingers, tickling the fish's belly until it becomes helpless with laughter. then it is easy to scoop the fish up out of the water and into your receptacle.

"One fish I caught laughed so infectiously and loudly that I kept him for a pet. He (or she, or whatever it was) has not only been a beloved pet but has made me a small fortune. You see, I made a tape of his laughter and have sold it to all the major television and radio stations. They use it a lot. If you doubt my work, just listen to the laughter on TV any night of the week. If the laughter sounds fishy, well, you can bet on it . . . that's the tape made of my pet fish."

"No thanks, Willie. I'll go look fer some mud wot ain't been used."
Bill Mauldin. UP FRONT.
Henry Holt & Co. 1945

The great American love for tall stories is strong in war and peace. Witness these three tales:

The good ship *Tuscarora*, in case you haven't heard, is the Paul Bunyan of the Navy. Any oldtime sailor or marine knows about her and talks endlessly of her mighty accomplishments. She was the biggest and best the Navy ever had, having forty decks and a straw bottom.

It was back in 1902 that I shipped aboard the *Tuscarora*. On reporting aboard as a private in the marines, I was looked over by the officer of the first deck, ad directed to report to the captain of the thirty-ninth deck for duty. I arrived on the thirty-ninth deck two weeks ahead of schedule, and the captain immediately promoted me to corporal, and put me to work at the old naval custom of chipping paint.

We had an interesting way of getting our food down there on the thirty-ninth deck. Just below us on the fortieth, we had a herd of Holsteins that grazed by day on the straw bottom and produced the finest of powdered milk. At night the herd was fed on hot water and the tar used in caulking the decks. this caused them to produce, the next morning, a liquid not unlike the coffee found on other naval vessels. Our vegetables and other food were raised on an eighty-acre farm tucked away forward under the Chief's quarters.

After I had been on the thirty-ninth deck for twenty years, I began to grow restless chipping paint. So I went to the executive officer to ask for a furlough. They were very hard to get in those days. Only once a year was a man granted a forty-eight-hour pass to take a shower and to shave. Our executive officer had been aboard for thirty four years, reporting as an apprentice seaman and working up from the ranks to lieutenant commander, so he knew the ways of the enlisted man. He wrote out a furlough for thirty days.

I had a wonderful time while on furlough visiting with my brother on the thirtieth deck. We spent many enjoyable evenings together, until he mentioned that I had been divorced by my wife ten years before. This I did not mind, but when he told me that she and her new husband were living on my allotment, I got sore.

I returned to my own deck, and immediately made application to retire on twenty years. Before my application could be acted upon, however, I was called to the first sergeant's office and told to report at once to the officer of the first deck. I packed my seabag and bid my buddies good-by, for I knew it would be many months before I would see them again.

By this time they had installed an elevator from the first deck to the tenth, so before leaving, I went to the quartermaster and received my transportation request and subsistence allowance for traveling on the elevator the last ten decks. I made this trip in record time.

On arriving topside, I reported to the officer of the deck, who, when I had seen him last, was a young ensign with not quite a year in the naval service. Now he was bearded and had been turned down on his last two forty-eight-hour passes and so had missed a couple of showers and shaves.

I gave him my name and he looked back through three volumes of the guard book to see why I had been sent up from below. He found what he was looking for, and rushed me to the captain of the ship. I had been reported for not saluting the officer of the deck when I had first reported for duty twenty years before. Since I had just two months to do before retirement, the captain only sentenced me to sixty days on bread and water, which was very light punishment for the crime I had committed.

I was on guard duty one night at Fort Armstrong in Hawaii, walking Post No. 2, which extends along the parade ground. It was very dark. I couldn't see ten feet in front of me.

All of a sudden I heard footsteps approaching across the parade ground. It was the officer of the day.

I gave him a snappy challenge and "present arms," since he was a new young looie fresh out of the academy. He seemed to be impressed. Then he asked me to recite my general and special orders for Post No. 2. "Oh," I said to myself, "a wise guy." But I rattled off the orders.

Still he didn't go away.

"Tell me this," he said. "What would you do if you saw a battleship coming at you across the parade ground?"

"I would fire a torpedo at it and sink it," I replied.

A gleam came into his eye. "And where would you get the torpedo?" he snapped. He thought he had me.

I came right back, "From the submarine, of course."

"And where," he said, "would you get a submarine out here in the middle of the post?"

"From the same place, sir," I said, "where you got your battleship."

The Navy's inshore patrol has developed such an effective method of capturing enemy submarines that the following details have been released to the public to satisfy civilian curiosity about the large number of warehouses filled with captured Axis undersea craft:

The personnel consists of one navy diver.

The equipment consists of one diving outfit, one underwater acetylene torch, one photograph of the United States battleship *Iowa*, and one long line.

After the sub is located, our patrol craft lies to directly over it, and the diver is lowered. The diver makes his way along the deck of the submerged enemy vessel and fastens the picture of the *Iowa* in front of the periscope. The U-boat commander spots the picture through the periscope and becomes frantically excited at the prospect of bagging one of the newest and biggest fighting ships of America's Navy. In his excitement, he orders all torpedoes to be fired at the battleship. The torpedoes, of course, explode harmlessly beneath the water.

In the meantime, the diver has sneaked around to the stern of the submarine and quietly proceeded to cut the propeller shafts with the torch. the crew of the sub then becomes completely flabbergasted. Not only does the *Iowa* refuse to sink – but their own vessel refuses to move.

While the Nazis are fighting among themselves as to who is the cause of all this mess, it is quite an easy task to pass a line around the sub and tow it into port.

Heifer Barn – A WAAC or WAC barracks.

A GI reported to the base psychiatrist. the physician asked him what the trouble was and the young soldier replied, "My sergeant is upset with me because of my taste in army boots."

"I don't see anything odd about that. I like a good fitting and stylish pair of army boots myself."

"Really, sir? Good to meet a kindred soul. But tell me . . . how do you like yours . . . with or without catsup?"

Another GI reported to the same psychiatrist. "My sergeant disagrees with me, sir. He makes me so damned mad. I used to think I was an Irish Setter but I don't feel like that at all, anymore."

"Well, it's certainly good that you have recovered," said the physician.

"I sure have. If you want proof of it just feel my nose."

Greasepot – The cook.

The GI was on duty in Germany, standing outside a building fronted by two huge statues of dogs. Two British tommies came by and one of them asked " 'ow often do you be feedin' the dogs, mate?"

"Every time they bark," grinned the GI.

They rescued Seaman Jones when he was just about drowned. They hauled him to the beach and pumped him as dry as they could. When he could take it, they brought him an enormous glass of smooth Scotch whiskey.

Seaman Jones took one look at the drink and said, "Turn me over again, fellows, and let's try to get more water out of me."

Corporal Peters awakened in a hospital bed after a long and wet night on the town. Groaning with the pain of his hangover he rolled over and saw his buddy, Jasper Jones, in the next bed.

"Oh, my head," groaned Peters. "What in the hell happened to us, Jasper?"

"You insisted on going up on the roof of the No Soap Saloon and you bet me you could jump off the roof and fly three times around the saloon."

"Oh my gosh," groaned Corporal Peters. "Why didn't you stop me?"

"Stop you! Hell, man, I had ten bucks bet that you could do it."

"What's wrong with you, soldier," asked the flight surgeon.

"It was two years ago, Sir, that I swallowed two fifty cent pieces and I'd sure like you to do something about it."

"Do something! Now? Why didn't you come see me two years ago."

"Well, sir, y'see . . . I didn't need the money until now."

Hindquarters Company – A corruption – derogatory, of course – of Headquarters Company.

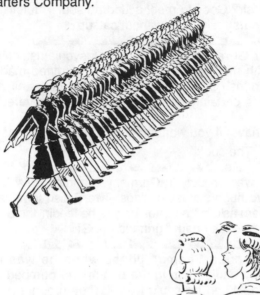

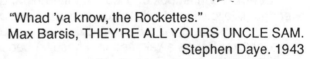

"Whad 'ya know, the Rockettes."
Max Barsis, THEY'RE ALL YOURS UNCLE SAM.
Stephen Daye. 1943

The battalion psychiatrist was very pleased with Sergeant Samuel's progress. "I must say, Sergeant Samuels, that you are doing so much better than Corporal Busch. He's going around telling everyone that he wants to buy the Chase National Bank."

"Really? He's still at that stupid effort? Why, sir, I've told him time and time again that I won't sell!"

Corporal Brown, stationed in England, had gotten used to drinking a potent Irish brew said to be strong enough to burn holes in a steel tank! After awhile, the soldier began to see many animals of several varieties. Being a shrewd fellow, he put up a sign reading: THE AMERICAN ZOO.

His top sergeant tried to talk sense to him, explaining that he was just imagining things. But nothing changed.

Meantime, to be convivial and gain the confidence of the GI, the sergeant had several drinks of the same brew. He finally staggered out and over to the office of the commanding officer. "Sir," he reported, "Don't worry about our nutty soldier, Corporal Brown. He's going to be just fine. He sold me half the lions and tigers, giraffes and hippos. That left him with too few to run his zoo and he's taken down the sign."

AFTERTHOUGHT

Of woman fair the poet sings,
Of lips and hips and other things;
Of warm and winsome weaker sex,
Of models barefoot to their necks;
How sad that beauty so symmetrical
Should frequently become obstetrical.

Sgt. H.E. George.
Puptent Poets. Stars and Stripes

An officer returned from a long term of combat duty overseas. He was given a desk job at the Pentagon and each day, for several weeks, he shifted the location of his desk. First this window, then that one, then in the center of the room, then beside the door. Never did he spend a day in the same place. At last, he settled in the men's washroom. And there he seemed content.

"He must be wacky, shell-shocked or something," the senior officers figured.

But when they asked him about his frequent moves and seeming contentment in the washroom, he replied, "That's the one place in this outfit where people seem to know what they're doing."

There was a camouflage outfit that had been hard and successfully at work for several weeks when one of those overbearing, self-important officers from headquarters came out on inspection. Nothing pleased him. "You men couldn't fool a blind Japanese with only one hand to feel with. Your work stinks!" And he got in his jeep and drove smack dab into the camouflaged headquarters tent. Now that's the poetic justice that comes all too seldom in the Army.

ARE YOU NERVOUS IN THE SERVICE

Are you nervous in the service, Mr. Jervis?
Do you wish that you were anywhere but here?
As the shells begin a-squealing
Do you get that empty feeling
That your life has been shortened by a year?
There are times at night when "butterflies" are fallin'
That you really wonder what it's all about.
Then a shell comes helter-skelter
And you dive for nearest shelter,
And once more you curse the dirty, lousy Kraut.
Are you nervous in the service, Mr. Jervis?
Are you frantic – don't know quite just what to do?
Well, please don't let it getcha,
For you'll find, if time will letcha,
That, though you're nervous, I am nervous, too!

– Pvt. Eddy Bendityky.
Puptent Poets. Stars and Stripes.

Discharge Stick – A crutch.

Dope Off – Used in polite company, but it means to fuck off.

Double-Slotted Kitchen Mechanics – A disparaging description of women absorbed in household duties.

Two pretty young ladies watched a shipload of marines sail away for foreign duty. "I sure hate to see them go," one of the girls said. "Such wonderful guys! I wonder what they'll be doing once they get there?"

"Doing?" remarked the other pretty girl. "It sure must have been a long time since you had a date with a marine!"

Stationed in Alaska, our soldiers never seemed to be accepted by the natives. Tough and courageous, as go-to-hell as any American soldiers have ever been, our men resented the disdain in which Alaskan-Americans seemed to hold them.

One evening, in a bar in town, a GI from Texas asked just why it was that the native population seemed disrespectful, even contemptuous of these American GI's

"Well, for one thing, up here we don't think you guys from the southern states are tough enough. You just don't seem to have any guts. You're soft, easy-going, indecisive. That kind of thing."

'It's just not so," said the GI. "Hell, our boys are as tough as they come. So give me an example of what we must to do convince you guys up here that we've got the right stuff."

"Well, there is a test we all go through," said the native. "First, you got to drink a quart of sourdough whiskey. Second, you got to track down a Kodiak bear. Third, you got to screw an Eskimo woman. Now if any of you pantywaists can do all three, well, we'll take you in as one of us."

So the GI from Texas said he'd show 'em how it was done. He left. The next night he was back, battered and bloody with a torn uniform.

"Holy smokes!" shouted the Alaskan. "What happened to you?"

"I got confused, friend," said the GI. "I managed to drink the quart of whiskey. That was easy. And I just finished with the bear. But where's this here Eskimo woman I'm supposed to track down?"

It was during a particularly muddy time in Vietnam and the going was tough. A GI was struggling along a mighty muddy road when he noticed a bayonet sticking point-first out of the mud of the trail. He bent down to pick it up, figuring that some GI had lost it. But a voice thundered up at him, "What in the hell are you doing, soldier? Let go of my bayonet!"

"Holy smokes," said the GI. "I knew this mud was deep but I never figured it *that* deep!"

"Hell, man, this ain't deep at all," replied the voice from down below. "I'm standing on another guy's shoulders, and he's driving the jeep!"

What do they call GI coffee? Mud that's been drafted!

The cops have a tough time of it in Times Square. It's not easy to keep the sailors off the waves.

A recently drafted soldier went to see the base medico. "Doc," he asked, "I'm new in the Army. This here is my first set of clothes, my uniform. Take a look at it. The trousers fit perfect, in waist and length. Shoes are just right. Shirt fits like it was made for me. So tell me, Doc, am I deformed?"

General Balzoff – The wonderful pun used to name imaginary generals. The full name was General Katya Balzoff. The best known of all was the Chinese officer, General Fak Kyu.

GFU – General Fuck-Up, the kind of GI who did nothing properly.

THE CORONA CAMPAIGN

Our Irish was up when our wave hit the beach.
We flipped back the bolt and threw one in the breech,
Expecting a welcome of hot, screaming lead,
But "Report of change due, please," met us instead.
We struggled with ammo and gas by the ton,
and dug enough foxholes for every last one,
Expecting a Heinkel or two up our way,
But no – "Your Status Report's due today."
At last a barrage! – of publications.
Reports, requisitions and recommendations,
Copies quintuplicate volley and thunder,
Letters and circulars bury us under.
So when we return from this war (soon, Lord, please!)
And our inquiring offspring climb up on our knees
With embarrassing questions like, "Papa, old chap,
Just how did you conquer the German and Jap?"
We'll spout, with chest out, and heroic leer on,
"My child, I replied by indorsement hereon!"
                              – Capt. J.H. Critton.
                        Puptent Poets. Stars and Stripes

HITLER'S ESCAPE

We are sorry they missed
As he should have been kissed
With a large hunk of steel in his head;
I think it's a shame
That it didn't have his name –
We'd be so doggoned pleased with him dead.
It tears hearts asunder
He's not six feet under
Making old Mother Earth his last bed.
(If you don't like this poem
Think up one of your own –
No one asked that the blamed thing be read!)
                              – Lt. Roy Johnston
                        Puptent Poets. The Stars and Stripes

CHICKEN FEED

Rain Room – The bathhouse.

A GI wrote his buddy a terse, self-explanatory note: "Long time, no she."

There was an argument at the soldiers' club as to which smelled the worst, a German infantryman captured in battle or a goat. Considerable sums were bet on the question. Finally, a master sergeant was made the judge of the contest.

First they brought in the goat. And the master sergeant fainted. Then they brought in the Nazi soldier and . . . the goat fainted.

Blivet – The things with which you hit a pest, usually "ten pounds of shit in a five pound bag."

It is amazing how a man's record in civilian life can be misinterpreted in terms of his military assignment. Consider the man assigned to the cavalry who was terribly inept at handling horses and scared half to death around them. When asked why he, obviously unsuited for the cavalry, had been assigned to it, he replied.

"Sir, I really can't figure it. I hate horses! But I *have* been a bookie most of my life."

The first day the recruit was ordered to the mess hall a sergeant gave him a knife and took him over to a mountain of potatoes.

"But Sergeant," the GI complained, "in this modern age you ought to have machines to peel these things."

"We do," said the Sergeant. "And you're it!"

Earlier in that same basic training course, a private was asked by the instructor, "Suppose yourself to be on night sentry duty. Suddenly you notice a figure creeping, crawling toward camp. What would you do?"

"Sir, I'd help the officer to his quarters."

Brain Box – A device which controls, monitors or operates a complicated mechanism e.g., a thermostat.

Bumf – A derivation of bumfodder (toilet paper) and indicates *unnecessary paperwork*.

Button Chopper – Laundry.

GI ingenuity at work. Talk about tall tales!

There is a story, sworn to be true by Private Mel Goofus, U.S. Infantry, about three of his buddies on maneuvers. It was summer so they disguised themselves as trees and waited all day in the field for the enemy. Their camouflage was so lifelike that one was attacked by termites. Another was unaware that a kid had come by and carved joined hearts and the message "Pete loves Jane" on his thigh. And they say that the third GI's camouflage was so realistic that he was cut down by a lumberman and is now a telephone pole on Route 55.

This tale is matched and – hard as it is to say it – even topped in describing the American art of camouflage. Consider this one from the Seabees.

It all started when these sailor boys camouflaged a fence so efficiently that a platoon marched through it. It took days for the repair crew to locate the damaged section. Of course, they put a man on guard at the place so they wouldn't lose sight of it before they repaired the break.

These same Seabees camouflaged a semi-trailer so effectively that all you could see coming down the road were the tires that were not camouflaged because they hadn't time to do it. Good thing too, because if they had, the semi never would have been discovered.

And there's more! These same Seabees had to hurriedly camouflage the base for an inspection. Well, they got to hurrying and camouflaged themselves with paint so that they were charged with being AWOL for five days! Can you imagine!

Then, to top it off, the inspecting admiral traveled clean across the country looking for the base . . . and couldn't find it. Finally, the crew painted a sign: WELCOME TO THE ADMIRAL. If they hadn't done that, he'd still be looking for that f---g Seabee base!"

SHADES OF SHAKESPEARE

When you think it's there and it ain't
That's known as a mirage
When you think it ain't and it is
We call that camouflage

The former we agree
Is an optical illusion
The eyes just playing tricks
That causes the confusion

The latter your instructor
Has very well explained
And if he missed a point
Being male he can't be blamed.

The story he has told you
About our mother Eve
Tho highly entertaining
I really don't believe

Even tho the mind of man
Is very very clever
In dealing with the female
Will he understand her? – never

The object of the fig leaf
Was never to conceal
But on the other hand
To — er — more charmingly reveal

And there is a well known fact
That simply can't be dodged
There'd been a different ending
Had Eve been camouflaged

Camouflaged by Shumake
Biggs Field Bigstuff

What Whoppers These Sailors Tell

"Recently my ship, an LST, was returning from a tour in the western Pacific and, due to a low cruising speed of ten knots, the trip took twenty-eight days. After two weeks at sea, the fresh meat was used up and the frozen and dried food started to taste all the same. The crew was becoming bored after watching the same unbroken horizon day after day. Some of the crew confided in me that they were beginning to worry the closer they came to the States, as they had spent all their money on a big celebration in Japan before sailing and hadn't saved any to buy presents for their wives and sweethearts. To add to my troubles, the chief engineer reported that a lube-oil leak had developed in the port main engine and that the lube oil reserves were getting critically low.

"One afternoon, while checking the noon position, I noticed that the ship was crossing the migration track for the sperm whales, and suddenly I thought I had found the solution to all our problems. I assembled the crew and explained the plan of action. A fire hose was rigged on the bow, pointing directly in the air, and a seaman was stationed at the valve. The port and starboard lifeboats were rigged outboard. The large bow doors were opened and the bow ramp was lowered into the water, exposing the 200-foot-long tank deck compartment which was located at the water line. The only remaining preparation was to station a lookout on the mast.

"Shortly before twilight, the lookout shouted, "Thar she blows!" and Operation Moby Dick went into action. The seaman on the bow turned the valve on and off, shooting a geyser into the air at regular intervals. The boats were rapidly raised and lowered along the side, simulating fins in action. The whale, on seeing the whale-shaped ship spouting away with fins flapping, thought it was his long-lost Marilyn McWhale and went for her at top speed.

"The rest is history. By the time the whale discovered the deception through his nearsighted eyes, it was too late. The combined speed carried the onrushing Romeo up the bow ramp and into the tank deck, where he lay gasping, his misspent youth flashing before his eyes.

"The crew dined on whale steak for the remainder of the voyage. The pure sperm oil restocked our lube-oil supplies, although the engine exhaust developed a slightly fishy odor. The whale bones kept the men busy for the rest of the trip; they were carved into bracelets, earrings and anklets, and the whale teeth were strung as necklaces. All the wives and sweethearts were very much impressed with their presents.

"I have one whale tooth left to completely verify this story."

Lt. Ronald A. Campbell

Swinging Dick – A male soldier whose dick (penis) is reputed to swing in tempo with the cadence call.

Chancre Mechanic – an enlisted medical corpsman assigned to a medical dispensary. Sometimes called pecker checker or penis machinist.

Chrome Dome – Bald head.

"Ya wouldn't git so tired if ya didn't carry extra stuff.
Throw the joker outta yer deck o' cards."
Bill Mauldin. UP FRONT.
Henry Holt & Co. 1945

They tell an interesting story of the hardships on Bataan. Especially was it true about food . . . there was scarcely any! And toward the end, the quartermasters began to serve cuts of tough old army mule meat.

It was hell to butcher them, too. Took bayonets to do it. and even after cooking, the meat was awfully tough. On one occasion, a steak of mule meat was being eaten by a corporal.

Playing games, someone hollered, "Whoa!"

That hunk of mule steak stopped cold and wouldn't go farther. The poor corporal fell to the ground and nearly choked to death.

One of the enlisted men, a fast thinker, hollered, "Giddap!".

The mule meat balked only a moment more and then proceeded dutifully on its way.

They tell this joke down in Texas. It seems that a recruit from the sidewalks of New York went for a walk around the army camp **where** he had just arrived. He returned with a set of rattles!

"Where in hell did you get them things?" a buddy asked.
"Off a woim. A curled-up very big woim," he replied.

THREE CHEERS FOR THE APO

Why is it that the mail I write
Gets home okay, without blight?
But all the mail that's sent to me
Takes ten damn months to cross the sea?

S-Sgt. Gray Wilcox, Jr.

Private Peters came to the hospital with a severely damaged foot. Asked how he had hurt himself, he responded:

"Ten years ago, I was being tested for a hotelkeeper's job . . . "

"Come, come, soldier," said the harassed medical officer. "I've got no time for stories . . . "

"But it deals with my foot!"

"So, go on."

"The boss had the most luscious daughter you ever saw. She came into my room, one night, when I had just got to bed and asked if she could do anything for me. I told her everything was just fine.

"The next night she came in wearing the sheerest danged nightgown you ever saw. Again she asked if there was anything she could do for me and did I want anything. Again I told her everything was jake.

"The next night she came in stark naked. Man, she was a picture. Pretty as heck. She asked if she could do anything for me and I said, 'Nope. Thanks anyway. Everything is 100 . . . '

Irritated, the officer asked, "Just what the hell does that have to do with your foot, soldier!"

"A lot, because this morning I finally figured out what she meant, and I was so dad-blamed mad at myself that I threw a ten pound hunk of steel ballast against the wall and it bounced back and hit me on the foot and that's what I came to see you about."

Blanket Drill – Sleep!

Drop Your Laundry – Prepare for sex!

The Eagle Shits – Payday!

Eight Ball – The guy (in almost every unit) who screws up and brings trouble to his outfit.

"Tell th' old man I'm sittin' up wit' two sick friends."

Bill Mauldin. THE BRASS RING.
WW Norton. 1971

SUPPERS ACROSS THE SEA
All the good things to eat that are far away
From the great dream of all my morale obtains:
What a tiger I'd be at the beef and the pork
Could I fight out this war with my knife and fork!

Puptent Poets. Stars and Stripes

The American infantryman had captured a German and, on the way back to turn him in, he discovered that the prisoner had a huge wad of money on him. That realization brought visions of Paris leave, great chow, great dames and one helluva time on the town. But he couldn't bring himself to just take the money.

He thought about it for a time and then he asked, "Kamerad, kanst du craps schutzen?"

The GI had been killed in combat. His body was brought back and delivered to his small-town home in South Carolina. At the cemetery, a large gathering came together to honor the lad, with family, friends and sympathetic acquaintances. It was a sad occasion. Finally the guard of honor fired the final salute and old Aunt Sadie, queen of the family, keeled over in a dead faint, just as the riflemen fired their salute.

There was a moment of complete, shocked silence and then a small boy yelled so that his voice carried over the entire crowd, "Damn, they shot Grandma!"

An Air Corps flying officer was getting a medical checkup. He was asked, "When was your last sex experience?"

"1955," answered the officer.

"So long ago?" queried the doctor.

The pilot glanced at his watch. "Well, it's only 21:20 now."

The officer of the day was questioning the rookie serving his first tour as a sentry. "Suppose," the O.D. asked, "Just suppose that you shouted "Halt!' three times and I didn't stop. What would you do?"

"Sir, I'd call the corporal of the guard," replied the sentry.

"What! And just why in hell would you call the corporal of the guard?"

"Only because I'd need help in hauling your dead carcass away, sir!"

Organized Grab-Ass – Calisthenics!

The sentry on duty, in the early morning relief, did his level best to stay awake. But, finally, he fell asleep on his feet. A slight noise awakened him and he saw the officer of the day looking at him.

The sentry didn't know what to do or say, he stood with his head bowed, trying not to panic. Then he had it. Slowly he raised his head and as the officer of the day began to snarl at him, said, "A . . . men!"

SAD SACK'S DREAM

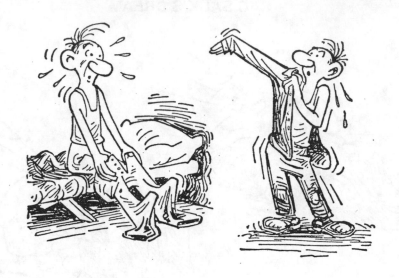

Sometimes the snafu of the Army is beyond belief! Consider the order of the U.S. Army officials, during a serious typhoid epidemic in Germany, that all water purification standards would be maintained. One order stated, "All ice cubes will be boiled before using!"

The naval medical school at Pensacola ran a test to determine the qualifications of aviatrix Jerrie Cobb. They did all the usual tests then wired for authority to do additional tests on her: "Request authority for civilian Jerrie Cobb to fly in naval aircraft for purpose of baseline studies to determine fundamental differences between male and female pilots."

The chief of naval operations replied, "If you don't know the difference already, we refuse to put money into the project."

A young sailor came home on leave and accompanied his family to the local movie theater. The newsreel section of the show presented the bombing of his very own ship. When the group left the theater, the show over, the young sailor was so shaken he could hardly walk.

His father remarked, "Son, you shouldn't have seen that newsreel. It must have brought back all the horror, blood and gore of the bombing."

"Pop, I got to tell you . . . I never was frightened till I *saw* that damn newsreel."

Poontang – Sexual intercourse.

In the hospital ward in England there was a buck private who was obsessed with questioning everybody and everything connected with the hospital. All the patients within earshot were sick and tired of it. Then, one day, the medical officer came around and this pest asked him, "Were most of your patients, in civilian life accident cases, Captain?"

"I don't know," the officer replied.

"How is it you don't know?" the soldier persisted.

"Soldier," the captain remarked as he walked away, "I was an obstetrician!"

A GI remarked to his buddy that he was looking for a nice girl, one that didn't smoke, swear, drink or have any other bad habits."

"Why?" his buddy asked.

Sometimes wives and sweethearts have to use true ingenuity to get around army regulations. Consider this one wife whose husband was in the Navy in WW II. She wanted to send him a telegram on their anniversary but wartime restrictions forbade sending any nonessential message. So she returned home and composed this dandy that went through at once: ANXIOUS TO CONTINUE PARTNERSHIP. DESIRE TO ENLARGE FIRM EARLIEST CONVENIENCE.

A noted European diplomat came to the United States for his first visit, soon after World War II. A group of reporters interviewed him and asked what he planned to do with his time.

"Well, the first thing I want to do is look up a famous lady about whom I've heard so much. She is a Mrs. Beach and she had an enormous number of sons in the U.S. Army. Such a prolific woman, and I do very much want to meet her!"

A new second lieutenant reported to his infantry company and was assigned to the front lines. As night approached, the soldiers began to dig foxholes and the green lieutenant asked his top sergeant, "Sergeant, where is my foxhole?"

"Lieutenant," the sergeant replied, "You're standing smack dab in it! Only you haven't yet thrown out the dirt, sir!"

A Pentagon general, certain that he knew more about technical matters than the authorities in such matters, had so interfered with the project that it was months behind. Realizing that he would have to account for the delays, he summoned his staff to discuss the matter. When they were assembled, he severely lectured them on speeding things up, streamlining the operation, eliminating bottlenecks. "I demand that you get rid of any and all bottlenecks," he demanded. "Any comments?"

"Sir," said one shy but determined junior officer, "in the course of my long and intensive research into the anatomy of bottles, I've noticed that the necks are always at the top!"

Paul Bunyan is the number one, the truer-than-life American hero. So Uncle Sam called him into service.

Now you must understand that old Paul is a modest man (even though he stands ten axe handles tall) and has allowed us to tell two of his great accomplishments. But we can tell you this, if you want to know more about what Paul Bunyan did, along with his great battalion of heroes like Pecos Bill, Kemp Morgan, Johnny Inkslinger, read all about them in PAUL BUNYAN IN THE ARMY by John Rogers Inskslinger (Tom Binford), Binford & Mort Publishers, Portland, OR.

The German Supply Line

The Germans had their communication lines worked out so well to the Russian front that their soldiers were kept well supplied with everything they needed. A modern army runs on its supply lines, so this gave Paul and idea. The second night he took Babe, the blue ox, and a pair of old logging tongs he'd brought along, and slipped over the German lines.

Paul knew Babe could pull anything that had two ends to it and some things that didn't have any ends at all. With the help of these logging tongs, which weighed 250 tons each, Paul hitched Babe to one end of the German railway lines. The tracks and junctions came flying into the air, and the Berlin Central Station was halfway over Poland before it fell to pieces.

Japan Gives In

Paul decided the quickest way to teach Japan a lesson was to drag their whole island up to the North Pole. He had Jim Liverpool throw the International Date Line around it. Babe gave a small preparatory tug. The Japs thought it was an earthquake and came running out of their houses yelling for help. The Jap admirals were powerless because they had no fleet; the Jap generals were powerless because their armies had fled in all directions; even the emperor was powerless, because his ancestors wouldn't come to his rescue. So altogether the Japs begged Paul to let the island stay where it was, and they'd do whatever they were told.

Paul scratched his head a minute and said, "Well, for a long time I've been wanting a pair of silk hose big enough for Mrs. Bunyan — you can start making those. After that, I reckon there'll always be plenty of constructive things to do."

To the World War II soldier, the B-29 was an enormous, unbelievably huge airplane. And one pilot's description encapsulates all the ohs and ahs of GIs everywhere about the size of the plane. "I'll tell you what it's like to fly one of those things," the pilot said, "it's like sitting on the front porch and flying the house."

"How ya gonna find out if they're fresh troops
if ya don't wake 'em up an' ask?"

Bill Mauldin. THE BRASS RING. W.W. Norton. Inc. N.Y. 1971

A GI began to read aloud an article on the ideal woman in an issue of the base newspaper. "A group of artists have created the ideal and perfect female," he began, and every ear in the barracks listened. "And that female has Brigitte Bardot's nose, Rita Hayworth's mouth, Lana Turner's eyes and Grace Kelly's lovely chin . . . "

"I shore do wish I'd had a chance at them parts they throwed away," groaned a voice from the rear.

While stationed in France, I was a chauffeur for a major who was a notorious wolf. One day as we were driving, he spotted a beautiful girl walking along on the opposite side. "Turn the car around, Sergeant! Quick!" I promptly stalled the car. By the time I started it, the girl had vanished.

"Sergeant," said the major, "you'd be a total loss in an emergency!"

"Could be, sir," I said. "But that was my girl."

Michael D. Boris. True

"Fresh, spirited American troops, flushed with victory, are bringing in thousands of hungry, ragged, battle-weary prisoners . . .
Bill Mauldin. UP FRONT. Henry Holt & Co. Inc. 1945

Air Farces

During our takeoff on a training flight, as I was tightening a loose hydraulic connection, suddenly I saw that an engine was on fire. Wrench in hand, I turned, tapped the pilot calmly on the shoulder with it and told him, "We're on fire."

He soon had us safely back on the ground, and a short time later I was modestly explaining my great presence of mind in a trying situation to an admiring audience. Just then two medics passed with our pilot on a stretcher. Startled, I called, "What's the matter with him?"

"Broken shoulder!"

Les Black

Presbyterian – A drink preferred by temperate officers. It was half ginger ale, half soda water and camouflaged with a few drops of Scotch whiskey for fragrance!

Prop Wash – Idle chatter, foolish talk, gossip.

SCRATCH, SCRATCH, THE BLANK BLANK CHIGGERS

A beast that's almost microscopic
Forms the soldiers' commonest topic.
This wretch is simply called the chigger –
A speck of dust is somewhat bigger,
But hasn't nearly as much venom
As this crawler-on-the-denim.
Two dozen types of sure removers
Fight the chigger on maneuvers,
But every single bivouac patch is
Crawling full of extra scratches.
Science says that human plasm
Gives the chigger a fatal spasm:
No matter what the soldier tries,
The chigger bites before he dies.
Each fingernail becomes a digger
To hold the teeth of every chigger.
Fifth columns are a threat, no doubt,
But this attack bores from without.

Val Brake
Fort Brady Lock Guard

Sin Hound – a chaplain.

Skull – A truly stupid GI who is solid bone above the neck!

Army pilots are known as the very paragons of truth-telling, accurate reports, utter honesty. But some become addicted to the tall tale (some call them windies). We present an unfortunate example, the case of Donald R. Gardiner.

"I would like to say a word about kindness to animals and our feathered friends and its rewards. I like to hunt for the sport, but I never shoot to kill. When fishing, I take a case of beer and no bait.

"While in the Air Force, I'd go goose hunting every morning, always using the same blind. Each morning, the same flock of geese would fly by, led by an old gander whom I called Old Granpap, named after a bottle of antifreeze which I had.

After a few mornings without a feather being touched, Old Granpap, recognizing my kindness, would fly by with a big wink. Seems I've seen that same wink somewhere.

"On the sixth morning, I was flying a practice mission and fell asleep in the waist of the B-24. Unfortunately, I was dreaming that the plane was on fire and, when the pilot rang for a bail-out drill, I jumped. Since I had neglected to snap on my chute, this was a bit embarrassing, and I closed my eyes, as I hate the sight of blood. Suddenly, I felt several tugs at my flying suit. There was Old Granpap and the flock, each with a beakfull of cloth.

"They flew me to the ground as gently as – pardon the expression – goose down.

"As you can see, kindness really pays off. So if you ever see an old, winking gooco, please don't shoot him. I still get goose bumps thinking of my escape.

Argosy Magazine.
Donald R. Gardiner.

NEW MILITARY DISEASES — NO. 1

The *Muldavian Crud* – a disease peculiar to the *Specie Humanus Militarius, Order Kitchenium Police,* first uncovered during the Revolutionary War in epidemic form. It quickly dies out following cessation of hostilities only to reappear along with other epidemic diseases at the beginning of the next war. It is characterized by a wide variety of asymptomatic symptoms!

Sometimes known as *ergophobia,* or fear of work, its etiology is baffling but often attributed to an endless chain organism known as the *pitypitypotpanosum.* Careful, oh most careful, precautions are taken by *Humanus Militarius* to avoid infection with *pitypitypotpanosum,* but since there are so many predisposing causes it is almost humanly impossible. Some of these causes are slight awryness of the tie, a dullness of the shoes, looseness of the tongue in normal intercourse with the non-coms, imbibition of *Spiritus Frumenti,* taking out the sarge's girl, *not* taking out the sarge's girl, excess contact with morpheus, etc.

The pathology of this peculiar entity is unknown since no one has ever died of it – although many a medical officer has come close to dying from too frequent contact with ye patients having this disease.

Symptoms are most alarming. The onset is almost always sudden, heralded in by sudden inability to unbend the back from the right angle position often assumed in mopping a floor, accompanied by sharp, lancinating pains originating in the same area and radiating to the subungual tissues of the left great toe and as far north as Forty-second Street and Broadway! There is a great heaving and a-sighing and inability to catch one's breath no matter how fast one runs after it.

An almost pathognominic sign is elicited when the doctor takes the pulse – the patient gets mad as hell if you forget to give it back to him! Occasionally, one will notice a two-sided limp with the legs spread far apart. This is due to bilateral inguinal hernia, suddenly arising during the lifting of a three-ounce potato. A peculiar aspect of this symptom is that all objective signs of hernia are absent.

Another interesting aspect of this disease is the oral temperature which often reaches the alarming height of 109.6 with slight help from a glass of hot water or a cigarette end while the nurse's back is turned. It is often wise to disregard such slight temperature rises.

The diagnosis is clinched by the amazing response to treatment. This consists of one of two timeworn procedures. One is the dorsal decubitis position with the right upper extremity outstretched making contact at its distal end with a similar extremity attached at its *proximal* end to the delectable shoulder of a Second Lieutenant, A.N.C., preferably under fifty (if one can be found). All symptoms abate immediately and completely.

The other treatment, more drastic but equally effective, is the introduction per os of three to six CC pills and a dirty look. You pays your money and you takes your choice – or cherce – depending on your early proximity to Brooklyn. The patient will recover sufficiently within two hours to become a leading contender in the latrine marathon and an eternal critic of the medical department, but a permanent cure is effected, lifelong immunity to the disease established and one more constant visitor to sick call bites the dust – to return nevermore!

Hippocrates J. McCorn, A.B., M.D., M.C.

A farm boy from the hills of Arkansas was taking his first day of training. He decided to look the place over and began to stroll about the grounds. A major happened to pass him and the lad said, "Howdy, partner. How ya doin' ?" The major bawled out the young fellow in the toughest language, informing him just how he was supposed to address an officer.

The kid listened patiently, turned his head, spit out a large cud of tobacco and said, "If I'd knowed you was to act so blame uppity, I'd jist not talked to you atall!"

The brother to the Arkansas boy above was inducted into the Navy. He was asked if he would like to try out for the submarine service.

"No, sir!" he replied hotly, "I ain't goin' on no ship that sinks on purpose!"

And here are a few sayings, definitions, aphorisms about war and peace:

Army – a body of men assembled to rectify the mistakes of the diplomats.

A **hero** is a man who has fought impressively for a cause of which we approve. – Dumas Malone.

Pacifist – A guy who fights with everybody but the enemy.

Patriotism, in some cases, is the willingness to make any sacrifice so long as it doesn't interfere with profits.

Peace treaty – A slight delay to allow the losing side to breed a new generation of soldiers.

War hath no fury like a noncombatant.

It is easy to be brave from a safe distance. — Aesop

They tell the story of the Western Union delivery boy who went into the Pentagon on a Monday and emerged one week later as a full colonel. They tell also of a visitor who sat down at a desk in the Pentagon merely to rest himself and suddenly found that he had been given a phone, blotter, desk set and a secretary plus an appointments book.

But most telling of all is the tale of the quite pregnant woman who stopped a Pentagon guard and demanded that he show her how to get out of the place. "Lady, what the hell are you, in THAT condition, doing here at the Pentagon?"

"I can only tell ya I wasn't like this when I came in!"

At the beginning of World War II, an Arkansas hillbilly appeared before the army recruiting sergeant. He asked, if he should enlist, would he have a jeep?

"Sure," said the eager-to-enlist-him sergeant. "You bet you

can have one. Just like those jeeps lined-up over there . . . "

"Oh-h-h," mused the hillbilly. "So them is jeeps. I done made a turrible mistake, Mister Sergeant. I thought jeeps was girly Japs."

"I'm sure the sergeant must have been wrong,
I can't find any lead in here!"

THOSE SULFA DRUGS

The Sulfa Drugs! The Sulfa Drugs!
  The boon to all physicians,
Are guaranteed to kill all bugs
  And cure the worst conditions.
    They make you fat, they make you lean,
    They save the hair upon your bean,
    Promote the dunce-to college dean,
      Those Sulfa Drugs!

The Sulfa Drugs! The Sulfa Drugs!
  No need for diagnosis;
Just slip them to the ailing mugs
  And leave it to osmosis.
    They clean the skin and swell the bust,
    They give the timid nerve and crust
    And clear the home of dust and rust,
      Those Sulfa Drugs!

The Sulfa Drugs! The Sulfa Drugs!
  What scientific wonders;
You get them tinned, in glass, in jugs,
  They cover doctors' blunders:
    Psoriasis, pneumonia, sprue,
    Pertussis, colic and the flu,
    They kill them all – and even you!
    Those Sulfa Drugs!

PENICILLIN

We lauded the sulfa drugs,
Death to infectious bugs,
  Even considered them ultra-selective.
Now comes a bulletin
Telling of PENICILLIN,
  How it is super oolossal protective.
    No more cachexia,
    Hyperpyrexia,
    Even alexia
      Yields to its will;
    Aching neuralgia,
    Pounding otalgia,
    Choking pleuralgia
      Now become nil!
Spinsters are clamorous
It makes them glamorous,
  No more passé, but objects of passion.
Hep cats and jitterbugs,
Down and out bitter mugs,
  Call for this miracle, number one fashion.
    Flagging potentia,
    Manic dementia,
    Spirochaete dentia,
      PENICILLIN halts.
    Pharmacological
    Swell biological,
    Physiological,
      Stronger than salts!
Best by comparison,
Field or in garrison,
  From the Canal to the streets of Bizerte.
Nothing is genuine
If it's not PENICILLIN,
  Staff of the asocial, shy introvert.

Heals paraphasia,
Checks cataplasia,
Bans euthanasia,
  (Deaf, dumb and blind).
Boon to the phthisical,
So metaphysical!
Why remain quizzical?
WOW! What a find!

Medicus

Hiya Dogfaces:

Hadda hair-raising experience out at Baker Hollow this past weekend. We was out there tactically indisposed, as the saying goes. It was night, black as pitch. Four of us, Flaptrap McGonigle, Gaptooth Smith, Slit-Lip McPherson, and me, we was in adjoining foxholes. Hours went by and then the fireworks started. Bombs was exploding, the white light of flares cut the darkness, and the whole place was going nuts with excitement. Then it happened. Flaptrap rose to his knees, the flares throwing a ghastly light on his upturned face as he murmured a short prayer to the heavens.

"For God's sake," muttered Gaptooth, "Shoot, man, shoot, there isn't much time."

"Don't get me rattled," grunted Flaptrap, "I must not miss!"

And then, slowly, Flaptrap drew back his arm. The muscles in his back and shoulders tensed. His knuckles were white with strain. Every eye followed his every move. Fate hung in the balance. Back, back, back came his arm, and then, like a tight spring released, it shot forward, with a power and speed beyond conception.

And there it was! MY LAST FOUR BITS ON THE LINE AND THIS GUY ROLLS EIGHT STRAIGHT PASSES!

THE GRUMBLING SOLDIER

There was a grumbling soldier
  Who growled the whole year long.
What wasn't was the "Ought to be,"
  What was, was always wrong,

He didn't like his station, and he made it plain to see
  That anywhere he wasn't was the place he'd rather be.
He didn't like his general: he cursed his captain, too;
  He saw no rhyme or reason in the chores they made him do,

He wished they would transfer him to some post across the sea,
  For anywhere he wasn't was the place he'd like to be.
They sent him o'er the ocean with his rifle and his pack,
  But no sooner had he landed than he wished that he was back,

He couldn't stand the tropics with the hot sun blazing down,
  The place to be a soldier was some good old Yankee town.
At last death's final transfer moved him onto realms afar,
  He drew a post in Heaven where the perfect quarters are,

But hardly was he seated when he passed around the word:
  IF Saint Peter could arrange it, he would like to be transferred.

Sergeant Cox
Camp Callan Range Finder

Army pay has never been what you might call lavish! And most GIs either write home – or wish they could – to their folks for a bit of the green stuff. One GI chose this rather pointed plea and got an equally pointed reply:

"Dear Dad:

"Gue$$ what I need mo$t of all? That'$ right. $end it along. Be$t Wihe,

"Your $on,

"Tom."

The father replied:

"Dear Tom:

"NOthing ever happens here. Write us aNOther letter aNOn. Jimmie was asking about you Monday. NOw we have to say goodbye.

"Dad."

CHANNELS

The colonel calls the major
  When something must be done.

The major calls the captain
And starts him on the run.
The captain then gets busy
And strives to make things suit
By shifting all the baggage
On a "shavetail" second lieut.
The said lieutenant ponders
And strokes a beardless jaw,
Then calls the trusty sergeant
And to him lays down the law.
The sergeant calls the corporal
And explains how things must be
And the corporal calls the private
And that, my friend, is ME.

Fort Slocum Casual News

Dear Annie:

What I am doing in this place is a secret.

But anyhow, I am in this place, and I am in this place with a corporal, which makes it twice as bad. Because a corporal is what they make of you if you do not pass your IQ examination. That IQ usually stands for "Intelligence Quota," but as far as a corporal is concerned, it stands for "Inertia Quality." And, believe me, Annie, a corporal has got plenty of inertia.

The fact of the matter is that the only thing a corporal worries about is chow and blondes. And he will not worry about chow if there is a blonde in the immediate vicinity.

And it was blondes that started the whole thing. I mean, as far as I am concerned, the only thing I know about blondes lately is pictures I see of them in **Esquire Magazine**. But this corporal is telling me that he is really rapid when it comes to blondes. So he is telling me about being a fast little goer with the blondes while we are standing at the bar having a beer. And I am paying for the beer. Because another thing that a corporal does not have, besides brains, is cash.

So he is telling me about his way with the women, and he looks on the counter and sees that my dollar bill is all in the landlord's till, so he suggests that we go.

We are coming out of this place, which is in a basement, and when we get to the head of the stairs, what should be standing there but a blonde. And right across from her are three civilian young guys with vaseline and curls in their hair. So the corporal walks up to the blonde just as proud as you please and starts giving her the old line.

Well, when I get to the head of the stairs, one of these civilian young guys says, "Hey, soldier, what are you doing talking to my blonde, hey?"

The corporal says "flub dub" or some such, because a corporal cannot talk very plain anyhow. So the young civilian guy walks over and is about to take a poke at the corporal when I jump in between and stop the argument. I stop it with my chin. When the smoke clears away and I get back on my feet, what is the corporal doing but holding the blonde's hand and telling the young civilian guy that the recruiting office is open Monday morning at 8!

So, now I have a very sore chin and about $1.50 in PX checks. Because the corporal borrows my last dollar just a few days ago so that he can go visit this blonde.

And all I can do is sit in the PX and listen to a lot of lies being told by a bunch of soldiers. And, after all, a PX is only a place where you go to buy something you are just out of.

But I've got to end this thing now, because the corporal just told me to report to the coal detail, and I feel very sad about the whole thing.

Hoping you are the same, I am
Pvt. Elmer Squitch.

Aberdeen Proving Grounds Flaming Bomb

A young wife was terribly disturbed over reports that her husband had fallen for the beautiful girls on the Pacific island where he was stationed. In a panic and deeply depressed she went to see her physician.

"I can't get over it, Doctor! He's always been so faithful but now I hear he's gone nuts over those pretty dames out there. What can I do?"

"Does he like fudge?"

"Oh yes, Doctor. He loves it."

"Then you do this. Make a big batch for him and lace it with saltpeter. Saltpeter is a chemical that reduces sexual drive. You send him a big box of fudge laced with saltpeter."

The worried wife took the doctor's suggestion and mailed her husband a large box of the doctored fudge. Eight weeks later, she got a letter from him. Beside herself with anxiety, she ripped it open, to read what had happened.

The letter began, "Dear Friend."

A British tar and an American bluejacket were exchanging lies. "Why, mate," boasted the Britisher. "Our flagship is huge, enormous, gigantic. Why, it does take the admiral nearly one hour to cruise about the deck in his limousine."

"So what!" rejoined the bluejacket. "Why the galley of our flagship is so big the cook has to go through the Irish stew in a submarine to see if the potatoes are done."

Dorothy trains for the M.P.

Max Barsis. THEY'RE ALL YOURS, UNCLE SAM.
Stephen Daye. 1943

An isolated Arkansas hillbilly from away back in the hills, one of those characters they call "okie," came to town on his semiannual visit for supplies. The storekeeper sat him down at the potbellied stove and proceeded to enlighten him on all the late news:

"Jeb," he said, "The Germans have invaded Belgium and France has got into it on the side of the British along with Russia and Holland. The Austrians have lined up with the Germans. Real bad battles are going on and it is just the biggest danged war in all history. Tell me, Jeb, what do you think of that?"

All eyes turned to see what Jeb would say. He thought about

it for some minutes, then rubbed his chin and said, "Well, they sure have got a purty day fer it."

In occupied Europe, a lieutenant summoned a sergeant to his desk and growled, "What is this they tell me about your being so drunk last Thursday that you pushed a wheelbarrow through the Dutch embassy?"

"You tell me, sir. You were in the wheelbarrow."

"Last night, after days and nights of trying, I finally got my girl to say "yes," the soldier reported.

His buddy responded, "So when is the wedding?"

"Who said anything about a wedding?"

A very pretty girl stood on the corner, waiting for the bus. She felt a tap on her shoulder, turned and there stood a handsome marine. He smiled at her and said in a charming southern drawl, "Excuse me, but would you happen to know a Johnny Green hereabouts?"

"No, I'm afraid I don't," she replied.

The marine grinned, blushed, cleared his throat, shuffled his feet and then asked, "Would ya like to meet him?"

"He's right, Joe. When we ain't fightin' we should act like sojers."
Bill Mauldin. THE BRASS RING.
W.W. Norton. 1971

AFTERTHOUGHT

Of woman fair the poet sings,
Of lips and hips and other things;
Of warm and winsome weaker sex,
Of models barefoot to their necks;
How sad that beauty so symmetrical
Should frequently become obstetrical.

           – Sgt. H.E. George. Stars and Stripes

Sugar Report – A letter from the girl friend.

They tell the story of a famous practical joker, now a draftee and stationed at an air base in Alabama, who was a legend with his zany activities. It seems that when he was given a desk in an office on the base, along with the furniture went report after report after report until he was sick of paperwork.

So he invented yet another report . . . a "flypaper report" that gave each strip of flypaper in the mess hall a special code number and then recorded the number of flies trapped, each day, on the strip. He then sent these reports to higher headquarters for review. Headquarters thought his notion was such a good idea that they put out a bulletin demanding the same report from the other bases in the command and insisted that these reports be sent in with unfailing regularity!

A self-important Air Force colonel, walking the halls of the Pentagon, saw a sailor and called: "Sergeant!"

The sailor acted as if he had not heard and the officer called again with the same result. Furious, he hurried to catch up with the sailor and asked why the sailor had ignored his call.

"Because I'm not a sergeant, I'm a chief petty officer."

"That doesn't make a damned bit of difference!" snarled the Air Force officer. "If you were in the Air Force, you'd be a sergeant."

"No sir," replied the sailor. "If I were in the Air Force, I'd be a colonel!"

A former Iowa merchant, who was a buck private in the infantry, received a three-day pass. He had just completed a four-day march and his feet were very sore. So he went to the beach intending to soak his feet to ease the pain.

When he got to the beach, he bought two buckets, walked up to the life guard whom he supposed was in charge of the water concession, and asked, "How much for two buckets of sea water?"

The guard caught on immediately but wanted to have some

fun so he replied, "Two bucks a bucket."

The GI paid him, filled his buckets and went back to his beach chair to soak. His feet felt so much better that, after several hours of soaking, he returned for more water. Again he handed the guard four dollars and was told, "Help yourself!"

The GI walked to the beach, to the water, then stopped in amazement. The tide had gone out and he saw just how far the water level had dropped. "Holy smokes!" he exclaimed. "What a business they got here!"

Latrine Orderly In A WAC's Barracks – An utterly useless GI who couldn't do so inconsequential a job as "latrine orderly in a WAC's barracks".

LUPUS SELECTIVE SERVICUS

The Wolf (lupus selective corvicus) is a two-footed, whisker-bearing mammal found in all parts of continental United States. He may also range, generally against his will, into the South Seas, Africa, or Europe. Since the **Dispatch** is essentially a family news-paper, (all right – we're one big happy family, aren't we?) this arti-cle is slanted at its feminine readers. The best defense against any predatory animal is to understand its habits. And in the case of this particular animal, its habits are all bad.

Every night is the Wolf's night to howl. His call is distinctive, commencing with a whistle and ending with a suggestive remark such as "Looks like they aren't rationing angels yet!" When the moon is at its brightest, thousands of Wolves may be observed slinking from barracks and hutments. Their eyes shine like cross-ing signals before the days of the dim-out, and their long, cruel teeth, bared in sensuous smiles flash as they move out, singly or in packs.

It is on nights such as these that Lupus Selective Servicus is dangerous. Despite the confessions of Little Red Riding Hood, lit-tle girls are forever running afoul of the creature. His bag of tricks is constantly changing to suit the situation and the terrain.

Except on weekends, the rough brown coat of the wolf is drab. On Saturday night he festoons himself with colored ribbons and shiny bits of metal designed to make himself attractive to the opposite sex. He may sport a yellow service ribbon as well as a red "good kids" ribbon, though the latter is probably stolen. He will have enough scrap iron on his chest to endow a couple of 75's. His hat will be a rakish air force chapeau, though he may be the humblest shovel-pusher in the cavalry.

To deceive his victim, the Wolf may whine that his sergeant doesn't understand him. He may even use a box of cheap candy or a bottle of dimestore perfume as a come-on. If the proposed victim does not immediately detect his dastardly motives, she may find herself borne off to a soft drink parlor and plied with ice cream sodas until she is mere putty in his hands – and darned soft putty at that.

The extreme wariness of this animal has made accurate observations as to his habits difficult. Should you trap what you believe to be a Wolf, handle him with care. Stupefy him with some anesthetic (other than alcohol) until help arrives. You can then make what allergists call the "scratch test," an infallible method of determining whether you have caught a genuine lupus.

Make a superficial scratch on the back of the brute's wrist and over it brush a crisp new marriage license. A bona fide Wolf will immediately break into a violent rash and run howling back to the hills. This test practically never fails. We know. We've been holed up here across the Nacimiento for three weeks, waiting for that babe to go away so we can come down.

Pvt. C.F. Bonham
Camp Roberts Dispatch

"Oh yes! I've heard a lot about you!"
Sgt. Leonard Sansone. THE WOLF.
United Publishers. 1945

Are you a wolf? Here are the symptoms: If you recognize the symptoms from the following poem, then send in your application. The poem, incidently, was composed after a brief session with a Burma Shave sign and six lessons from Madame La Zonga:

> If you park your little flivver
> Down beside the moonlit river,
> And you feel yourself aquiver,
> Buddy – you're a Wolf.

> If you say she's gorgeous lookin'
> And her blue eyes set you cookin',
> But her eyes ain't where you're lookin',
> At ease, Buddy – you're a Wolf.

> If you say she's quite delightful,
> Then your hands begin to trifle
> And your heart beats like a rifle,
> Rest, buddy – you're a Wolf.

But if she holds you in her power
Rousing passion by the hour,
While you her burning eyes devour,
Watch out, brother – SHE'S the wolf!
>> Aberdeen Proving Grounds Flaming Bomb

Stupor Juice – A type of high-powered booze devised by GIs in Normandy.

CLUB FORMED FOR WOLVES IN SHEEP'S CLOTHING

Are you a Wolf?

You know darn well you are, brother. And for years you've assumed your most innocent expression when accused by some sweet young thing. You've been looked down upon, scorned, shunned by the weaker sex. You've suffered.

That's all over now. For the Camp Roberts **Dispatch,** that representative of the downtrodden dogface, is opening a chapter of the Benevolent and Protective Order of Wolves of the World . . . B.P.O. WOW! for short.

The organization, ingenuously founded by Fort Ord's newspaper, the **Panorama** intends to make the term Wolf a compliment. It will raise wolfing to a dignified and honorable pastime, respected by all womankind.

No longer will a soldier blush when some lovely gal accuses him of being a Wolf. No, he will raise his head proudly, whip out his membership card, whisk it in front of her face, and exclaim, "You're darn right I am!"

The membership application blank (see following page) should be filled out and mailed to the Camp Roberts **Dispatch,** Building 103. The card is designed to help the soldier in his wolfing activities. It will contain his name, home town, how long he has been in the Army and the usual information that normally takes up 15 minutes of the Wolf's operating time. After she reads the card, the soldier can get on with more important matters.

Remember, though, that the membership card is not a license. A member cannot walk up to a girl, knock her down and then show her the card. The soldier's gotta be smooth. The B.P.O. WOW! is going to raise the standards of wolfing. A B.P.O. WOW! has technique and will never stoop to the old line, "Come on, baby, be nice to me because I may be sent overseas tomorrow."

"How do you know she's not your type?'
Sgt. Leonard Sansone. THE WOLF.
United Publishers. 1945

The password of the club is simple. Just say, "Hello-o-o-o-o." And make it a howl that would do justice to a four-legged wolf.

Members will be divided into suitable classifications:

1) *Married Wolves* have a chapter to themselves. There, however, won't be any telltale identification on their membership cards to make things tougher than they already are.

2) *Commissioned Wolves* will be handicapped five yards. Those bars give them a headstart, anyway.

3) *Timber Wolves* like to work out in the open, especially under a full moon.

4) *Were-Wolves* are those whose membership blanks bear the signatures of more than two women.

5) *Mere-Wolves* are those members who do not fall into any of the above classifications.

6) *Coyotes* are those who can get only one signature.

" . . . I've lived here a long time, soldier – but I've never heard of *that* custom before!"

Sgt. Leonard Sansone. THE WOLF.
United Publishers. 1945

```
APPLICATION FOR MEMBERSHIP IN B.P.O. – WOW!
Name _____    Rank _____

Branch _____    How Long in Service _____

Home town _____    Married _____

What type of Wolf are you (See story for description of vari-
ous classifications) _____

Address _____

        Following lines should be signed by two girls who can
testify you are Wolf material. I hereby certify that I am person-
ally acquainted with the above named applicant, and that I con-
sider him a Wolf, either real or potential.

(Signed)                         Phone Number (Aw, please!)

_____

_____
```

Camp Roberts Dispatch

Buy A Farm – To crash!

PAY DAY BALLAD

Now Private Jones
He rolled the bones
A good deal more
Than his small store
Of cash on hand
Could quite withstand.
In consequence
His opulence
All flew away
The day of pay.

Now Private Smith
Was lucky with
The self same bones
That rolled poor Jones.
His dice were hot
He won a lot
And came away
With both their pay.

But just the same
When pay next came
(And here's the joke)
They BOTH were broke.

Pvt. Larry Miller
Aberdeen Proving Grounds Flaming Bomb

"I hate to discourage your sniping at the enemy, but all the
local farmers are complaining!"

Dave Breger.
The Pilot Press. London. 1944

A shipwrecked sailor managed to swim until he sighted an
island. Wearily he swam toward it, hitting the beach, at last, in a
state of exhaustion and terrible thirst. He pulled himself up on the
sand and lay there panting.

A shadow caused him to look up and there before him stood
a voluptuous girl, scantily dressed, smiling, altogether lovely to
behold. "Sailor boy," she murmured sweetly, "I've got just what

you've been dreaming about ever since you left the shores of the U.S.A."

"You have," he gasped. "Now how in the heck did you find a bottle of cold beer on this godforsaken island?"

GI Jesus – A chaplain.

Two soldiers had been buddies for over a year. The younger man was married but childless; the older had four kids. One day they were discussing their home life and the one with kids asked his buddy, "I don't mean to pry or anything like that, but with kids being so dang much fun, how come you never had any?"

His friend blushed, then said, "Well, it's like this. A few nights before we were married, I suggested to Mabel that we go to bed together and make love. "Well, I'll tell you . . . that sweetheart of mine got so damned mad, so furious and upset that I never had the nerve to bring up the subject again!"

An American officer was stationed in London and billeted on the sixth floor of a hotel that the Army had taken over. It rained and rained and rained as it generally does in England. The American was fed up. Looking out his window, one gloomy day, he noticed several barrage balloons floating high in the sky.

"How come they don't just cut the ropes on those things," he asked, "and let the damned island sink!"

Then there's the true story of the American sailor who was asked what he had done with his pay. He replied, "Part went for liquor, part went for women, and the rest, damnit, I spent foolishly."

Always a topic of discussion, a group of GIs were talking about what they would do when discharged from the Army.

"The very first thing I'm going to do," one GI said, "is bust that sergeant right on the nose."

"Yeah," said another, "well, you'll just have to take your turn like the rest of us."

Garrison Cap – The common headcovering of officers and men, shaped something like a pocket. Also called *piss-cutter cap, go-to-hell-cap, tit cap,* etc.

In England you must be careful about the use of the word, bum because as these images illustrate, there are different meanings:

And should you run out of gas while driving a jeep, command car or the like, it is wise to know what to ask for when you pull up to a gasoline/petrol station.

RAIN-SOAKED

Rain-soaked . . . my bed and my baggage,
It's happened before, or I'd cry:
But I think maybe it's worth it
For I feel so damn good when I dry.

— Lt. Rose C. Craig, ANC

The brand new recruits were in formation for their first review and the officer in charge stopped before one sad sack.

"You didn't shave!" the officer shouted. "And your boots are filthy and unpolished. You've buttoned your tunic wrong and your fly is open. How in the devil did a man like you ever think he could be a soldier?"

"Well, sir," the sad sack said meekly. "I never did think I could be a soldier. But my draft board disagreed!"

General George Patton had a favorite story. It went like this. It seems that a valuable officer under Napoleon had a brain tumor and submitted to an emergency operation. The surgeon unscrewed the officer's skull, took out his brain and laid it on the table.

About that time a message was delivered that the officer had been promoted to general! With a howl of happiness the sick officer jumped down from the operating table, slammed his cranium in place and headed for the door.

"Hey! Wait a minute," yelled the surgeon. "You forgot to put your brains back inside your skull."

"Never mind, Doc," the officer called back. "I won't need them now!"

Everyone knows how strict is our army censorship. So to give his family some idea as to his whereabouts, the young sailor wrote three letters. The first read: "I cannot tell you where I am, but yesterday, I killed a polar bear." His second letter read, "I cannot tell you where I am, but last night I danced all evening with a hula gal." His third letter read: "Of course you know I can't reveal my location, but this morning the medic told me I'd have been better off if I had danced with the polar bear and shot that hula chick."

The Moocher

The moocher has a greedy paw,
The longest reach you ever saw,
And when he gets a box, he'll hide
Until he's stuffed it all inside.
But when others get the same
He considers them "fair game."

Private Estes put in an urgent request to see his commanding officer, and it was granted.

He entered the colonel's office, halted, snapped off a firm salute and said, "Sir, I got to have a three-day pass. Urgent!"

"You're not due for one, Private Estes, but tell me why you are so disturbed and I'll listen. But you better make it good!"

"Sir, it's like this. My wife is in the WACs and, by golly, she just got promoted, to master sergeant. Well, sir, I now have that unique opportunity to do what every American soldier has dreamed of doing for the last 100 years."

Fruit Salad – What a soldier displays when he wears a chestful of service and decoration ribbons.

An American GI was leaning against a London building observing the girls. One pretty lass happened by and a gust of wind lifted her dress up above the level of decency!

" A bit airy," remarked the friendly GI, smiling and touching his hat in salute.

To which the English girl replied, " 'Ell yes, Yank! What did you expect . . . feathers?"

When home on leave, stout Sergeant Reaves
Would say, w'thout blinking an eye,
The SECOND thing I want, by jing,
Is a piece of pumpkin pie.

Back from a twenty-mile hike, the exhausted men stood in ranks listening to an officer ask for volunteers for an additional ten miles reconnoiter. "All those too tired to march will step three paces forward," he commanded.

All the men stepped forward except one, a private who stood his ground. The officer was disgusted with the entire company. "No guts!" he growled. Then he walked over to the one man who had failed to step forward. "Congratulations, Private James. You are a credit to the Army. You, soldier, are the only one willing to march twenty miles more."

"Who, me?" muttered the GI. "I think you misunderstood me, sir, I couldn't even march those three paces forward!"

Red Ass – Anger, irritation.

The sergeant was about out of his mind trying to teach a batch of stupid rookies. He stopped the drill and faced them, hands on hips, his face a study in frustration. Then he spoke to them in a sad and tremulous voice.

"When I was a little shaver," he began, "my mama gave me some wooden soldiers to play with. A few days later they disappeared and I ran crying to her.

" 'Never mind, son,' she said, 'you'll get them back some day. Don't worry. I promise! You'll get them back.'

"And you know something, men, I never knew until now, just now, how right my mother was."

The GI is beset with difficulties galore, in any war. But there are difficulties beyond those encountered in and out of battle. An example is that of language, of making yourself understood in even your native tongue when stationed in outlandish places like England or, even Australia. Here are a few examples of the problems encountered in even so civilized a place as England.

Picture a GI speaking sweet words of love to his beloved in England. It used to go like this in World War II:

"Listen, Rationed Stuff, even if you are strictly from Piccadilly and I'm a citizen of Brooklyn, I've got you figured as bein' zipped to the hip, see? You're as mellow as a cello and a solid sender. If you dig my jive, I'm just pernting out you're one dish that's delish — but delish! Me and you could be out of this world if we'd just middle-aisle it and yes the ecclesiastical welder. Am I cookin' with gas, Lass?"

Or just suppose the word belt came up. How would a GI handle it?

Or place the GI in an English barracks and see something of his problem:

Or suppose the GI told his sweetheart he was a bowler. Could you blame her for thinking him nuts?

"Hit th' dirt, boys!"
Bill Mauldin. THE BRASS RING.
W.W. Norton Co. Inc. N.Y. 1971

Rear-Rank Rudy – An inadequate soldier, hence placed in the rear ranks where he won't be noticed.

War – A time that starts with paying off old scores and ends by paying off new debts.

War paint – The red smear (lipstick) on a married man's collar.

Draft Board – The world's largest travel agency.

Military expert – He tells you what is going to happen next week – and then explains why it didn't!

Chaplain – An army official who works to beat hell.

An elderly captain of a destroyer had a ritual each morning while at sea. His lieutenant commander noticed that his boss would go to the wall safe, take out a piece of paper, bow his head and murmur a few seemingly pious words. This went on everyday for many months during the war.

Finally, the commander retired and his lieutenant commander was promoted to fill his place. The very first thing the lieutenant commander did was to open the safe and take out the wrinkled pieces of paper. He read these words:

"PORT . . . Left. STARBOARD . . . Right."

When the recruit complained of "a pain in his abdomen," the medico said, "Young man, officers have abdomens. Sergeants have stomachs. You have a bellyache!"

A flyer, whose wife was expecting, was asked just how soon the great day would be. "Don't know," he replied, "but if it ain't soon the doc will have to bring it in on instruments."

A selectee shouted to members of his draft board, "They can't make *me* fight!"

One of the board replied. "Maybe not, but they can take you where fighting is and you can use your own judgment."

Over the bunk of an exhausted GI, just returned from a three-day pass, hung a sign: "Temporarily Out of Ardor."

"Who the hell put those flowers on the table?" the mess sergeant yelled.

An orderly replied, "The captain."

Then the sergeant said, "Purdy, ain't they?"

Army nurses who came into wards to give hypo injections often yelled, "Bottoms up." One popular nurse's patients chipped in at Christmas to buy her a present which they tagged, "To the best rear gunner in the outfit."

Just as the landing barge hit the Normandy beachhead on D-Day, a GI bent over in great pain, groaning, "I'm hit in the belly and I'm dying!"

A nearby medic had him strip at once but could find nothing wrong with the soldier.

"My belly, my belly!" the wounded lad kept moaning so the medico got out his stomach pump and put it to work on the lad.

Everything seemed to be working fine and the medic was amazed to see what was coming out . . . tadpoles, crabs and a lot of small fish whose normal habitat is the Normandy coastline.

As the medic was trying to figure just how all this was happening, a GI buddy suggested, "Doc, I think you might get a better test with that pump if you'd move Joe. He's sitting in the water."

A very pretty young lass stood watching the precision work of her boyfriend's company. Suddenly a rifle volley rang out and it took the young lady by surprise so that she screamed wildly and fell back into the arms of a young soldier.

"Oh," she said, blushing, "I was so frightened by the rifles. Won't you forgive me?"

"Nothing to forgive you for, ma'am," said the GI. "But let's you and me go over and watch the artillery."

Wishing to do something for the soldier boys stationed nearby, an old maid sent an invitation to the captain to bring some of his men over to her home for an afternoon cocktail party. The captain arrived with fifteen of his troops but they were shocked to discover that the old lady was serving only pink lemonade and platter after platter of chocolate chip cookies. The cookies were good but after ten or fifteen for each man, the fun of eating them began to lessen. At last there was only one cookie left on the big platter.

"Goodness me!" sighed the old lady, "there is only one cookie left on the plate. What in the world are we going to do with it?"

The captain immediately spoke up, "I warn every man here that the first one to answer that question will be court-martialed!"

Then there is the persistent story of the marine wrestling with a Jap in a foxhole.

The GI managed to gasp, "Where at is you from?"

The Jap moaned, "Yokohama."

The GI replied, "Then what in hell we fightin' for? Ah'm from Tulsa."

Captain Edward was arrested for chasing a nude girl down a hotel corridor in England. And he was as naked as she.

His lawyer won an acquittal by citing the following army regulation: "It is not compulsory for an officer to wear a uniform at all times, as long as he is suitably garbed for the sport in which he is engaged."

Every enlisted man will appreciate this once-in-a-service-time opportunity. A major in command of a battalion was the son of a famous U.S. Senator, and he was forever letting the men in his battalion know it. On one occasion, he was bawling out a simple soldier from the Arkansas hills. In the course of chastising the young soldier, he let loose his usual "Soldier, do you know who my father is?"

The GI cleared his throat, then replied, "No, suh! Don't you?"

No-Clap Medal – The Good Conduct Medal.

"Tell him to look at th' bright side of things, Willie. His trees is pruned, his ground is plowed up, an' his house is air-conditioned."

Bill Mauldin. UP FRONT.

Henry Holt & Co. Inc. 1945

A GI returned to camp after a long furlough and eventually received this poem from his girlfriend:

M is for the many times you had me,
O is for the times you tried.
T is for the tourist cabin visits,
H is for the hard things in your eyes.
E is for eternal love you professed,
R is for the rooster you seemed to be.
Put them all together, they spell MOTHER, and that is what I'm sure I'm going to be.

At once, the GI replied with his poem:
F is for the funny little letter,
A is for my answer to your note,
T is for the toothsome occasions,
H is for the hope that wrote the note,
E is for the ease with which I laid you,
R is for the rat you thought I'd be.
Put them all together they spell PAPA,
But you're nutty if you think it's me!

Twink – A second lieutenant:
Twinkle, twinkle, little bars,
How I wish that you were stars.

Deep Shit – To be in deep shit was to be in more trouble than a man was able to handle as, "we're in deep shit, men, up to our ears in it!"

Swabby – A Navy man of any rank.

A colonel in the field artillery took sick and was hospitalized in the officer's ward. He was just about the most demanding, officious, unbearable patient the hospital had ever had. When he wasn't sleeping, he was demanding this or that, bawling out this one and giving hell to that one. Everyone hated him.

It so happened that in the process of taking a rectal he was ordered onto his stomach. He turned over and just then an orderly entered to tell the nurse she was wanted at once at the front desk.

She left and the orderly made the insertion in the colonel's rectum, then left.

Nearly an hour later, a nurse came by and stopped, shocked at what she saw.

"Colonel!" she exclaimed, "what in the world are you doing?"

"Why, they're taking my temperature," he growled. "Anything wrong with that?"

"Oh dear me, Colonel," the nurse moaned. "With . . . with a *daffodil?*"

The physician was asked why he gave a certain WAC a medical discharge. His reply: "She was hit by a guided muscle."

An elderly lady riding on the train was doing crossword puzzles. But one word stopped her; she simply couldn't place it. She groaned, shuffled her feet and kept switching around in her seat while she endeavored to solve the difficult word. She turned to the soldier beside her for help.

"Young man," she asked, "could you help me with this puzzle? It's got me stumped."

"I'll try. Shoot."

"What is it that is a four letter word ending in the letters "IT" It says that it is found in the bottom of a bird cage and that our President is full of it."

"Well, that has got to be . . . GRIT!"

"My goodness, you're right! It is GRIT. Do you have a pencil with an eraser?"

Sleeping Dictionary – A live-in native woman in a foreign country.

At an infantry officers' training camp there was one intolerably tough, unrelenting captain hated by every candidate. But at graduation, the new second lieutenants all contributed happily for a present to the disliked officer.

They gave him a framed picture of Lassie. And neatly inscribed were the words, "With love from your mother."

A Marine veteran was approaching the time of his discharge. He signed up for a course in electrical engineering and was puzzled by a question on the application: "How long has your present employer been in business?" The marine wrote "Since 1776."

A sailor returned from the north Atlantic was recounting his experiences. "It was a terrible time for me. I was shipwrecked and had to live ten days on a can of sardines."

"Remarkable," said the fellow next to him at the bar. "How ever did you keep from falling off?"

A sergeant in the American Army was entertained by a duchess in her baronial mansion. When he got back to the barracks the boys flocked around him to find out what it was like.

"Well," the GI said, "if the water had been as cold as the soup, and if the soup had been as warm as the wine, and if the wine had been as old as the chicken, and if the chicken had been as young as the maid, and if the maid had been as willing as the Duchess, likely I'd not have come back at all."

Paper Asshole – A term used to describe a stupid, sad sack, goof off, as "you act like a guy with a paper asshole!"

A GI assigned to camouflage school was given his final exam. He was charged with doing his room in yellow, everything in yellow so that the examining officer could not differentiate bunk from trunk, or any other object in the room. He passed the exam.

However, the poor GI got yellow jaundice and had to go to bed. To complicate matters, the medico came to his room to treat him but . . . couldn't find the sick GI!

Now THAT's camouflage!

Bomb Disposal Daddy, my little powder caddy,
You're a most exciting and explosive gent.
Your future is behind you; do I need remind you
That on very shortish notice you may well be heaven sent?
When you're fiddling with torpedoes
And those ton (or more) blockbusters,
Which, like grapes, are there in clusters,
You may find yourself blown higher than a kite.
Since a cigarette is naught without a light,
You're a poor insurance risk, so I'll be curt and brisk,
And tell you I am seeking someone else.
So take a powder, laddie,
Strop your fuze and shake your paddy,
I'll try and get along without you fine,
Bomb disposal Da-ha-dee of mine.

Pvt. Dale Armstrong
Aberdeen Proving Grounds Flaming Bomb

On the civilian front, in World War II, eggs were scarce as hen's teeth. One store was forced to conserve the supply by erecting a sign beside the eggs. The sign read, "These eggs are for expectant mothers only."

A young woman stopped before the sign, read it gravely, nodded and then said to the clerk, "I'd sure appreciate it if you'd just put a dozen of those eggs away for me. I'll call back for them tomorrow morning."

They tell the story on General Stillwell, known as "Vinegar Joe" to his troops in CBI. The General prided himself on his ability to speak Chinese and to write it.

One day a lad from San Francisco's Chinatown asked him for his autograph. The General spelled it out for him in Chinese, and waited to hear the kid's surprised remarks about his talent.

But the kid only said, "Holy smokes! A five-star general and he can't even write English!"

PRIVATES' PRIVATE LIVES

Reader. If you think this poem is frivolous . . . just ask a soldier.

We privates have no private lives.
Our privacy is *nil*.
We're stripped of clothes and modesty
At any Medic's will.

I can not give the full details,
I'd blush if I'd begin to,
But *nothing's sacred* in this life . . .
Each item is gone into.

Cold prying eyes and instruments
Seek out each nook and cranny
We stand in line as bare as eggs
From head to toe to fannie.

It does no good to shrink and cringe
From spatulas and tweezers.
We "take 'em off" as we are told
Like masculine strip-teasers.

We're stabbed with needles in the arm
And scratched with blades unfeeling.
We mutter "ahhh" and gurgle "erp"
Until our brains are reeling.

And when the outside has been viewed
In summer heat or blizzards
The X-ray seeks the inner man
And photographs our gizzards.

Our teeth are scanned with closest care
For cavities that rot 'em.
Our ears, our eyes . . . oh, everything
Is searched from top to bottom.

We privates have no private lives
(a fact to cause dejection)
We *never know* when we must face
That so-and-so inspection.

Don Blanding. PILOT BAILS OUT.
Dodd Meade & Co. 1943

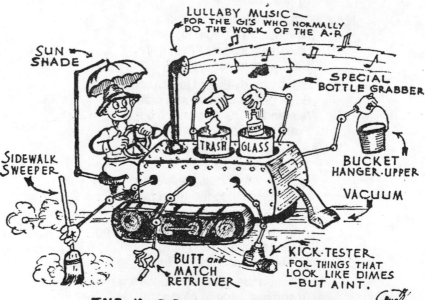

One of the most often told stories pertains to a ski trouper who, after many months of combat, was given a furlough home. He was gone a week and, when he returned, was asked by his buddies just what was the first thing he did when he got home. "I won't tell you that, but I will tell you the second thing I did."

"What was that?"

"I took off my skis."

Mail never comes often enough for GIs on overseas duty. But in this one case, the soldier got highly scented, beautifully decorated mail every week or oftener. Each letter was read by the guy, then filed in a bundle with all the others.

Well, one day this guy was away on duty and several of his bunkmates swiped the package of letters. One guy began to read them aloud to the others. In sequence the salutations of the letters began something like this:

> Dear Mr. Hart
> My Dear Mr. Hart
> Dear Eddie
> Dearest Eddie
> Dear, dear Eddie
> My Very Own Eddie
> Dear, dear Eddie
> Dearest Eddie
> Dear Eddie
> My dear Mr. Hart
> Dear Mr. Hart
> (end of the letters!)

There is the ageless story of a retired general who while visiting his old Army base, watched a parade of troops. The general was 92 years old but in excellent condition. As he watched, a beautiful young lady walked past him. She was wearing a tight-fitting, low cut and generally provocative dress. And could she swing those hips! The General carefully watched her move down the way until she turned a corner and disappeared.

"Well, well, well," he sighed. "What I wouldn't give to be eighty again!"

Orgasm In Place – A fit of temper, as the C.O. got mad at us. He liked to have had *an orgasm in place.*

Max Barsis. THEY'RE ALL YOURS UNCLE SAM.
Stephen Daye. 1943

A colonel, a major and a captain were discussing love. The colonel was certain that making love was 50 percent hard work and 50 percent fun. The major was equally sure that it was harder than that . . . at least 60 percent work and not more than 40 percent fun. And the captain was vehement in asserting that making love was 75 percent work and only 25 percent fun. Just as the discussion waxed hot, an orderly appeared at the door and the colonel suggested that they allow the orderly to decide the matter.

Quietly the orderly listened to all the arguments, then answered with absolute certainty. "Making love is 100 percent fun. I'm sure of it!" he said.

"What makes you so sure of it?" the officers asked.

"Sir, if there was any work in it, you officers would have us GIs doing it!"

Sometimes GI humor can get wild and wacky . . . like these three specimens.

A lieutenant entered the officers' mess, sat down at the table, looked across it and was astonished to see another officer reading a newspaper upside down. He couldn't figure out how this could be.

He stood, walked around the table, leaned over and whispered in the officers' ear, "Pardon me, Captain, but do you realize you are reading your newspaper upside down?"

"Your damned right I realize it!" growled the Captain. "Do you think it's easy?"

Private Pete Jones speared his sixth pork shop and his fifth baked potato.

"Hey, man, you sure do like your chow," laughed the man next to him.

"Not especially," Private Pete replied airily. "It's just that I am passionately devoted to bicarbonate of soda."

When Private Jacobi did not answer roll call one day the NCO discovered him seated on his bunk writing a letter. "I suppose you are writing a letter to the commanding general?" the noncom asked sarcastically.

"Nope. I'm writing to myself."

"Yeah? And just what in hell you got to say to yourself?"

"How could I know that?" the soldier replied. "I won't get the letter till next week."

Smoke Jumper – A GI who crosses the color line sexually.

⚓ ⚔ ⚓ ⚔ ⚓ ⚔ ⚓

But to get back to more rational, sensible stories, here's one about an applicant for enlistment who was asked if he had any special qualifications for the military.

"Well," he bragged, "on my father's side, I'm descended from Thomas Jefferson and on my mother's side from Cotton Mather, and my Uncle was a Rockefeller . . . "

"Never mind all that crap," interrupted the recruiting sergeant, "We want you for fighting, not breeding!"

⚓ ⚔ ⚓ ⚔ ⚓ ⚔ ⚓

An aged farmer stood by his mailbox near the highway. A truck stopped and the driver said, "Sir, could you tell us . . . "

"What'd you say?" asked the farmer, cupping his ear. "I didn't hear you."

"Where is Fort Riley?" the GI driver asked, louder.

"Speak up, soldier, I can't hear you. I'm a little deef."

"I'm lost," yelled the driver at the top of his lungs. "WHERE . . . IS . . . FORT . . . RILEY! "

"Thanks, anyway," said the farmer. "But we already got one of those."

The exasperated driver drove off only to stop a mile or so down the road at another farmhouse. He went to the house, knocked and a lady opened the door.

"Ma'am, I 'm . . . "

"Go on this same road, just the way you're heading" she snapped, "for two miles, turn left and go on to Fort Riley. Soldier, I heard you the first time!"

⚓ ⚔ ⚓ ⚔ ⚓ ⚔ ⚓

A recruit from the Ozark hillbilly country was on his first duty as guard at the entrance to the base. The post C.O. appeared and the rookie stopped him, questioned him and ordered him on. The C.O. had gone only a few paces when again the rookie guard halted him.

The C.O. was surprised, turned about and yelled, "What's wrong with you soldier? I just did identify myself."

"Sir, I got my orders and I'm adoin' 'em. They told me to holler "halt" three times and then shoot. Sir, you are on yore second halt now!"

⚓ ⚔ ⚓ ⚔ ⚓ ⚔ ⚓

Retired officer: "I was in the Army myself when I was younger."

Eager young lieutenant: "Really? And what was your capacity, sir?"

Retired officer: "Three or four quarts a day."

A bloody mess, the GI staggered back to his barracks to explain his condition as follows: "This jerk in Company B got mad at me and I challenged the bastard to a fight. So we started. I stuck my nose solid in his mouth and threw him heavily to the ground right on top of me. I kicked him in my balls and then punched him in this left eye of mine. I bet that bassard ain't going to make me no more trouble for a long time."

Then there's the tale of the armless man who was drafted. He was so surprised that he was speechless until he reached Camp Lee. There he protested to the clerk that he could do the Army no good, given his condition.

The clerk told the armless GI to look out the window. "Take a look at that soldier out there pumping water into that bucket. You go out there and tell him when it's full. He's blind."

Manhole Inspection – Physical checkup of WACs to detect VD.

Nappy – The company barber.

New Guinea Salute – Waving the hand over the mess kit to keep off flies.

A tiny slip of a girl came to the recruiting office of the WAVES and requested an examination for service.

The officer looked her over and told her, "You want to be a WAVE, do you? Why, baby, you couldn't even be a ripple!"

TRUCK DRIVERS

A female hitchhiker from Bari
Had legs that made truck drivers tari
It wasn't the beauty
That kept them from deauty
They just were exceedingly hari.

– Lt. Owen Cooper
Puptent Poets
Stars and Stripes

Wistful Thinking

I'm patriotic as can be,
I've gone all-out for victory.
My step is sure, my eyes are clear,
I'm Uncle Sammy's little dear.
I'm quick to bed and quick to rise,
I do my breathing exercise,
I get along without the sweets,
I eat my spinich, peas and beets.
Of coffee, I take half a cup;
It's plain to see I'm building up.
Oh, peacetime will be great, I know,
I'll help to kiss the boys hello,
I'll see the whole thing through, and then
I think I'll fall apart again.

Alice Hamilton – Puptent Poets.

SEE HERE, PRIVATE HARGROVE

The most popular book produced to date in the present war by a member of the armed forces is the spirited and delightful SEE HERE, PRIVATE HARGROVE. *It has been featured in* **Life,** *condensed in* **Reader's Digest,** *and is headed for screen immortality by the MGM studios. Its author is now a corporal, attached to the editorial staff of the Army newsmagazine,* **Yank.** *How he ever won a promotion will be a complete puzzle to the reader of his memoirs – but, in the words of Louis Untermeyer, "he has provided unflinching humor throughout a long, hard summer."* (from a contemporary review.)

"As if I didn't have enough trouble on my hands with payday," said Top Sergeant Tate, "now I have to be exposed to the sight of you. Be brief."

"Sergeant," I began, "when I hear people say a soldier can't live on the pay he makes, I'd like to show them myself as a living proof that he can."

"Quit beating your gums," he said, "and get to the point. You didn't come in here to compliment the Army on its pay. And take your cap off when you're in the orderly room."

"I didn't come to compliment nobody nor nothing," I said, laying my cap on the corner of his desk. "I just came in to see if the War Department is mad at me. They haven't given me a cent of salary since the first of October."

"What in the sweet name of heaven are you talking about?" the top kick hooted, handing me back the cap. "We've had two regular paydays, including the one today. And we've had two supplementary payrolls for people who missed the regular paydays."

"Mind you," I put in, "I'm not complaining. I eat regularly and I have a roof over my head. I can get haircuts and movie tickets and cigarettes and shoe polish on credit, but I certainly would like a little cash spending money from time to time."

"Well," he groaned, slapping his desk wearily, "here we go again! Hargrove, the boy who makes a top kick's life exciting! Hargrove the hopeless – the sloppy bunk on inspection day, the soap in the soup, the thorn in the side. Hargrove, the boy who can take the simplest problem and reduce it to its most confusing form. Now let's start at the beginning and take the whole thing slowly. You haven't been paid since October first. How come?"

"That was because when the November first payday came around, I had just got here. I signed the October payroll in my old battery."

"All right," he said patiently, counting off a finger. "That's one payday. That brings us up to November tenth, the day of the supplementary payroll, when you should have got the pay you missed on the first. Did you sign the supplementary payroll for that occasion?"

"Yes, sir," I insisted. "Then when the supplementary payday came around, something happened. Or to be more correct, nothing happened. I still didn't get paid."

"That's two paydays you missed," the sergeant sighed. "I will check into the second later. Now – what about today's pay?"

"I missed out on that one too. The battery commander couldn't find my signature on the payroll."

"Isn't that just too utterly delightful?" he cooed. "Couldn't find your signature on the payroll! You know, I'll bet some nasty old thing came along with ink eradicator and erased your signature from it! If your signature wasn't on the payroll, Private Hargrove, it was because you hadn't signed the payroll!"

"That makes sense," I conceded.

He patted me on both shoulders, a little heavily, and I cowered. "Wait just a minute, Private Hargrove," he said sweetly. "Let sargie-wargie see what he can find out about the nasty old payroll!"

He returned in a few minutes, frowning wearily. "Private Hargrove," he sighed, "dear Private Hargrove! You didn't draw your pay on the tenth of November because you weren't here on the tenth! You were on furlough! And you didn't sign the payroll for today because you were on furlough while it was being signed. Your modest pay for October has been in the battery safe for three weeks, just waiting for you to get around to picking it up!"

He took a small envelope from behind his back. "Twenty-one dollars for services rendered through the month of October. Harrumph! Minus two-forty for theater tickets, minus a dollar for haircuts, minus seven dollars for canteen checks. Private Hargrove, I present to you your October wages – ten dollars and sixty cents!"

I took the money, looked at it tenderly, and crammed it into my pocket.

"And Private Hargrove," said the top kick, "in a few days you will see a notice on the bulletin board asking all men who were not paid today to come in and sign the supplementary payroll. When you see that notice, Private Hargrove, I want you to come right into the orderly room so I can explain it to you. Then I want to watch you while you sign the payroll, so that we'll be sure to get it right. Will you do that much for your old top sergeant?"

"Yes, sir," I promised. "May I go now, sergeant?"

"Yes, Private Hargrove," he sighed. "Please do."

Marion Hargrove. SEE HERE PRIVATE HARGROVE.
Henry Holt & Co. 1942

A congressman once received the following letter from a soldier in basic training. Part of it said, "And the food, sir, I can only describe it as slop. Why, sir, I wouldn't feed such slop to pigs because if I did they'd die of it or, at least, get sick to their stomachs. No self-respecting garbage man would consider hauling it. And the worst of it is that they serve such dinky, little portions."

It seems that Admiral Nimitz and General MacArthur were in a small boat, enjoying a round of fishing when a large wave overturned them. They floundered about until they reached the boat and laboriously climbed back into it.

When he'd caught his breath, the Admiral said, "I'd appreciate it if you kept quiet about this incident, Mac. Y'see I'd feel terrible, disgraced if the men knew I couldn't swim."

"Not to worry," said General Mac. "I'll never mention it again. and if you think it a worry, well, consider the fix I'd be in if it ever got out. It'd be awful if my men knew I couldn't walk on water."

It has often been remarked that the Ten Commandments are clear, brief, concise, direct and to the point. It has also been remarked that the reason for this is that they did not come through the military chain-of-command!

Twelve men were assigned to bury their beloved army mule and to erect the following inscription upon the headstone:

"In memory of Susie who joyously kicked one general, two colonels, a passel of majors, a clutch of captains, thirty-two sergeants and, alas, one bomb."

No Hair Off My Ass – GI indifference as, "You want to buck the C.O.? So go ahead . . . it's no hair off my ass!"

The One-Seventy – A drink that was half champagne, half cognac, probably derived from the German's long-range 170 MM gun.

One A-Shootin', Ten A-Lootin' – GIs who were loath to fight but eager to loot after the fight.

The big city lad was inducted into the Air Force. Now, this man had never been in an airplane, was afraid of them, and angry because they had put him in the Air Force.

"Sir," he stuttered to the inducting officer, "I ain't gonna like this job no how, no way. I jist don't like them airplanes. I'm scared to hell and gone!"

"That's probably because you've never been up in one," said the officer.

"You're right, sir. Never!"

"Then let me send you up for a flight and you'll see how much fun it is. Then you can judge properly. Report back to me when you land."

An hour later the lad returned to make his report to the officer.

"I hope you enjoyed your flight, soldier," the officer said in a friendly manner. " It *was* fun, wasn't it?"

"Well, I got to tell you that I didn't especially like it, either one of them."

"Either one? What are you talking about? You only had a single ride."

"Nope, two! My first and my last!"

Dan was a black man reporting for recruitment in the Army. The sergeant began to ask a whole series of questions.

"Your name, soldier."

Dan told it.

"Age?"

Dan gave it.

"Race?"

Dan was puzzled at first, then grinned. The sergeant looked up and smiled, then checked off in the proper place.

"Now for the last question, "Who do you want your remains sent to?"

Dan didn't reply at first, just studied the question, then said, "Well, Sergeant, if'n it be all the same to you, I expects to bring 'em home myself."

"Them buttons was shot off when I took this town, sir."
Bill Mauldin. THE BRASS RING
W.W. Norton Inc. N.Y. 1971

At Pecos, Texas, a B-29 training base, state authorities asked the commanding officer to cancel all leaves and passes until a critical water shortage ended and the supply returned to normal. The drought in west Texas was that bad! And the C.O. accepted the civilian request and banned all leaves. But a group of flying officers under the command of their Captain O'Toole, broke the ban and stormed Pecos, Texas, only to be arrested by the military police and returned to the base.

The captain was brought before the commanding officer who demanded to know whether O'Toole knew of the order.

"Yes, sir! I did, sir."

"Then how come you didn't obey orders?"

"Sir, I figured that order was not applicable to us."

"And just why did you consider yourselves exempt?"

"Because, sir, my men don't drink water when they go to town!"

Lung Warts – Female breasts.

A group of sailors were seated in a restaurant watching a seductive, beautiful waitress as she jiggled and twitched her way between tables. When she got to their table, one of the boys asked, "Do you take orders to go out?"

"You bet we do!" she said.

"Good," the sailor said, smiling happily. "Go get your coat."

A candidate with terrible eyesight was examined by the draft medico and placed in 1-A.

"There must be a mistake," groaned the candidate. "My eyesight is awful. I can't see anything."

"Never mind that," said the doctor. We don't examine eyes any more . . . we just count them!"

Dumb soldier jokes are always popular in the armed forces. Here are two examples.

A GI returned from his furlough and he looked terrible. His face had the green color of Roquefort cheese and he trembled, breathed fast and seemed near collapse. "What happened to you, a bunkmate asked. "You look like death itself."

"It was that damned train ride from home to the base here. It was awful. For five hours I road backward in a stuffy coach. And I get sick as hell when I ride backwards."

"Why didn't you ask the folks sitting across from you to change seats with you?" his buddy asked.

"Hell, man, I'd of been happy to . . . only there wasn't nobody sittin' opposite me."

An officer returned to his quarters late one evening and found a GI crawling around under a lamp post just outside his front door.

"What are you looking for, soldier?"

"I lost a silver dollar a block down the street," he replied, slurring his speech.

"If you lost that buck a block away, why in hell don't you try going back there where you lost it?" asked the officer.

"The light's much better here."

An officer accepted a pair of brightly shined boots by his orderly. "Soldier, you've brought me a black and a brown boot. Can't you see that you've brought me the wrong pair?"

"Sir," the orderly replied, "your other pair is exactly the same as this."

A young American officer met a pretty English lady and was invited to spend the weekend with her at her estate. Naturally, he accepted and had a wonderful, if tiring, time of it. The English beauty seemed to want to spend all her time in bed with him.

Well, as with all good things, the weekend finally concluded and the happy but tired officer prepared to leave.

As he approached the door, the lady surprised him with her, "How about a bit of the folding stuff as a token of our friendship?"

The American officer was taken aback, but for only a moment. Then he responded, "Lady, an American officer never accepts money from a woman."

Kickapoo Joy Juice – Brandy produced by distilling wine.

The question was raised at an American base in England as to why a certain German general had ordered a glass-bottom boat. Nobody seemed to understand it.

Then a GI came up with the logical answer: "He ordered the boat so he could inspect his air force!"

A cavalry officer looked over a group of draftees. "They've transferred my orderly out from me. And so, I need a new man, one who understands horses and has spent years working with them. Do any of you men qualify for the job?"

A long, lean, soldier stepped forward and the officer put him through his paces, ordering almost every conceivable act a horse was capable of. The volunteer did fine and the officer said, "You must have had a lot of experience, soldier."

"I have," the man replied. "I even think and act like a horse. I've been around them and worked with them so much. Why, I recall a time at the races at Belmont Park. Just before the sixth race, I leaned over to tie my shoelace and some nearsighted fool jockey comes along and puts a saddle on my back."

"And what did you do about that?"

"What could I do? There was only one way to proceed. I came in second."

"He was mentioned in his home-town paper!"
Dave Breger. PRIVATE BREGER IN BRITAIN
The Pilot Press. London. 1944

CLOSED FOR DURATION

A Lost Soul stood by the Gates of Hell
And watched the Devil carefully spell
The words he was painting in flaming red.
"Closed for Duration" the bold sign said.
The Lost Soul asked, "A little vacation?"
"Hell, no," said the Devil, "my reputation

IS shot t'Hell. The folks these days
Snicker at my 'old fashioned' ways.
They loll at ease in my hottest rooms
And sniff the vapors like rare perfumes.
'Why, this ain't nothin',' one fellow said,
"They're usin' poison-gas . . . overhead.'
They smile at my chorus of screaming imps
And say, "Those yammering little shrimps
Should hear the screech of a falling bomb.
It makes their music sound like a psalm.'
I call on the best of my Torture Staff
But the racks and the thumb-screws make folks laugh,
"Say, after the things that we've been through . . .
Hitler has made a "sis" of you.'
They jeer and heckle with scornful mirth,
'We've *been* through Hell . . . *real* Hell on earth.'

"I got ideas from the Last World War,
But I guess it's worse than it was before.
So, all you sinners will have to wait
Until I bring Hades up to date."

Don Blanding. PILOT BAILS OUT.
Dodd Meade & Co., Inc., N.Y. 1943

As soon as the words were out of her mouth, the officer fainted dead away. She threw cold water in his face and soon he revived to see her kneeling beside him.

"I understand why you'd be saddened by my refusal," she murmured, "but I never thought it so severe as to make you faint."

"It wasn't your fault," the officer protested, "but you got to understand that I've been in Washington for several months and this was the very first time that I got a definite answer."

Khaki-Wacky – A girl who is crazy about military guys from any and all branches of the service.

Gizmo – Anything that could be labeled equally well as watchamacallit or thingamajig.

Grease – Butter.

AN INTERVIEW WITH A NAUTICAL CLICHE EXPERT

Q. Tell the court your name, please.
A. My name is Zilch. But nobody calls me that.

Q. What do they call you, Mr. Zilch?

A. They call me "Shanghai" or "Gunboat" or "Salty." Sometimes they call me "Jughead" or "speedy."

Q. You are an expert in the use of the nautical cliche' — the overworked word as applied to the sea?

A. Aye, aye, lad — I am, indeed.

Q. When a man is a veteran sailor, how do you describe his career?

A. Why, man and boy he has sailed the sea for forty years. He is a plank owner. He has wrung more salt water out of his socks than you ever sailed over. And he has passed more lighthouses than you have telegraph poles. He —

Q. I believe that is sufficient, Mr. Zilch — I mean Mac. When you say he has sailed the sea, what sea do you refer to?

A. The seven seas. The wide salt sea. The cold gray sea or the bright sea or the bounding billow. Sometimes you mean the briny pond.

Q. How does this man walk?

A With a roll — a deepsea roll. With the swing of lifting decks.

Q. Or, if he is an officer — ?

A. Oh, if he is an officer, he walks with that indefinable something which can be acquired only at the Naval Academy, or on the broad quarterdeck of a man-o'-war.

Q. Thank you, Mr. Z — I mean thank you, Bulkhead. Now, how does he enter a place?

A. He barges into a place. He may be cruising down the sidewalk when an old shipmate heaves into view two points off his starboard bow. They — do you want me to keep going?

Q. Please do.

A. Well, one says to the other what's cooking, and the other says whaddya know, and then the first one asks howya doing. Then they barge into this place, which is a waterfront joint called Snug Harbor over to the bar and pound on it with tattooed fists — with their horny hands. They drink grog and talk about the bilge water swishing around in their holds. The first thing you know, they are spending their money like a dr —

Q. There, there, Spitkid — we will skip that portion of your testimony. What happens then?

A. Then? Oh — well, a marine, or sometimes forty marines, hit the place. Only you don't call them marines. You call them gyrenes or leathernecks. They are bronzed by tropical suns. They are hard-bitten, two-fisted, grim-jawed fighting men. Well, there is a beef.

Q. A beef, Eight Ball?

A. Yes – an argument. Nobody knows what for. But –

Q. Come, come, Rebel, you know what the argument is over! Tell the court.

A. Well, maybe it starts over Mabel, the tavernkeeper's buxom daughter. And if it isn't, it is probably over somebody else's daughter.

Q. And what happens then, Skee?

A. All hell busts loose. Fists crash against jaws. Men go down, swearing and grunting. they roll under the tables in tangled heaps. There is the tinkle of glass as bottles splinter against skulls, and the furniture is broken. The shrill whistles of the shore patrol knife the din, and both the sailors and gyrenes leave for –

Q. *Please,* Mr. Zilch? *Leave?*

A. Pardon me – they shove off. They all shove in a hurry. They snap out of their hop and shake it up chop-chop. They make a speed run. They make plenty miles, and –

Q. *Miles?*

A. Knots to you.

Q. Yes, and knots to *you,* too. By the way, how long have you been in the outfit – in the Service – in this man's Navy?

A. Who, me? Listen, bud, I ain't in the Navy. I just write for *Sailor Stories Magazine* . . .

Lt. Com. Allan R. Bosworth.
Our Navy Magazine.

The Nazis caught an American and accused him of being a spy. He was sentenced to death.

"You have a choice, filthy American," the Nazi officer told him. "Choose whether you want to die by being shot . . . or hanged!"

"If you don't mind," the American grinned, "I'll choose old age."

SAFU – Self-adjusting fuck-up. Initial confusion that, somehow, ends with all in order.

Samshu – An Asiatic beverage reputed to have been made from concentrated garbage with hoof parings off the floor of a farrier, that's been distilled in a brass radiator from a 1914 Model-T Ford.

Swindle Sheet – Company payroll.

Screwed, Blewed and Tattooed – To get a raw, unfair deal!

Upset because her American boyfriend was drawn to the Australian lassie, she wrote: "How dare you talk so lovingly of those Australian girls. What have they got that we haven't?"

"Nary a thing," her boyfriend wrote. "But they've got it here."

An astute, watchful M.P. stopped a GI who was staggering down 5th Avenue, obviously drunk. The M.P. took out his report book and said, "I got to report you for this, Soldier. You're drunk. Let me have your name."

"Alexander, Ebenezer, Winniporker, Archibald, Delano, Xavier, Mephitabel," began the GI.

The M.P. closed his book. "Well, soldier, don't let me ever catch you again!"

Everybody knows that GIs love to tell tall tales. But the feller that told this one says it is true! He saw it happen!

New Jersey is known for its enormous mosquitoes, especially around Fort Dix. This GI actually saw one of these monster mosquitoes turn over a fellow's dog tag and read the statement to determine whether his blood type was sufficiently appetizing to warrant making a meal off him.

Yop! He swears it's true!

There was an awful racket going on over at the officers' quarters and the commanding officer asked his adjutant what was the cause of it.

"Oh, sir," said the adjutant, "that's just our chaplain, Lieutenant Burns, busy at reciting next Sunday's sermon. You see, he's unique. He's practicing what he preaches!"

Corporal Smith had a two-week furlough granted so that he could get married and have a short honeymoon. Two days before his leave expired, he wired his commanding officer, "It's fantastic here. Request one week's extension of furlough."

The C.O. wired back, "It's fantastic anywhere! Return to base at once."

An American soldier and a German corporal met suddenly, face to face on the field of battle. The GI hauled out his bayonet and made a quick and hard swipe at the Nazi's throat.

"Ho!" exulted the German. "You missed!"

"Yeah?" rejoined the GI. "Try movin' your head!"

Dirty Gertie from Bizerte – In the north African campaign, Dirty Gertie represented the available female as:
Dirty Gertie from Bizerte,
Hid a mousetrap 'neath her skirty,
Baited it with fleur-de-flirty,
Made her boyfriend's fingers hurty.

Pvt. William F. Russell.
Puptent Poets. Stars and Stripes.

Hugh Garvey enlisted in the Navy and was told to report to Ellis Island. He got to the dock just as the ferryboat he was to take pulled out but, ignoring the warning shouts of the deck hands, he grabbed his suitcase and jumped for the ship. He made it all right but fell and hit his head. When he came to, the boat was at least one hundred yards from shore. Hugh took a look at the shore line and in great surprise cried, "I'll be damned if I thought I could jump *that* far!"

One of the oldest most often-told tales involves a Scotchman and his wife who were working the fields on their farm. A U.S. Army plane made a forced landing and the old Scotchman helped the young airman repair the plane and get ready to resume the flight. Suddenly the old man asked if the aviator would take him and his wife for their first plane ride.

"Sure, glad to," replied the aviator.

"How much?" the wary Scotchman asked.

"Nothing. So long as you keep your mouth shut. But if either of you say so much as one word, even a 'Gee' or 'Hey', it'll cost you $100 donation to the Red Cross."

Well, the couple gladly accepted the ride and up they went. The pilot put his plane through every trick he knew — dives, loops, rolls, slides and more. Finally he landed the plane.

"I got to hand it to you," the pilot said, grinning. "To go through all that on your first ride and say not a word. *That* showed real guts."

"Aye, ye kin say that agin, mate. But ye almost heard fr-r-rom me . . . when me wife fell out."

A marine was interviewed on a national radio hookup. In the course of the interview he was asked if he'd ever done any heroic acts while at sea.

"You bet I have," the marine replied. "One time I saved the whole crew of my ship."

"Really? And how did you do it?"
"I shot the cook," explained the seaman.

A certified public accountant who had worked in a watch dog agency for the government, was drafted into the field artillery. During firing practice, he hung back from firing his cannon, arguing with his commanding officer until the latter lost patience. "Damnit, man, when I say 'fire!' you fire! And don't give me that guff about how much it costs the taxpayer for every shell!"

If you think that excessive paperwork is a contemporary phenomena, consider this story in **The Orange Judd Farmer**, May 15, 1920:

Excited young man at lunch counter: "Gimme a hamburg steak, gimme a hamburg steak, gimme a hamburg steak."

Counter man: "What's the matter, young feller? Shell shock?"

Excited young man: "Shell shock, nothing. I used to be a company clerk and we always made out our requisitions in triplicate."

"Miss Logan, just where did you learn how to take temperatures?"
Dave Breger. PRIVATE BREGER IN BRITAIN
The Pilot Press. London. 1944

For the battalion he'll do or die,
Every GI hates his roar.
He's the apple of his mama's eye,
But rotten to the corps!

Slipping Your Clutch – "You, sir, are slipping your clutch (talking too much!).

Kiss Ass And Take Names – The work of non-commissioned officers (NCO).

The instructor of airborne troops had been told that, above all, he must not do or say a single word that could cause the trainees to spook out, to suffer fright. It was stressed that the psychological approach was indicated in every tight situation.

And so, when they lost an engine during a flight and the other gave every sound and the appearance of joining its mate, the instructor tried the psychological approach. He walked to the hatch door, adjusted his parachute and said, "Nothing to be frightened of, men. Keep your cool. I'll just step out of this little old door and go for help."

A GI stationed in Alaska wrote home and, in the letter, tried to describe the intense cold. "Folks, it's so danged cold up here that the inhabitants have to live somewhere else!"

"I gotta hand it to ya. I didn't think that buried treasure rumor would work."

Bill Mauldin. BILL MAULDIN'S ARMY. Presidio Press 1951

SPAM

SGT. GEORGE BAKER

THE HUMOR OF
THE KOREAN WAR
1950 – 1953

Humor among servicemen may be raucous, gentle, sarcastic, or profane, but it is always present on the battlefield. It may be directed at the enemy, at the situation "back home," at each other, or at life in general. But always it springs from that intense, close association of one man with another which is found only in combat.

Here life is stripped of the niceties of custom and the walls of conventionality that man erects around himself in a more "civilized" existence. Here the realities are life and death, and the facts of life are reduced to their simplest terms – sorrow and joy, heat and cold, bravery and fear, hunger and a full stomach, love and hate. And here, too, I think, man experiences both the zenith and the abyss of his emotions. There is no elation greater than the exultation of wresting a hilltop from the enemy. There is no cold more penetrating than that of a winter battlefield. There is no experience more ennobling thanthe deep affection, quiet understanding, and fierce loyalty of a marine for his buddies. And neither, I think, is there a brand of humor more genuine than that of the fighting man.

Battlefield humor may be slapstick, but it is not contrived; it may be sophisticated, but it is not effete; it may be satiric, but not sadistic; it may be bawdy, but not really dirty. And this also ought to be said: Whether his jests are delivered as bluntly as a tank or as delicately as a rapier, they are equally devastating.

As any military man will tell you, humor is a necessity on the battlefield. Man would be hard put at times to keep his sanity if it were not for his innate funnybone. When a fighting outfit loses its ability to laugh, its morale is at a dangerously low point. Without high morale, there is no real will to fight, and without the will to fight there can be no victory.

Brigadier General Homer Litzenberg
U.S. Marine Corps
(From the preface to LEATHERHEAD IN KOREA)

GI's Can Laugh Even In Korea
Somehow, men in the field manage to indulge a rather caustic wit under tough conditions.

SOMEWHERE IN KOREA.

One of the minor marvels of the war in Korea — a war with no Paris or Rome behind the lines, no wine cellars to liberate and no pretty girls to fraternize with — is the ability of the American soldier to find something funny in it. A lot of GI humor in Korea, as elsewhere, is both pungent and unprintable, and all of it is directed either at the soldiers themselves, at the country they are fighting in or at their officers. There are some overtones of bitterness in it, but nobody ever claimed war was a picnic.

Somehow it becomes evident in defeat as well as in victory. Early in January the capital city of Korea, Seoul, gave the uniformed jokesmiths something to work with. The Communists were approaching the city and it was known that they could not be stopped.

Someone remembered the "panic button" in an airplane that is pressed when it becomes time to abandon ship. Signs reading "panic button" were shortly found on light switches throughout Seoul. Better known was the sign left by the GIs when they evacuated Hungnam: "We never wanted the damned place anyhow."

The GI is no less sardonic when he is winning. After the Inchon landing a colonel of the First Marine Division was approached by a correspondent and asked why he was fighting. "I am fighting," he replied forthrightly, "for $700 a month."

Two of the things constantly on the American soldier's mind are (a) how much he disliked being in Korea and (b) how to get rotated out of it, even if it is only for a couple of days. The following dialogue is classic:

First GI: "How long you been in Korea!"
Second GI: "Dunno. Nobody'll tell me."

In the infantry the favorite comment on rotation is "Wish I could get rotated back to the artillery."

And in a card game one day someone fished out a $10 bill. Another man asked him, "What do you think you're doing with that funny money?"

"I know a place," said the first GI, "called America."

The roads in Korea are so bad that Japan is often referred to as "stateside," and the marines lined roads with signs reminding drivers that enemy bullets could not be held responsible for the dozens of trucks lying on their sides in ditches. Nearing

Hongchon, following the capture of Hoengsong, the roads got so bad that the marines gave up trying to write rhymed signs indicating just how bad they were. They simply staked out large exclamation points.

Official language is a rich source of both GI gripes and humor. When our troops were falling back last year there was a great deal of derision aroused among the men over such pronouncements as "retrograde motion to the rear" and "redeployment of troops to the south." The soldiers began to talk about "retrograding on the double" or "redeploying to a foxhole well to the rear."

"We've been looking for the enemy for six days," one marine officer said tersely. "Now we've found him. We're surrounded."

In the early days of the Chinese invasion, when the highest military authorities were referring to Chinese "hordes" or to hundreds of thousands of the enemy engulfing our troops, both officers and men began to be gripped by a deep fear. But as the enemy advance slowed, the attitude became one of scorn. "Communist hordes!" said one officer to a correspondent. "How many hordes make a platoon?"

The communications situation in Korea is, to put it mildly, haphazard, and Army message centers are always working on a backlog. One officer in charge of a center — they are usually located in squad tents that move once a week — began to dream up a lightning messenger service manned by winged turtles in sneakers. Whenever someone stuck his head in the tent demanding immediate service he would answer, "Yes, sir. I'll turn it over to the turtles right away, sir."

In any army food is a mint source of humor, and the Army in Korea has a lot to work on. Aside from the coffee that tastes like iodine and the meat that breaks teeth, there is the outfit of helicopter pilots that hunts deer from the air with carbines, lands to pick up the quarry and removes it to the home base for venison parties. This story, there is reason to believe, may be true.

Allied to food stories are liquor stories. And some of these, too, are true. There is little doubt, for example, that the GIs and their allies drank a brewery dry in Yongdungpo. In this land of won, yen, occupation dollars and sometimes greenbacks, the bottle of whisky is the most subtle currency. To begin with, it is true that jeeps have been bought for a case of Scotch, but the best booze story of all goes like this:

A GI sold everything he had, excepting absolutely essential gear, on the Korean black market for occupation dollars. With some of his own money added, he then bought a couple of dozen bottles of whisky. By making judicious gifts of the liquor, he wangled five days of R. and R. (rest and recreation) in Tokyo. Once there, he talked his way aboard a plane to Seattle, where he lived, and returned to his outfit in five days.

Once the war ends, the humor that arose in Korea among the soldiers may take on a gentler, more nostalgic aspect. It may have already, among those GIs rotated back to the States. But right now the laughs are sharp, more often sardonic than not, and almost always the result of some situation a man wouldn't put up with for ten minutes in civilian life — much less make jokes about.

Stars and Stripes

Don't Shit The Troops – "Tell me the facts, the truth, the way it really is!"

An army cook, stationed in Korea, wanted to create an impressive letter to his girlfriend. But he wasn't quite sure how to go about it and still tell her the truth. Then, one day, the solution came to him while he was preparing eggs.

"As I pen these inadequate words to you, keeping in mind the regulations of the censor, shells are busting all around me."

A carousing GI in Korea, fell out of a sixth story window and hit the street without any damage. A bunch of his buddies rushed over and one said, "What the hell happened, Smith?"

The fallen GI got up very slowly, painfully, dusted himself off and said, "I sure as hell don't know, fellas, 'cause I just got here myself!"

A bored-with-it-all captain, stationed in Korea, complained in a letter to his wife that he missed all the good books and music of home. And even more did he miss her. To complicate his boredom there were all those beautiful South Korean dames who made a pest of themselves and did nothing but try to get to him.

"Maybe, if I had something to do, a musical instrument, or something, I'd be less bored and homesick for you," he wrote. "Even a harmonica would help a lot."

So his wife sent him a harmonica.

When her captain returned to the States, she met him at the airport, took him home, seated him and then demanded that he produce the harmonica. He did.

"All right! Now let me hear you play it!"

The tall tale or, the impossibly possible, is the most common persuasive and funniest form of American humor. Of course, such whoppers find their way into the military where the form reaches its ultimate funniness. Witness this dandy.

Sgt. Norval Packwood, Jr. LEATHERHEAD IN KOREA.
Marine Corps Gazette. 1952

"You certainly do impress me, June."

OUT OF LINE.
Stars and Stripes. 1952

Head – Civilians refer to this as "Rest Room," "Washroom" or "Bathroom."
Captain Of The Head – The gentleman who is honored with the job of cleaning same.

I could really go for a good case of bedsores about now!

OUT OF LINE.
Stars and Stripes. 1952

Slickee Boy – A clever thief, so able he could slip a wristwatch off a GI without him knowing it.

Suckahachi, GI Watcher – Offer of a Korean whore to perform for the price of a watch.

"We'll have to fight like hell, guys," said the captain to his company in Korea. "They outnumber us four to one."

The engagement started and everyone was in it, fighting for the life of them all. That is, all but one were in it . . . and that one was Private Estell. He was found sitting on a tree stump a safe distance back of the battle.

"Dammit, Estell!" the captain yelled back to him. "What the hell are you doing back here?"

"I done got my four, sir," said Estell.

There was a sign at a marine base in Korea that read: "MANY HAVE BEEN COLD BUT FEW HAVE BEEN FROZEN."

Tell It To The Chaplain – Shut up!

Skivvy – A prostitute. A skivvy house is a house of prostitution.

"Most amazing case, colonel. What stumps us is how he removed his helmet."

SLAUGHTER
3° Inf Div
KOREA

Furnished?

If Communist forces plan to repeat last year's drive against UN forces, marines have a surprise for them.

The marines plan to stay.

Captain Olen Price, a marine pilot now serving as a forward air controller with the ground marines described the manner in which front line marines were dug in.

"I found one bunker that looked like a Far Eastern Waldorf-

Astoria. They had the dirt walls lined with ponchos, photos of Marilyn Monroe were pinned all over the place, and woven straw mats were spread over the dirt floor."

"They even made me take off my shoes outside before they'd let me in!"

1st Lt. Jack Lewis
1st Marine Air Wing

Gizmo and 8-Ball are to the soldiers of the Korean War what the famous Sad Sack (the creation of Sgt. George Baker) was to the GI in World War II. No matter what these GIs did, they ended with a face full of s--t (mud)! Nothing they did ever turned out satisfactorily. And, of course, as in civilian life, everyone loves to see a funny pratfall by a Gizmo or a Sad Sack . . . providing it isn't THEIR prat!

Here is the Korean misfit, Gizmo and his buddy, 8-Ball, the two of them having a total of four left feet! You'll recognize them. Every unit has at least one!

THE COLD WAR

Leatherneck Magazine.

Salty – Has little, if anything, to do with the flavor of foods. But it does describe a remark which is "hep," or a person wise in the ways of the Marine Corps. A "salty" marine uses every word in this glossary as if he had been born to the language.

Down – Used as a verb, meaning to pass something. "Down the joe!" Translation: "Please pass the coffee."

R & R – Rest and Recuperation leave. In GI talk, it meant *Rape and Restitution* or *Rape and Ruin*. In short, R & R was a five-day pass called *Little R* to distinguish it from Big R, or rotation.

Pogie Bait – Candy bars exchanged for . . . pogie!

Pongo Honcho – A GI who exudes excessive gas . . . and noisily. From the Korean word for flatulence – *pongu*.

Pucker Factor – The tightening of the anal muscle caused by sudden danger. It results in being unable to defecate, or to be "too scared to shit!"

HMMMM !

OUT OF LINE.
Stars and Stripes. 1952

There's a general sentiment among the NCOs in Korea that a GI is not to be considered drunk until he tries to take his pants off over his head.

It had been a long, hot, tough march through tough terrain followed by a hard fire fight in which the infantry company had not done well.

"Damned if I know what to do with you jokers," the company commander said in disgust. "You guys fought a lousy fight back there. Lousy!"

"Well, sir," spoke up one of the troops, "till you do, there's a mighty cool grove of trees over there and . . . well . . ."

"Yeah, I see 'em. But I ain't got any rope with me."

Boot – A recruit, newcomer, green hand. Some marines are boots throughout their entire lives.

Pogie – The female genitals, from Korean slang.

Purple Shaft – a royal screwing, or, very harsh treatment. A play on the *Purple Heart* decoration, as "He got the order of the purple shaft with barbed wire cluster."

OUT OF LINE.
Stars and Stripes. 1952

Medical Officer: "How's Sergeant Jeremiah today?"

Nurse: "Better sir. He regained consciousness and before we knew it, he tried to blow the foam off his medicine."

The cute barmaid, the first sergeant's regular girlfriend, watched him leave the bar to go on an errand that might take an hour or more.

A handsome young GI with no rank at all, remained seated at the bar, drinking his beer, his glass almost empty. The sergeant's girlfriend leaned over and brushed her lips against his, saying, "Ooh . . . ahh . . . Now's your chance, Handsome."

So the private soldier reached over, took the sergeant's glass of beer and gulped it down.

"Sir, we've come across a reservist with a very unusual problem."

OUT OF LINE.
Stars and Stripes. 1952

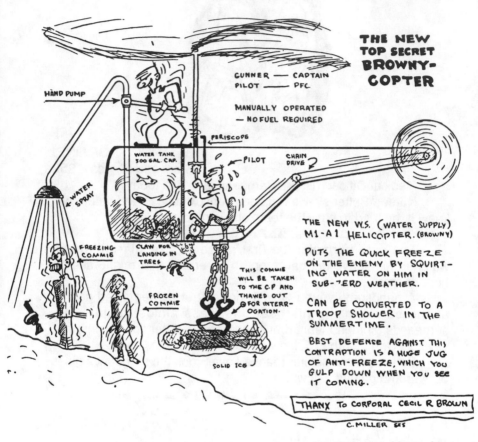

THE NEW
TOP SECRET
BROWNY-
COPTER

GUNNER — CAPTAIN
PILOT — PFC.

MANUALLY OPERATED
— NO FUEL REQUIRED

HAND PUMP

PERISCOPE

WATER TANK
500 GAL. CAP.

PILOT

CHAIN DRIVE

WATER SPRAY

FREEZING COMMIE

CLAW FOR LANDING IN TREES

THIS COMMIE WILL BE TAKEN TO THE C.P AND THAWED OUT & FOR INTERR-OGATION.

FROZEN COMMIE

SOLID ICE

THE NEW W.S. (WATER SUPPLY) M1-A1 HELICOPTER. (BROWNY)

PUTS THE QUICK FREEZE ON THE ENEMY BY SQUIRT-ING WATER ON HIM IN SUB-ZERO WEATHER.

CAN BE CONVERTED TO A TROOP SHOWER IN THE SUMMERTIME.

BEST DEFENSE AGAINST THIS CONTRAPTION IS A HUGE JUG OF ANTI-FREEZE, WHICH YOU GULP DOWN WHEN YOU SEE IT COMING.

THANX TO CORPORAL CECIL R BROWN

C. MILLER SF5

Leatherneck Magazine.

The new arrival in Korea was shaken awake by his sergeant after a long first night in the barracks.

"Get up, soldier! Its four o'clock!"

"Four o'clock!" moaned the new man. "You better get to bed right now, sergeant, 'cause we've got a lot to do tomorrow!"

The Korean veteran was to attend a reunion of his old outfit. He thought he'd wear his old uniform. He tried it on, looked at himself in the mirror, then murmured, "Hey man! If you think old soldiers just fade away, try getting into your old army uniform."

Pull A Hank Snow – to run for your life. To bug out.

"He asked me opinion of da chow and I told him..."

OUT OF LINE.
Stars and Stripes. 1952

"Hell!! It's only candy, cake and cookies!!—Not a single can of flea powder"!!

Blow Out Patches – Pancakes, hotcakes – which may also be used in the manner described. Also collision mats, shoulder pads.

OUT OF LINE.
Stars and Stripes. 1952

On Your Horse, Amigo? – The GI form of saying . . . How are you? From the transcribed Korean greeting *annyong hasipnika.*

Peon – The Air Corps term for anyone not airborne.

Boondocks – Any remote or isolated place. Rough terrain, jungles, mountain country – or simply someplace that is 50 yards away from the nearest slopchute, women, showers and other comforts of civilization.

Boondockers – Heavy service shoes worn while boondocking.

Warning On GunTotin' Kids

(EDITOR'S NOTE – The public information office of the 24th Division has prepared this article to help adjust rotatees to some of the unexpected features of civilian life. They pose here a "minor" problem, the solution of which should be of some value to any married man expecting soon to hear little exemptions patter across the nursery floor.)

With the U.S. 24th Div. —

If, within the near future, you plan on a little Stateside duty, there are a few things you should be warned of beforehand. American kids aren't exactly "Little Lord Fauntleroys."

The advent of the television screen has turned once loveable little tykes into youthful, gun-slinging Roy Rogers, Hop-a-long Cassidys and Gene Autrys. The living room has been turned into a stable and ole dad has become the "varmint of the range."

Taking advantage of this fad, toy manufacturers have produced a bigger and more fearsome ordnance selection. The "hardware" the kid next door now wears nonchalantly strapped to his lean hips is enough to destroy the minds and nervous system of any battle hardened Korean war veteran.

This well dressed juvenile cowhand is helmeted with a snap brim, jam smeared sombrero. An authentic looking fringed leather vest hangs loosely from his widening shoulders and around his neck is tied a dust-cutting silken bandana. Riding chaps with the bowed legs built in and high-heeled cowboy boots complete the effect.

His armament, which he takes off only at meal times, consists of a pair of ivory handled long barreled pistols that "bang" smoke, recoil and create a concussion that will knock hats off at 30 paces.

Enough about the ranch-type breed, we will now attempt to tell you about another breed of TV-affected kids. They are the Buck Rogers and Flash Gordons of the 19th century.

Usually these conquerors of Mars can be identified by a long flowing cape, a rocket belt —(for short flying trips around the earth) — strapped to their backs and a pair of the ole man's long johns neatly converted into a space suit.

How this new situation will affect the home coming Korean veterans depends on the conditioning he received before debarking. Steel yourself against sudden loud noises. Learn to take in stride the sudden appearance of a weirdly garbed "Space Patroller," or a gun flashing deputy marshal. And above all, control that temper.

Leatherneck Magazine. 25 Nov. 1951

Numbah Ten – The worst, as opposed to numbah one (as the Koreans pronounced it). The numbers go up to the very worst, as labeled "*Numbah ten thousand*."

Old Joe Chink – Chinese communist troops.

Out In The cold – The miserable state in which an ex-marine finds himself after he has been discharged. He may have to beat his gums for four years, but once he is out in the cold, he can hardly wait till he gets down to the post office so that he can ship over for another four years. There are exceptions to this rule, but every ex-marine is out in the cold. There are even some authorities who claim that there is no such thing as an ex-marine. They say that so-called ex-marines are merely temporary civilians, or marines doing penance between enlistments.

A friend was showing me through her new home. On the wall in her four-year-old twins' bedroom hung a picture of their father being presented with a Korean War combat decoration.

"Is that to remind the children about being brave?" I asked.

"Oh, no," she giggled. "It is to remind their daddy when he has to put them to bed that he has fought and survived bigger battles."

– Mrs. A.H. Small
Frances E. Warren AFB, Wyo.

KISS – Keep it simple, stupid!

To Move On – To run like hell.

Armed Forces Gestapo – Military police.

Banjo – A toilet.

"Yes, he's back—but I'm afraid it's going to take awile before he's adjusted . . ."

Out of Line. Stars and Stripes. 1952.

Up For Office Hours – This means that a Marine has been scheduled to appear on-the-carpet before the commanding officer for alleged infractions of rules. It is regarded as a period of deep meditation, during which the culprit tries to think up excuses.

LEATHERHEAD IN KOREA. Ssgt. Norval E. Packwood, Jr.
Marine Corps Gazette. 1952

Fouled-Up – Comes from the nautical expression meaning that a line (rope) has become tangled. Fouled-up describes any person or situation that is hopelessly involved, mixed up, confused. A bitter drill instructor likes to tell his platoon of knuckleheads that "You are as fouled-up as a Chinese fire drill." A deplorable combination of circumstances, a mess.

The sergeant strode into the bar and stopped short when he saw Private Gonzales seated at the bar, a glass of beer, a shot of whiskey and a large glass of gin before him.

"Gonzales!" thundered the sergeant, "you're an alcoholic, dammit, and you are required to stop all, I repeat, all drinks."

Gonzales replied, "Well, you don't see any getting past me do you?"

Brig Time – A period of *very* deep meditation, during which the accused ponders the error of his ways. This sometimes follows Office Hours.

"I wasn't that good, was I?"

OUT OF LINE.
Stars and Stripes. 1952

Caught In The Rain – When one happens to be out of doors at the time the flag (colors) is raised or lowered, one must stand at attention and salute. Marines are meticulous and proud in executing this duty, yet they will refer to a man as being "caught in the rain."

Back in the States, love and babies were still being made.

In fact, at Brooks Field, Texas, this particular medical corpsman had been on 24-hour duty in the obstetrical ward and had had so many deliveries that he'd had little time to sleep and eat. To show the true condition of things, especially the morale of the corpsman, he posted a sign at the entrance to the maternity ward: MAKE WAR, NOT LOVE!

OUR LATEST SECRET WEAPON!!!
IT'S THE NEW, TOP SECRET "COMMY TRAP", WHICH
WAS UNVEILED RECENTLY ON THE EAST WEST
CENTRAL FRONT

SAYS INVENTOR
R.D. SMART
"I GOT THE IDEA WHEN MY MOTHER IN LAW YAWNED WHILE READING A PEEP MAGAZINE (SHE CAUGHT A FLY)."

HERE'S HOW IT WORKS
PHONOGRAPH ① PLAYS "CHINA NIGHT" WHICH COMES OUT OF LOUD SPEAKER ②, FAN ③ BLOWS AROMA OF HOT RICE ④ KEPT HOT BY BURNERS ⑤ THROUGH HOLES ⑥. CHINESE SOLDIER ⑦ HEARS MUSIC, SMELLS RICE AND SEES PAINTING OF A CHINESE GIRL ⑧. HE MAKES A FLYING TACKLE BUT DOESN'T SEE TRAP DOOR ⑨, CRASHING THROUGH IT, HE IS RABBIT PUNCHED BY STEEL ARM AND FIST ENCASED IN BOXING GLOVE ⑩ HAMMER ⑪ COMES DOWN AND HITS HIM IN BACK OF HEAD, KNOCKING HIM THROUGH TRAP DOORS ⑫ INTO HOLE ⑬ "COMMYTRAP" OPERATORS MUST HAVE AN I.Q. OF AT LEAST TEN AND GO THROUGH FIVE MINUTES OF INTENSIVE TRAINING. OH YES, ⑭ IS THE OPERATOR.

LEATHERHEAD IN KOREA.
Marine Corps Gazette. 1952

One of the new seamen had a superb talent for fouling up on anything he was assigned to do. If you can imagine it, this one time he
set out an American flag in an upside-down position. Finally, they
got it all set to right but the chief in charge was called on the car-

pet about the endless bad reports concerning this inept sailor.

He explained it in this way. "Having that sailor posted to duty is just like two good men being absent."

_⸜⸜_ _⸜⸜_ _⸜⸜_ _⸜⸜_

Snow Job – an extension of the truth. Not actually a bald-faced lie. Yet, "it ain't necessarily so." On the other hand, it may happen to be the absolute truth — which no one believes. It is often told by marines to the so-called weaker sex — under soft lights. Snow jobs have been known to get a marine into serious difficulties, such as marriage, tougher duty assignments, etc. Most marines are adept at concocting amazingly convincing snow jobs.

_⸜⸜_ _⸜⸜_ _⸜⸜_ _⸜⸜_

SEA GOING SALTS

This social study has nothing what-so-ever to do with marines who have gone to Sea School and have been assigned to duty aboard a battle wagon, flat top or other ship rating a Marine detachment. It is concerned primarily with the common, garden variety marine who finds himself in the FMF and, aboard a transport bound for assorted boondocks in foreign lands.

Once this type of marine staggers up a gang plank under the weight of a bedroll, full pack and rifle, (and/or the plate of a mortar tube) his entire personality changes. He is no longer a landlocked Marine with the dust of PI and Pendleton in his eyes. At the first sniff of an ocean breeze and a slight roll of the ship, he takes on new and sometimes startling characteristics. Psychologists call this change a "personality deviation" or, "split-personality." In other words, a guy is simply not himself. He is somebody else.

SALT, SEA GOING M1,
(Pfc Christopher Columbus Jones)

This fellow is often called The Navigator. Before the ship has left the harbor, Jones may be found hanging over the bow taking soundings. He argues with the Sailor on watch, claiming that the ocean floor is scraping the bottom off the ship. He swears that the skipper is headed in the wrong direction and, that they will end up in Kansas unless they change course immediately.

Fifteen minutes out of San Diego, he sights land. "Land Ho!" he cries. It is San Clemente Island.

Down in South Pacific waters, along the equator, he sights an average of three icebergs a day.

At night, he insists that the radar has fouled up the movements of the planets and, that every star is out of place.

The private opinion of the Navy is that this character should be set adrift in a small boat — without compass — and allowed to do his own navigating.

SALT, SEA GOING, M2, (Pfc Roger ILL)

Roger wasn't cut out to be a sea-faring man. He was born in the middle of the Mojave Desert and should have stayed there. The moment he steps foot on a Navy pier, he begins to get green around the gills. On board ship, give him a wide berth. Clear all gangways! The ship is tied up at the dock, not moving an inch, and he swears it's about to capsize.

No matter how smooth the crossing may be, Roger may be found, throughout the journey, hanging by his toes off the starboard rail. You can't get him near the galley. He claims the mere odor of food is like a poison gas to his sensitive stomach. Doctors claim that his gyro-compass is off the beam – that he lacks a proper sense of balance. Roger ILL gets sea sick watching a gold fish do flip-flops in a bowl.

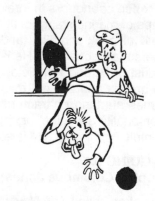

Pfc ILL belongs on Mojave Desert

SALT, SEA GOING, M3, (Sgt. Gordon M. Brainy)

Brainy should have been a great medical man. He knows more about sea sick remedies than the Mayo Brothers and the whole United States Navy Hospital Corps put together. Just mention that you might possibly feel a little bit upset when the ship gets under way, and Brainy comes up with a remedy.

Brainy's treatments for seasickness range from a chew of tobacco to standing on your head in the crows' nest.

He'll spot some poor guy leaning against the bulkhead, trying his best to forget the whole thing. Brainy will slap the fellow on the back and say, "It's all imagination, Mac. Just go below and ask the cook for a hunk of salt pork . . . " By this time, the sick man is back at the fantail screaming for mercy.

Brainy himself insists that he never gets sea sick. But when the going gets rough he's hard to find!

SALT SEA GOING, M4,
(Pfc Milton L. Coma)

Ashore, this man is a plain, ordinary Sack Rat. When he gets aboard ship, you never see him again until several days after the ship has docked at its destination.

Even General Quarters will not rouse him. Scientists say that Coma is very much like some hibernating animals which store up enough food in layers of fat to last them throughout the winter. At any rate, Coma never shows up at chow time. He hasn't the slightest idea where he is going — and furthermore, he doesn't care.

When a detail goes below to police up Marine quarters, they just stack him against the bulkhead with the rest of the extraneous gear.

SALT, SEA GOING, M5,
(Pfc Phillip Lungwell)

Lungwell is a fresh air fiend, a Nature Boy. While everyone else goes below to fight over the best sacks, he finds himself a place on deck. Generally, he spreads his gear all over the fantail, although he has nothing against occupying a well traveled passageway.

He thinks he is camping out in the High Sierra Mountains, where pitching a tent and trout-fishing is OK with the trout and any other wild life in the area. Aboard ship, the wildlife objects — especially the crew. Two hours before reveille, when the crew starts swabbing down, Lungwell is sleeping soundly. Even when they turn the hose on him, he just rolls over. He thinks it's one of those mountain thunder showers and he loves it.

Throughout the day, when other people are trying to get from here to there, Lungwell is rooted to the deck. Climb over him, step on him, and he stays firmly established in his little home-away-from-home. He has a couple of shelter-halves, and six ponchos, rigged up in such a way that they resemble a Mongolian obstacle course.

SALT, SEA GOING, M6,
(Corp. Crumley O. Washout)

Corp. Washout saves up all his dirty laundry for at least six months before he goes aboard ship. As soon as the ship gets under way, he starts tying together little bundles of skivvies, dungarees, socks and handkerchiefs. Then he fastens this collection to a line and tosses the whole thing overboard. Nine times out of ten, he forgets to secure the line on the rail. But he doesn't care; he has a plentiful supply in reserve. When the line is secured, it drags at least two miles in the wake of the ship.

This method of washing clothes drives the boys back at the Depot of Supply completely nuts. They simply can't issue gear fast enough to keep up with Washout's losses. Once, they considered sending out a Navy diving party to salvage some of the lost clothing, but gave up the idea when it was discovered that Corp. Washout had traveled all over the Pacific Ocean and part of the North Atlantic.

Directives were sent out from Washington, but the laundering corporal still insisted that his way was the only way to wash clothes.

Now and then, he will even talk some other guy into letting him do his laundry. The guy's clothing either sinks to the bottom of the ocean or his best pair of khaki trousers come up looking as if the sharks had been playing tug-of-war with them.

SALT, SEA GOING, M7,
(Sgt. Myron Yukmust)

Sgt. Yukmust is the guy who organizes all those shipboard entertainments. And he is the star performer. He gives imitations of actors, Edward G. Robinson, Lionel Barrymore, Donald Duck and Marjorie Main. They all sound alike and just like Yukmust.

He also plays a ukulele, a harmonica and a beat-up set of tap drums he found down in the engine room. He plays all these instruments at once, which doesn't improve the selection. If anybody encourages him, he will recite "The Shooting of Dan McGrew," followed by a rendition of "Yes Sir, That's My Baby" in the supposed Frank Sinatra style.

This idea of entertaining the troops is entered into with mixed feelings on the part of those concerned. Usually, Yukmust promotes one of these parties at a time when you are in the midst of a good pinochle game on the Number One Hatch. That's just the spot he wants to use for a stage, so you have to break up your game. Or, you are comfortably curled up against Lifeboat No. 6 reading a good book, and along comes Yukmust with his Hollywood production and you have to shove off to make room for Genius-on-the-March.

His jokes are all fugitives from a radio show you heard five years ago. But there is no stemming his enthusiasm. "Must cheer up the troops," he says. "Going into combat and no telling when they'll see a good show again!"

The noise and excitement of combat would be a pleasant Sunday School picnic compared with the agony of having to sit through one of Yukmust's performances. But on board ship, there is no escape. You can't dig a foxhole in a steel deck.

SALT, SEA GOING, M8,
(Pfc. Winchell Herstly)

Herstly is the lad who starts all those rumors. This character gets all information from scuttlebutt, the source of all world-shaking news. He cuddles it for awhile, nursing little tidbits of information into gigantic whoppers. Then he adds his own interpretation and passes it onto the troops.

With a perfectly straight face, he will tell you that the ship was surrounded last night with a pack of hostile submarines. The only reason the ship wasn't sunk was because we were clever enough to have the equator moved to a more convenient location to evade enemy action.

He will also inform anyone who will listen that, (a) all Pfcs are to have a pay raise beginning the first of the month – which will put them in the same income bracket as Texas oil tycoons and brigadier generals; and (b), that all 782 gear, from now on, will include built-in sun lamps and collapsible swimming pools.

When Herstly is on the job, there is no need for a G-2 Section. He gets *all* the straight dope and is only too glad to pass it on — slightly bent.

At least his talents do more to while away the many boring hours aboard ship than a dozen well-meaning entertainers like Yukmust.

SALT, SEA GOING, M9,
(SSgt. Henry J. Windsok)

On the land, and in the air, Windsok is strictly a Fly-Boy, as buss-happy as they make 'em. How he manages to get himself mixed up with the infantry on board a transport, is anybody's guess. At any rate, there he is, entirely out of his element and, acting as if he owned the ship and was just lending it to the Government.

Because of his exalted rank and, perhaps because there is no other way to keep him out of mischief, he is made sergeant-of-the-guard. That means he stands at the head of the chow line, (which extends three times around the ship), and cheerfully lets in all his friends. When you come along, after standing in line since daybreak, he grabs you for mess duty.

In between chow times, he stations himself at the only head

having fresh water showers and chases everybody over to the one marked Salt Water Shower. After you spend thirty minutes working up a slight lather with a piece of soap the size of a dime, Windsok comes in and turns off the main valve.

You are willing to admit that perhaps he does hold all fresh water rights in the state of Texas.

But it's pretty hard to believe that the whole ocean is his personal property — even though it is piped into *his* ship.

After awhile you begin to hope that this guy will remain with the infantry — at least until you can get him up at the front line.

– Lee Ruttle

Scuttlebutt – Gossip. The word is derived from the drinking fountain aboard ship, around which the boys gather to exchange commentaries. Scuttlebutt is another form of truth which has undergone a considerable amount of rough treatment by being passed from one person to another. When it reaches you, it is a ragged and disheveled bit of fact. In spite of that, you believe every word. Eventually, it becomes folklore.

"Yes, George, I know how you marines slept in Korea—now will you please come to bed!"

Marine Corp Gazette. 1952

Gizmo – Any gadget, thingummy, who-ziz or thing-a-ma-jig. May also be applied to a person whose name is unknown or difficult to pronounce. Gizmo is as handy a word as you'll find in any man's language.

LEATHERHEAD IN KOREA. Ssgt. Norvel E. Packwood, Jr.
Marine Corps Gazette. 1952

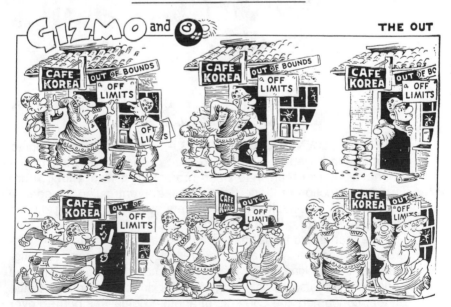

Leatherneck Magazine.

About midnight when the temperature outside dropped to ten below zero the bunch in our tent had busted into four groups, the social types who were outside dancing with a broom and pretending it was a Red Cross girl, the sporting types who had a high price crap game going, the music lovers that were singing with a guitar, and the tired ones that were trying to sleep. A big colored gentleman with sergeant's stripes was doing real good with the dice. He wrung me out in about eight throws and I was forced to join the music lovers, since I wasn't sleepy and I hadn't been in Korea long enough for a broom to look like a girl.

BILL MAULDIN IN KOREA.

WETTING DOWN THE CHEVRONS – This was a time-honored ceremony indulged in by enlisted men of the Old Marine Corps whenever one of them had been promoted. It was a long, hard road to promotion in those days and the event called for special observance. The lucky man, his new stripes gleaming on his sleeve, was escorted to the nearest slopchute by his fellow NCOs. He was then placed in a chair in the center of the room while others proceeded to buy up all the beer in the establishment. At a signal from the ranking NCO, the drinking marathon began with the honored guest also participating, drink for drink. But for each bottle of beer consumed, the contents of another bottle was poured over the head of the newly promoted marine. The pouring was done in precise cadence and was accompanied by song; each man taking his turn at leading the singing.

"Aha," they told me, "that's the difference between the navy and the army. We treat all our patients like officers, even if they're enlisted men."

This may or may not have been propaganda, Willie, but they looked in my ear, diagnosed it in triplicate, and gently held me down while they punched a hole in my eardrum to let the steam blow off, which made me feel better right away, and shot me in the rear with penicillin. The navy corpsmen even gave a painless shot, that's how nice they treated me. They slap you on one side of the tail and stick you on the other and you never feel the needle.

They kept me at Yokosuka for a few days, bunking me in a nice room with a view near the hospital so I could check in for my daily ear stabbing and needle jabbing until I was cured, and that's how I got acquainted with the Navy.

Bill Maudlin. WITH THE MARINES.

Secure The Butts! – The job is done. It is time to shove off, go home, quit work. On the rifle range, this command is given after "cease fire," and means that the men in charge of targets are to fasten them down. It is always a welcome command. At this point, it may also be welcome. Secure the Butts!

Asiatic – A person afflicted with a 1000-yard stare — in a ten-foot room. This may result from extensive periods of overseas service.

KOREA ORGANIST PLAYS RAGTIME
AT WRONG TIME

With U.S. Second Division — A congregation of soldiers couldn't believe their ears when an organist at the 72d Tank Battalion opened a Sunday chapel service with "Alexander's Ragtime Band."

Chaplain (Captain) Donald E. Trump, Petersburg, Va., was equally amazed.

Several days before the service, Chaplain Trump had to hire a new organist because the regular man was too ill to play. The substitute was a Korean houseboy who had often bragged about his musical ability.

With his heavy schedule Chaplain Trump didn't have time to worry about whether the lad could really play.

On Sunday though he was annoyed at not hearing any music as the hour for the service approached.

"Play! Play anything," he called to the organist.

The Korean beamed, and gave out with his "hot" rendition.

The rest of the worship service was conducted without benefit of organ music.

Stars and Stripes. Nov. 12, 1951.

A CHRISTMAS CAROL

"Twas the night before Christmas, and all through the tent,
Was the odor of fuel oil (the stove-pipe was bent).
The shoe packs were hung by the oil stove with care;
In the hope that they'd issue each man a new pair.
The weary GIs were sacked out in their beds,
And visions of sugar-babes danced in their heads;
When up on the ridge-line there rose such a clatter,
(A Chinese machine gun had started to chatter).

I rushed to my rifle and threw back the bolt,
The rest of my tentmates awoke with a jolt.
Outside we could hear our platoon sergeant Kelly,
A hard little man with a little pot belly.
"Come Yancey, come Clancey, come Connors and Watson.
Up Miller, up Shiller, up Baker and Dodson!"
We tumbled outside in a swirl of confusion,
So cold that each man could have used a transfusion.

"Get up on that hill-top and silence that Red,
And don't you come back 'til you're sure that he's dead."
Then, putting his thumb up in front of his nose,
Sergeant Kelly took leave of us shivering Joes.
But we all heard him say in a voice soft and light:
"Merry Christmas to all – may you live through the night!"

Stars and Stripes. Dec. 22, 1951.

AND THEN FOR MY FINALE...I DO A TERRIFIC
BIRD IMITATION!...I EAT A WORM!...I TELL
YA BOB, WITH ME IN THE TROUPE YOU'LL BE
A SMASH!!..

Oh, oh! I have a feeling my boy friend is back from Korea!

"*Wish those guys at the peace conference would hurry it up, my feet are gettin' cold.*"

"*I don't care if he does say 'sho nuff,' 'right smart,' and 'you all,' I still think he's a North Korean.*"

Brig – Jail, hokey, pokey, hoosegow, stir, jug, prison. The place where Brig Time is spent.

An army NCO was sent home from Korea for a most unusual reason. Neither wounded nor ill, he was allergic to wool and it was too cold in Korea to wear cotton!

WEEK-END CRISIS

The average guy who becomes a GI
Is one on whom you can depend
To do his job well; come high water or hell,
He will carry on right to the end.
But one thing, you can bet, will bring out a cold sweat
On even a man such as he:
The terrible fear that his name will appear
On the roster for Sunday K.P.

– Roy K. Kline.
"Reprinted by permission,
The American Legion Magazine, Copyright 1952."

"So I sez to the old man, I'd rather be a private in Korea than a corporal in this chicken outfit.'"

OUT OF SIGHT.
Stars and Stripes. 1952.

Blacklist forty – Code name for Korea where, once a GI smelled those rice paddies, he felt he'd been blacklisted.

OUT OF SIGHT
Stars and Stripes. 1952

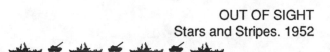

A lad from the hills of Arkansas was crouched in a foxhole alongside his buddy. They started to talk about how each came to be in service. The hillbilly kid was asked how come he joined up.

"Well, 'twas like this," George replied. "They was this feller come down to us and said if we was to want to work for the governmint we was to git in his truck. So I said 'yes' and got in his truck and he hauled us to the city. Then them fellers in khaki hauled us to this long shack near the water and there a feller come up and told us to walk into this here shack and sign up. Well, we walked through that there shack and come to a leetle plank. We stopped but this geek in khaki motioned us across it and another geek takes us through a iron door. When we all got inside, this gent slammed the door and that there shack jist sailed away! And here I am."

To Butterfly – To bestow sexual blessings! "You butterfly me, GI?"

Chargee – Korean pidgin; name for the penis.

Choggie-Choggie – To hurry up!

HOME REMEDIES FOR MARINES

Since marines are a unique branch of the military service, as well as unusual specimens of humanity, it has been suggested that some sort of "home remedy book" is needed to care for their lesser ailments. Research has proved, however, that the regulation sea bag is not large enough to hold a full-sized Home Remedy Book. Therefore, we have prepared this handy condensed version. It may be clipped from this book and pasted on the inside of a locker box.

The purpose of this information is to relieve the pressure on overworked corpsmen in the local sick bay. It is believed that a resourceful marine can really take care of himself in most cases by merely referring to this guide. More serious ailments should, of course, be handled by an experienced medical man.

STRIPE DISEASE

Symptoms – After making Pfc, the patient shows a marked tendency to sew stripes on his skivies. His voice changes. It takes on the deep sonorous quality of a master sergeant. Even his morning gargling sounds like a DI pack in full cry. In most cases, a noticeable swelling occurs in the region above the ears.

Treatment – Remove all stripes and place patient in a cool, well ventilated galley. Put a swab in his hands and a bucket of hot soapy water beside him. Then permit the patient to swab decks until he has recovered.

BACKACHE

Symptoms – A marine may be heard to utter, as if he were in great pain, "Oh, my aching back!" This means that he has probably been called out on a working party just when he is comfortably curled up with the latest copy of **Adventure Comics**. Moaning and groaning accompany the above remark. Slow movement of the feet and an expression of agony on the face are also common symptoms.

Treatment – Invariably, a trip to sick bay will reveal that the backache exists only in the patient's mind. In order that the patient may enjoy his backache in peace, it is suggested that he do one of three things: 1. Hide in the head to avoid the working party; 2. Tell the police sergeant that he is just about to go on guard duty; 3. Tell the police sergeant that he has just come off guard duty.

SORE ALIBIS

Symptoms – The patient first sees a red flag waving before his eyes. He then checks his windage and finds that he is breathing hard. Elevation is normal and pulse is rapid, especially in rapid fire, prone position at 300 yards. Other marked symptoms include the conviction that his coach has given him bum dope and that the guys in the butts are out to disqualify him. He also believes that someone pulled the target just as he squeezed off a round.

Treatment – Allow the patient to hold up the entire range party while he argues with the range officer. Then, give him a clip of ammo and let him take pot shots at the cow which always wanders across the line of fire. If he hits the cow, he is satisfied and — he is cured.

FURLOUGHITIS

Symptoms – The patient believes that he needs a furlough. He hangs around the company office, telling anyone who will listen that his poor old grandmother in Washout, Mississippi is suffering from an acute case of swamp fever and that he must go home to drain the swamps. This same type of patient has been known to have as many as 12 grandmothers, all suffering from the same complaint — which occurs whenever the patient, himself, feels an attack of furloughitis coming on.

Treatment – A 72-hour pass will generally make the patient feel better. In extreme cases, a transfer to recruiting duty may effect a cure. Recruiting duty is believed to be quite like a permanent furlough.

GUMBEATERITIS

Symptoms – The patient's jaw becomes unhinged and waggles continuously. Loud, braying sounds come out of his mouth at frequent intervals. His teeth show marks of severe chipping. This is known as "chipping the ivories." The patient is also very fretful and complains about everything from the free movie at the Post Theatre to last year's Christmas dinner.

Treatment – Remove patient's belt from his trousers and drape it over his head. Buckle tightly, under his chin.

LIBERTY FEVER

Symptoms – First signs of this ailment usually occur the morning after a strenuous liberty. The patient is unable to focus and his eyes resemble bursts of anti-aircraft fire against a deep black sky. He claims that thousands of tiny men, wearing lead shoes and wielding sledge hammers, are jumping up and down on the tin roof of his brain. Acute loss of appetite and memory accompany this disorder.

Treatment – Four hours of close order drill under a hot sun. Uniform-of-the-day: steel helmets, starched dungarees, tight leggings and full packs.

LOCKJAW

Symptoms – This form of lock-jaw has nothing to do with Tetanus. No shot in the arm will prevent or cure this particular ailment. The condition is generally observed the moment the patient stands before the commanding officer during office hours. The patient is totally unable to speak. Complete loss of memory and a violent trembling around the knees is also quite apparent.

Treatment – Allow the patient to rest quietly in a well guarded brig until his memory has been restored.

THOUSAND-YARD STARE

Symptoms – This disease is common among marines who have been overseas too long. It is sometimes called "Asiatic

Stupor" or, in the Old Marine Corps, "Tropical Freeze." The patient sits for hours under a coconut tree, dressed in his greens, mumbling to himself. His eyes are glassy and, they are apt to reflect visions of well-known Stateside pleasure resorts. He keeps his sea bag fully packed at all times and carries it around with him wherever he goes.

Treatment – Lead the patient gently to the top of the highest cliff in the area so that he can look out over the horizon and watch for approaching ships. A stout rope should connect him with the nearest tree – this guy will jump at the sight of a native canoe!

– Lee Ruttle
Leatherneck Magazine.

KIMCHI

Kick-A-Poo joy juice (sigh) may make the world go 'round in Al Capp's "Lower Slobovia." But in Korea (sob) it's Kimchi.

For the uninitiated, Kimchi is the Korean national dish. Its ingredients remained a mystery to marines until recently, when Lieutenant John A. Buck filed this report with the division food director.

"The national dish of Korea is known as Kimchi; a delectable food composed of many diversified materials, objects and occasional pieces.

" Ordinary' Kimchi," he continued, "includes these necessary ingredients:

"Four Chinese cabbages

"One white radish (sliced into two-inch shoe-string pieces)

"One pint red (sob) pepper (ground)

"One quart trepang (pickled in salt)

"Four bulbs garlic (grated)

"Four roots ginger (grated)

"One quart salt

"One-half pint sesame (sigh).

" Special' Kimchi," Lieutenant Buck continued, "includes those items plus the following:

"100 bulbs (ugh!) garlic (grated)

"four pears (sliced)

"When these ingredients are assembled, they are put into a porcelain, china, or wooden barrel and seasoned for approximately one week," he added.

Buck warned that almost invariably, extraneous matter, such as spiders, crickets and other insects wander into the Kimchi barrel during the seasoning process.

"These foreign bodies so introduced are immediately and completely dissolved, adding immeasurably to the high protein content (sigh) of Kimchi," he added.

Buck also filed a report with a Marine Corps equipment board praising the salutatory effects of Kimchi in combat operations.

"In unadulterated form, Kimchi protects the consumer from trench foot, frost-bite, body odor, gout and normal digestion.

"It is therefore concluded that Kimchi, canned in one-half tins, will provide an excellent assault ration," Buck concluded.

A copy of Lieutenant Buck's report also was filed with the division of graves registration section.

First Marine Division. June 1951

Gook – Any brown-skinned folks with whom we're on bad terms! Possibly from the term for a Korean man: *Hanguk-saram* . . . the guk (gook?) in Hanguk.

Luke The Gook – A North Korean soldier. Also, a North Joe.

Payday – The day before you're broke again!

A Korean civilian employee came down with a bad toothache. He called the base dentist and asked for an appointment. The dentist first asked, "Two-thirty all right?"

"The Korean replied, "Tooth hurtee, all right. What time I come?"

"Man! Dig that crazy television antenna!"

"Voodoo, hoodoo, whatever you call it, I still don't see how that will help you get even with the first sergeant."

OUT OF SIGHT.
Stars and Stripes. 1952

Stars and Stripes

A United Nations spokesman hinted not long ago that our forces in Korea might be facing a "new enemy." Corporal David X. Sharpe, a Marine combat correspondent, thinks he knows who that new enemy is.

Monkeys.

"Got it straight from the G-2 (intelligence officer),"Sharpe gravely told friends in a machine gun section. "Straight dope. The Chinese have trained battalions of monkeys to fling grenades and shoot .45 automatics. A regiment of Chink-trained monkeys like to have wiped out a ROK outfit."

Fascinated machine gunners, at a loss for anything else to talk about, went along with the gag.

"Better train the gun on them poplar trees, Jake," said one. "If they come swingin' through them trees, Jake, we'll cut 'em down."

The marines were dug in on the south bank of a river flowing across the central front. Several nights earlier, the Chinese counter-offensive had begun.

"Yessir," continued Sharpe. "We have three Chinese corps on our division front. Nobody's worried about them. But, we have the Zamboanga 45th Independent Commando Battalion facing us. Monkeys, all of 'em except the company commanders and first sergeants. They're full-fleged apes."

"Monkeys run and dodge real good," said a rifleman, mock worry on his face. "I don't know if I can hit a dodgin' monkey."

No marine has seen a monkey in the battle lines of Korea. No company has been overrun by chattering legions of monkeys. Nor have long-tailed creatures inflicted any casualties on United Nations troops. Nevertheless, the whimsical rumor has cropped up persistently for several weeks.

As Sharpe strolled away to spread his intriguing news in other quarters, the machine gun section leader advised his men: "I'm sending home for peanuts and bananas. You guys do the same. Those doggoned Chinks! Ringing' monkeys in on us . . . !"
> – Technical Sergeant James C. Jones, Jr.
> The Leatherneck.

A GI was hunched down in his foxhole, peering out at the gooks when one of those odd Korean hens zoomed past him with a rooster after her.

All at once the rooster slid to a stop and started to eat crumbs from the GI's sandwich he'd thrown away.

"Damn!" said the GI in wonder. "I hope I never get that hungry."

Joe – Coffee.

Sea Gull – Chicken

SWAGGER STICK TYPES

A swagger stick has been adopted as an optional item of uniform for all male officers.
Marine Corps Memorandum Number 121-52

Drum Major Type   Artistic Type

Gung Ho Type   Life-of-the-Party Type

"I think it's a trap." Leatherneck Magazine.

Staff Sergeant Kardiake was ill, so ill he died and arrived at the entry gate to his eternal rest home. He looked through the gate and remarked, "By golly, I never thought heaven would be so dad-blamed like Texas." He beamed at the prospect of his coming life.

"Young man," said the fellow at the gate, "this ain't heaven!

"What the hell we going to do if they find out this thing's a fire extinguisher?"

"No, no, no . . . ! I said bring up the B. A. R.!"

— Virgil F. Partch. Here we go again.
Duell, Sloane & Pearce, 1951

Easy Cure

A stiff wind was blowing across the black Korean waters as Captain Arthur W. Rawlings brought the transport helicopter slowly down out of the darkness.

On the lighted deck of the hospital ship, the officer helped unload the two wounded marines he had flown in from the front lines in the night evacuation.

As he watched Navy hospital corpsmen carry the stretchers away, a doctor looked at him with a note of concern.

"You don't look well," remarked the surgeon. "Did you have a rough trip over the mountains?"

Rawlings shook his head, "Gotta get off this damned ship," he muttered. "I'm getting seasick!"

— 1st Lt. Jack Lewis
1st Marine Air Wing

"Oink!"

THE FEET THAT SHOOK THE CORPS

That pair of feet was unbelievable — even when you saw them. So how could I ask you to believe what I'm going to say?

But there's been a lot of scuttlebutt about those feet, and for Jones' sake I want to give you the straight scoop just as I saw it happen. It began at boot camp.

Jones was the sorriest-looking recruit you ever saw, a big, bony, red-headed eightball who was always puffing, as if he'd just double-timed around the Parris Island parade ground toting a field marching pack. I discovered him standing near the window where the boots draw their first gear. He was asking for four pairs of boondockers instead of the usual two.

"Who do you think you are?" I boomed in my best D.I. voice.

He puffed desperately, then drawled, "It's just that both my feet's the same."

I was about to chew him out, but I couldn't help glancing down. I gulped. There, side by side like a couple of amtracks, were two huge, bare left feet. And they were attached to one pair of legs!

A man gets to see some strange things during a dozen years in the Corps, but the sight of those two grenade-sized big toes aiming off in the same direction almost flipped me.

"How long you had those?" I snapped. It was a stupid question, I know, but anything else would have sounded just as crazy.

"All my life, suh. Everybody back in Tennessee heard 'bout me. Folks call me Lefty-Lefty Jones."

At ease, Sergeant, I told myself desperately. A good NCO is supposed to keep cool in any emergency. I stalled for a time by continuing to peer at those fantastic feet.

There was nothing wrong with Jones' legs, except that they were long and knobby. But his right ankle was turned inside out, and below that, where his right foot should have been, swooped that other left foot.

Not only were his feet both lefties, they were gigantic. His size turned out to be 14 1/2 triple E, and there were only two pairs of boondockers in stock that would fit him.

"You're lucky I had those," growled the supply man. "Nobody's supposed to have feet that big."

He probably would have dropped if I'd told him the other oddity about Jones' feet. While Jones climbed into the left shoes, I chased away the other recruits, who were beginning to sense something unusual. I had to keep reminding myself that this was really happening. It was a problem for the Old Man, I decided. Leaving my assistant in charge of the platoon, I marched Private Lefty-Lefty Jones over to the company office.

Lieutenant Wilson was even more shook than I.

"Have you had your salt tablet today, Sergeant Stone?" he asked, eyeing me closely. "Did I hear you say you have a man outside who has two left feet?"

"Yes, sir. I know it's crazy, but I saw 'em! You can see for yourself."

The lieutenant slowly raised his bulk from the swivel chair, assumed one of those "you'd better not be snowing me" expressions, and ordered Jones in.

Now, Lieutenant Wilson and I were together at Tarawa, and I know him for a mighty cool customer. But this time he nearly lost control of himself.

"Incredible!" he gasped as soon as Jones stepped into the office. Lieutenant Wilson removed his glasses, carefully breathed on them and wiped them off with his handkerchief, put them back on, and stared again.

"Absolutely unbelievable! Young man," he growled right in the recruit's sweating face, "do you know that you're scientifically impossible? Two-headed calves, yes; midgets, yes; Siamese twins, yes. But two left feet? No!"

When the office staff began to crowd about, Lieutenant Wilson remembered who and where he was, and calmed down. He began making phone calls, pausing now and then to gaze at Jones' feet and mumble something to himself. He had to keep repeating the same words over and over into the receiver:

"Yes, sir, I know it, sir, but I'm looking at them right now, sir. No, sir, I don't need a 30-day leave . . . . "

After hanging up for the last time, he sighed, then wagged his head sadly.

"We've got to keep him. Nobody can figure out how he passed the physical, but then nobody can figure out why he shouldn't pass, at that. As the colonel pointed out, there's nothing in the Marine Corps Manual that says you can't have two left feet."

He ordered Jones to wait for me outside.

"Sergeant Stone," continued the lieutenant gravely, "we've got to keep this hushed up. No telling what may happen if Congress finds out about it. We're to treat Jones like an ordinary recruit until the general has time to check with the Commandant. I'm swearing my staff to secrecy under pain of court-martial, and I want you to do the same."

"Incredible!" gasped Lieutenant Wilson, staring. Lefty-Lefty Jones just stood there stiffly with his other left foot protruding like a sore thumb.

"I'll keep it strictly within the squad-bay, sir," I promised.

As I turned to leave, Lieutenant Wilson cleared his throat uneasily. "By the way, have Jones report to the battalion office in half an hour. The general's coming over and wants to see it himself."

While the general and the other wheels examined the left feet, I picked up a book called "Strange Freaks of Nature" at the post library. I was reading it that night in my room when I heard three heavy raps on my door. It was Jones. After the usual preliminaries, I gave him permission to speak man to man.

"Suh," he complained, "I know my feet look powerful strange to some folks, but suh, I'll be in boot camp all my life if everybody's got to see 'em."

"Nobody'll bother you any more, Pvt. Jones."

"Suh," he continued earnestly, "I just got to get to Korea fast. I gotta be a hero."

"A hero!" I snorted. "Listen, Jones, you'll be a hero if you live through boot camp." I dropped into heavy sarcasm. "Just why do you have to be a hero?"

The gangly recruit, who had been staring straight at the bulkhead all this time, looked down in embarrassment. "For my pappy," he said simply as his ears reddened. "My pappy told all the folks back home that my brother and me were going to Korea and would sure come back heroes. Only my brother went in the Army, so . . . ."

"Okay, okay, Jones." I strode over and poked my nose under his jaw. "Jones, you'd better not give the Marine Corps a bad name. You WILL go to Korea and you WILL be a hero! Do you HEAR me?"

His wide face lit up like a rocket battery at midnight. "Yuh, yuh, suh!"

"Now, shove off!"

If you've never seen a man with two feet trying to do a right about face, you've missed a rare spectacle. Excited as he was, Jones whirled wildly around and hit the deck nose first. Somehow, I kept from guffawing until he had scrambled out of the room.

Next morning the word came from Lieutenant Wilson. Headquarters, Marine Corps, had classified Private Jones as a secret! Orders were going out to all posts and stations, wherever Jones might be transferred, to keep the knowledge of his second left foot strictly within the Corps. If it got out, the marines would be the laughing stock of the Pentagon. But everybody knew it would be impossible to keep some scuttlebutt from floating around.

In the meantime, I had a lot of drill-busting to do. Lefty-Lefty Jones turned out to be a good man, sharp in map-reading and combat formations. He was nearly as clumsy as he looked, though, especially when it came to flanking and facing movements. The rest of the platoon considered Jones a freak, naturally, but I worked them so hard they didn't have much time to think about him.

They dared to laugh only once. That was the day I fouled up myself. The troops were in greens for the first time, and I was giving facing movements outside the barracks before marching to evening chow. They went through without a hitch until the very last command.

"LEHF' face!"

The green-clad recruits shifted as smoothly as a Notre Dame backfield. Except for one big clown in the rear squad. He had spun the wrong way.

"Your OTHER left!" I roared automatically.

Then I saw it was Jones. I didn't have the heart to stop the platoon from laughing, especially since I was doubled up myself.

As I say, although Lefty-Lefty was a good marine, the other recruits were always kidding him because he was good-natured enough to let them get away with it. On graduation day he seemed proudest of all.

Before he left on boot leave, Jones thanked me for not making fun of him like the rest, and promised to be a credit to his D.I. in addition to being a hero for his pappy. It made me feel good, even though I didn't expect to lay eyes on his two left feet again. He was bound for Pendleton and Korea, while I figured to retire from P.I.

As it turned out, I did see Lefty-Lefty Jones again, and in Korea. But in the intervening months the stories about him really got around. The way I heard it a couple of times, there was a big guy out at Pendleton with two left feet plus two left hands. Whoever passed out the yarn never failed to warn that it was strictly hush-hush on orders of the commandant.

By the time they finally shipped me to Korea, it was the summer of 1952, and the dug-in war was on full blast. I felt right at home when I found out my company commander was Captain Wilson, my old CO at P.I. He had further news for me: one of the corporals in my squad had two left feet, size 14 1/2 EEE.

"Not Jones!"

"Who else?" grinned the captain, appearing philosophical about the whole affair.

I found Jones sitting glumly in a bunker, examining the sole of one of his huge left shoes. When he spotted me, he was as happy as a liberty-hound on payday.

"Sarge, Sarge!" he pleaded, puffing anxiously, "you've got to help me!"

"Why the sweat, lad?" Jones brought out the fatherly part of the D.I. in me. "You've been here long enough to be a hero, haven't you?"

"No, Sarge," he wailed. "Nobody gives me a chance to be a hero for my pappy."

Lefty-Lefty Jones spouted all his trouble like a grease gun spewing lead.

In the first place, although he arrived the previous winter, he had just managed to get to the front. It was all because of his feet. There wasn't a pair of those Mickey-Mouse cold-weather boots in the Far East big enough for him. They kept him in reserve all winter.

Now that he was in the lines, with only three weeks to go until rotation, he was still cooling his big heels. Although everybody liked him, they still thought of him as a freak. They never sent him out on patrols, because they figured a guy with two left feet must be unsteady with them.

"And now I've got to go back in reserve again," groaned Lefty-Lefty, waving one of his boondockers under my nose. "Look, suh, they're worn out, and . . . .

"I know, they don't have your size in stock."

"That's what they say, Sarge, but that ain't all."

What really had Jones worried was his brother, who he had heard was in an Army outfit up the line a way. He was afraid the brother might do something heroic while he was back in reserve.

I offered Jones sympathy, but there wasn't much else I could do.

"They should have some boondockers for you in a couple of weeks," I said hopefully as I shoved off.

Then I had other matters to think about. The gooks kept sending out combat patrols that seemed to have a special hankering to hit our sector. It took us two weeks to find out why, from a prisoner. It seems a new Chinese brass hat wanted to see for himself how tough the U.S. Marines really were.

The old man was worried. We had been having supply troubles, and right then we were pretty low on ammo. If the Commies hit us in any strength, we'd have it rough.

In the middle of all this, Lefty-Lefty Jones showed up again in his bright new boondockers. He had found his brother. The brother hadn't won any medals yet, and Jones was anxious to beat him to it, especially since he had only a few days left. He expected me to come up with a scheme that would win him the Medal of Honor.

"Okay, Jones," I said, trying to get rid of him for a while. "Here's what you do. Go out and scare those gooks into leaving us alone long enough to get some decent sacktime. And get it done tonight."

Instead of sulking, Jones appeared to like the idea fine.

"Thanks, Sarge," he beamed, "that's just what I'll do."

He took off at high port. Sometime later the enemy started pounding our positions with everything they had.

I don't know when Jones returned, because by that time the ball had taken a bad bounce for me and I was in a rear area aid station with a few shell fragments in my leg. A couple of days afterwards, who should be brought in but Captain Wilson, with the same kind of ailment, and he had a wonderful story to tell:

The Chinese had been planning to hit us all right, but at the last minute they chickened out. A trembling P.O.W. explained: the gook scuttlebutt was going around that now the marines were seven or eight feet tall, and some were as big as horses, with fur feet, at that. They had figured all this out from the size and spacing of some strange footprints found in a muddy gully near their positions.

"Wait a minute, Captain," I protested. "Four feet? You mean Lefty-Lefty . . . . "

"Exactly," grinned Captain Wilson, "but his . . . . "

"Wait a minute! Those two left footprints would confuse the gooks, but how could it scare them?"

"Because you've heard only half the story. You see, it turned out that Lefty-Lefty's brother is his twin. Only, guess what? The brother has two RIGHT feet, he's a corporal, and the Army's classified him top secret, and they call him ...."

"No!" I moaned. "I don't believe it!"

"Righty-Righty. I saw them with my own eyes. And do you know how the Jones boys did it? They met that night at the mouth of this gully and dog-trotted together for a few hundred feet. Made it look like . . . . "

"Don't tell me, Captain! I'm going Asiatic now!"

"Okay, but there's more. They were out there alone, and their dangerous mission stopped the enemy from attacking. Both I and the Army commander wanted to recommend the twins for a Silver Star. But we can't, because both the Army and the Marine Corps want to keep the feet business secret."

"Nobody'd believe it anyhow, Captain," I shrugged.

"No, Sergeant," he agreed, "nobody would believe it."

— Fred de Luna. Leatherneck Magazine.

FIGMO – "Fuck It I Got My Orders," or "I've been reassigned (or I've got my separation papers) so don't bother me any more!"

Frozen Chosun – An apt description of winter in Korea.

A wounded GI, in hospital, had not written to notify his wife of his condition. A nurse with whom he had grown friendly tried to persuade him. "It's good to keep those home fires bright and warm, you know," she told him.

"But we never do write each other," the GI said. "Seems kind of silly to start now."

"Why not give it a try? Just start out with something simple to cheer her up, like 'My sweet, darling wife'."

"Nurse, let me tell you! That sure as hell would cheer her up. Why, that'd make her laugh like nothing else could!"

Boom-Boom – Sexual intercourse.

Old Salt – Any marine who has been in the Corps over twenty-four hours. A designation which implies that the bearer of the name has more than completed the period of boot training. Sometimes, it really is a person who is well integrated in the ways of the Marine Corps. At least, he may *think* he knows all the answers.

Leatherneck Magazine

"After de Doc examines me, I says, 'T'anks', and here I am!"

Leatherneck Magazine.

Chicken – It means a young Marine who has not quite gotten around to shaving the peach fuzz on his cheeks.

Sea Dust – Salt (the kind used at the table).

Buzzard – Turkey.

Slum – Beef stew.

Axle Grease – Butter.

Brightwork – Brass or other metal which *must* be polished.

To Cut A Choggie – To retreat. To move away fast.

General McToffreer was organizing a special awards ceremony for infantry officers recently returned from Korea. In the process of assigning duty for the occasion, he called Private Leroy Jones, and instructed him on how to introduce the officers. "Now Jones, as the officers approach one-by-one to receive the award, I want you to call everyone's name. Got that? Call names."

Private Jones slowly grinned. "Do you mean that, sir?" he asked. "Boy! Sir, that'll be a gas. I served under some of them guys for near onto two years. But, General, you'll make sure I don't get tossed in the guardhouse for doin' it, won't ya?"

The indispensable sergeant takes a beating at the hands of jokesters. Perhaps it's inevitable, given the feeling of the lower ranks, but the humor reflects the American custom of resenting higher authority. Here are some examples:

1st Sergeant: "You guys wish I was dead, don't you? Then you could spit on my grave."

GI: "No sir! Not me. I hate to stand in line."

Or this one:

Hi diddle diddle, the cat and the fiddle,
    He called the sarge a goon.
The MPs laughed to see such sport,
    Court martial – tomorrow noon.

And This:

Private: "Sir, the first sergeant just hung himself."
CO.: "How awful. Did you cut him loose?"
Private: "No sir! He hasn't quit wigglin' yet."

"THE LOUSY ARTILLERY GETS ALL THE BREAKS ... A SWELL HOUSE TO LIVE IN!"

Ssgt. Norval E. Packwood, Jr. LEATHERHEAD IN KOREA.
Marine Corps Gazette

"Yeh, yeh, that's it, now erase the necklace next."

SWEATING IT OUT

Leatherneck Magazine.

A Chinese soldier surrendered voluntarily to a company of infantrymen. During the interrogation, the captive was asked why he had surrendered and what the handful of surrender leaflets that he was carrying meant.

"I cook breakfast for 75 soldiers," the Chinese chef replied. "After breakfast, soldiers go out to fight Americans. Nobody come home for supper. Me think me better be on your side!"

"How many points you got?"

Leatherneck Magazine.

Fidelis to Whom?

Prunella Pastine
Wed a handsome marine
Named Otto, from the town of Chehalis.
Knowing Latin, she knew
That the lad would be true
For his motto was "Semper Fidelis."

But the lady, demure,
Was never quite sure
If this handsome young devil-dog fella,
Would only be true
To the Red, White and Blue,
Or would he be true to Prunella?

– Burge Buzzell
Leatherneck Magazine.

New Classification

Before World War II, a guy overseas too long, was termed "Asiatic," then along came the war and the island-bound marines were called "Rock-Happy" – today in Korea – you get "Korea

Conscious."

It's applied to marines who are beginning to carry baskets, stray timbers, or what have you on their heads like Korean women.

However, a marine who can carry a pail of water balanced on his dungaree cap, still rates stares of pure admiration.

– First Marine Air Wing
Leatherneck Magazine.

THE CAPTAIN'S VALENTINE

Moral: Don't trip your own booby trap when you send a comic valentine sealed with a hiss.

Ever been a company mail clerk? I was — once. It was a pretty soft touch, now that I think about it. But, like working in a bank, it has its own temptations.

The guy who invented Valentine's Day was no saint! And as far as I'm concerned you can knock the year down to 11 months and skip February.

I'm not sentimental but I used to get a nice, warm feeling when the guys got an extra special letter. Being a mail clerk has its advantages, too; I always knew exactly who had a supply of home-baked cookies and fudge. And that made up for some of the headaches like trying to convince Goober Dumbrosky that I wasn't holding out his wife's mail.

It all started when Goober Dumbrosky grabbed me by the stacking swivel one day and threatened to beat a regiment of small knobs on my skull if I didn't come across with the daily letter from Effie, his wife. Goober's one of those guys you just don't argue with — nearly 200 pounds of him crammed into a six-foot-two frame like a Sherman tank. His blue eyes are flashing and his thick, blond head is shaking and his mouth is firing little threats at me like a machine gun.

"Take it easy, Goober," I tell him. "There just isn't any letter from your wife today."

"She writes me every day," he explodes.

"Maybe the Pony Express rider got tied up in traffic yesterday," I suggest.

Goober's kinda dumb. "There ain't no Pony Express in Detroit — them postmen use trucks now."

"Okay . . . maybe the truck was struck by a thunderbolt or something."

"There weren't no storm yesterday."

You just can't argue with the guy — and him with a 70-pound weight advantage. So I invite him in to shuffle through the mail and have a look. He does just that. He still ain't satisfied.

"You're hiding that letter someplace," he shouts.

"Look, Goober, whatinthehell would I want with a letter from your wife?"

Goober doesn't think very fast, and since he hasn't got an answer for this one, he starts to shove off to brood about it.

But he turns, sights in on me with his bulls's eyes and issues a wild order. "You'd damnsite better have two letters for me tomorrow or I'll rip off one of your arms and beat you with the bloody stump."

Goober is a very tough fellow.

Like I say, the job can be rough, guys like Goober wear me down. I have to hit the sack for a couple of hours. That's where I get my very unbright idea. Valentine's Day is only a week away and stowed in my locker is a cache of comic jobs left over from last year.

I can't wait to get up and dig out those valentines. What a collection. I've got just the right one. It's a picture of a hefty babe with buck teeth and a wart on her nose and it says:

> Roses are red,
> Poison ivy is green,
> You're the biggest mess
> I've ever seen.

With this ammunition, my 14th of February will be bigger than the 4th of July. Luckily Goober gets his two letters the next day and the twin envelopes keep coming in regularly so I don't have any more trouble with him for a while. Then one day he gets three letters – all from Effie! A special delivery job is in order and I trot out to look for Goober.

Unfortunately the captain grabs me on the way and asks me to take care of some mail for him. I like Captain O'Brien, but he is a writer of many letters — so many that I have a hard job finding time to read them all so I can keep track of what goes on in the outfit.

By the time I get out of the captain's office, I've got over a dozen letters including a couple of his personal ones. Of course, I'm too honorable a guy to think of reading those he writes his wife and personal friends — if they don't concern the company. Anyway, with so many of them I don't have enough time to read them and I've still got to find Goober and deliver his mail.

I finally locate Dumbrosky cleaning his M-1 over at the steam rack and he beams on me for a change — after I deliver the letters.

Usually Goober gets one of the guys to write his replies since he's not so good at writing. I take advantage of my current good favor and tell him, "With that many letters, you'd better write Effie a good one back."

"Yeah," he mumbles, eagerly reading the letters.

"Say, Goober, I'm not going to be doing anything much this afternoon . . . how'd you like me to type a letter for you?"

"Yeah," he answers — still reading on.

So I stand by and wait — reading a couple of the captain's letters about some new training manuals and a new clerk to replace an eight-ball on the roster. I scan the letter in a hurry, looking for the name of the clown.

I find it.

It's not me.

I breathe again.

Goober wades through the three letters and looks up. "What's that you were saying, kid?"

"I just thought that since Effie has written so many letters this time, you ought to get a reply off pronto . . . and since I'm not going to be busy this afternoon, you might like to have me write one for you." I try to camouflage my eagerness.

It takes a while for him to think this over but he finally decides that it's a good idea.

I am reading the last of the captain's letters that afternoon when Goober comes in and, putting important matters first, I sit down to give Goober my very best service. He dictates a lot of mush and tells her what a big wheel he is while I type the words on a hunk of paper. I finish typing his "love and kisses" ending and he takes the letter and reads it through with a proud smile on his ugly kisser.

"Nice letter, ain't it?" he asks.

"You sure know how to write 'em," I lie. "Now, tell me the address and I'll type the envelope."

That job done, he insists on sealing the letter and dropping it into my mailbox. This is a handicap I don't plan on, so I set my coffee pot on to boil. As soon as Goober leaves the mailroom and the water in the pot comes to a boil, I get his letter out of the box and proceed to steam it open again.

Just as I finish, the captain comes in and I think maybe he

has caught me in the act. But evidently he didn't see what I was doing because he just asks if the mail has gone out and if I have sent the letter to his wife yet.

I dig it out for him and he tears open the envelope. "Got to add a note," he explains.

He takes out his pen, adds a quick postscript and then hands the letter back to me and asks me to address an envelope and send it.

I get all of the mail taken care of and then bring out that special valentine I have selected. I type "To My Valentine, Effie" at the top of it and then enclose it with Goober's letter. Luckily, there is still enough goo left on the envelope flap to reseal it so you can't even tell that it has been reopened.

"That'll thin down Goober's mail for a while," I tell myself with pleasure.

I am feeling mighty proud of myself for the next few days as I await the reaction from Effie. The letters keep coming regularly and Goober is still happy.

Then one day I notice Goober has evidently had some bad news. "The wife giving you a rough time?" I asks.

"Aw, she's mad at me for forgetting to send her a valentine," Goober answers.

"For forgetting to send her one?" I say, somewhat amazed.

"Yeah, I completely forgot women expect such things. Say, how about writing her another letter for me?"

This snows me. I think, for once, I have gotten the best of big Goober, but the jinx is still on me. I don't have to wonder what happened for long, though.

I am passing the captain's office the next morning when I hear a woman's voice – she is screamin' mad! Now, who am I to eavesdrop? But I think maybe there is some mail in the next room for me to pick up, so I go in to check.

Through the wall I hear this gal throwin' real trouble at the captain. "So, you think I'm the biggest mess you've ever seen, do you?" she shouts. "Well, let me tell you, I turned down a glamorous Air Force pilot and married a stupid moron like you. I'll make you pay . . . "

But Effie," pleads the captain, "I tell you I didn't send you that valentine . . . I didn't . . . I swear . . . "

Well, I don't have to tell you I'm no longer the mail clerk. In fact, I'm not with Captain O'Brien any longer. He seemed to think the Marine Corps needed my services out here in Korea. Funny thing though, I gave the rest of those comic valentines to Goober before I checked out and he sent one to his wife. It had a picture of a witch and read:

> I took a little drink
> It went to my head
> I married you
> Now I wish I was dead.

Saw him over here the other day and he said his wife got a big kick out of it . . .

– Lt. Dick Hodgson

During the Korean War, an officer was showing a group of women through the large army base. They paused before a large baking oven where a cook was rolling dough into huge slabs, then he cut out small portions that he pressed against his belly button. Then he put the small, round portions in a baking pan.

The ladies were puzzled. "What in the world is he doing?" one of them asked.

"He's making cookies, ladies, and impressing an attractive design on each one." the officer explained.

"Well! That's the strangest thing I ever saw!" remarked one of the visitors.

"You think that's strange?" said the officer. "You should see how he makes doughnuts!"

"I'd probably be a SFC today, Algy—but the Army don't have a brewer's M.O.S."

KOREA—LAND OF THE MORNING CALM!

THE HUMOR OF THE VIETNAM WAR 1964 – 1973

The Vietnam War was unique in several ways, one of which was the humor of the GI.

In all our previous wars, GI humor was upbeat, appropriate, funny and derisive of the enemy rather than of themselves. But Vietnam humor was sardonic and sarcastic as well as self-critical to an extreme. Vietnam humor has come to be regarded as "black humor".

Accordingly, the humor of our last war evokes only a somber smile, an agreeable grunt or an understanding nod. Rarely does it provide the side-splitting, knee-slapping hilarity evoked by the humor of earlier wars.

There were exceptions to the preceding statement in cartoonists such as Tad Foster, Tony Zidek, Jake Schuffert and the Marines generally upbeat humor in LEATHERNECK MAGAZINE. But these exceptions proved the rule that GI humor in Vietnam was as different as the statewide view of that war.

Thus, Vietnam WAS a unique war. The GI in Vietnam produced an exemplary military record in spite of the mixed support he received from home, from "the land of the round doorknob". He fought a good fight and deserves a salute of gratitude from every American. "He seen his duty and he done it".

We hope the following humor does him justice.

"Keep your eyes open Claude—
These babies are pretty
good at camouflage!"

Leatherneck Magazine.

My wife had a Pekinese dog and she thought it was the smartest animal alive. I was of the opinion that chimps were smarter than dogs, and just about as smart as people. I bet her a new dress, payable after the baby was born, that I could prove chimps are smarter than dogs.

We got a newborn chimp about two weeks after the baby was born and raised him as if he were a twin to my son. He grew up pretty much like any other kid, except that he went through rather more combs and brushes, learned to shave about fifteen years earlier, and had to be admonished about his posture more often than the average child.

He reached his teens in the early sixties. Outside of being a little shorter than average, (and having to have jeans special-made with pockets near the cuffs) he looked very much like all other youths of his day.

He joined the Navy in 1968. When they measured him for a uniform in boot camp — size three hat and a size forty-four shirt — they made him a bosun's mate. Because his classification scores were so much higher than the average, he was sent to an advanced school to learn all the intricacies of the rating (three days at the Marine Corps submarine base in Pittsburgh, Pennsylvania). He got out after six years because of constant squabbling with his superiors about hair regulations, and the fact that his knuckles were always sore from the detergent the Navy uses on its decks (actually, a lot of bosuns have this same problem).

I could get many sworn statements from my friends at Pappy's Bar to prove all of this is true, but I don't want to jeopardize the boy's chances of winning the congressional seat he is running for up in central Alabama. Also, we've never told him or the other kids that he is adopted (he rather favors several of my wife's relatives).

Truly yours,
Dave Dunlap

P.S. Just a few days ago my wife reminded me of the bet, and, since the boy is running for Congress as a Democrat, I went out and bought her the damned dress.

Viet-Speak – A mixture of slang, patois and odd terms from Oriental language drafted into English and used in Vietnam. An example follows:

Little Red Riding Hood Is leaving her hotel with a basket of chop-chop to take to her home for her sick grandma-san. As she puts the basket near the bed, she does a double-take, exclaiming "Choi-oi! What big eyeballs you have!"

"Yep!" says Mr. Wolf, "the better to see you with."

"And your ears are filled with onions," remarks Miss Hood.

"Sho! You bet! All the better to hear you with," etc.

Ping – To criticize constantly; to nit-pick.

Plat-Daddy – A platoon sergeant.

One of the most hated master sergeants on the base was giving a lecture to a group of PFCs on the basic requirements for promotion to the grade of sergeant.

"Consider what it takes to make a topnotch sergeant, men, a truly superior one, an unparalleled one. Well, you think about it for a moment and then I'll tell you."

He paused for two or three seconds, then continued. "Here's what it takes . . . well . . . I'll tell you what it takes . . . well, well, y'see . . . he's got to be born that way. Understand?"

There was a moment's silence, then a voice chirped from the last row, "In wedlock or out, Sergeant?"

Two young flying officers had had too many drinks in the local tavern. On their way back to Chanute Field they got lost.

Suddenly one of them stopped and said, "Hey, Joe, we'ze ina shemetery. Here's a gravestone."

"Whosh is it?" asked Joe.

The aviator lit a match, looked at the stone, and said, "Don' know hish name, but he sure wash an old man. Says hunert and twenty.

"Wow," exclaimed his buddy. "Maybe he wash Methuselah?"

The aviator lit another match. "Nope" he reported. "It was shum guy named Miles to Chatham."

Captain Smith commanded a company of the Fourth Infantry Division. One day he was asked the derivation of the term "Dink," used to describe hostile troops during the war in Vietnam.

"I never did like the name Charlie for those guys," he replied. "Y'see, I had an Uncle named Charlie. And my best friend in college was Charlie, too. So you can see why I figured that Charlie was just too goddam good for those bastards. Well, I got to figuring just what these little jerks are really and truly like and it seemed to me that the name, Rinkydink, fitted them just fine. But it was too damn long, don't y'know. So we reduced it down to size. And that's how come we call 'em Dinks."

Sir Charles – Mister Charlie, a Vietcong, or North Vietnamese soldier.

Cheap Charlie – The bar girl's taunt, as, "You numbah fuckin' ten, Cheap Charlie GI! (Cheap Charlie was a fair-priced restaurant in Saigon).

Cherry – A new, innocent and unused soldier. The derivation is obvious.

There was this kid in our outfit from Middletown, Illinois. He read the *Stars and Stripes* carefully, every day, checking to see who had been killed and where they were from. He didn't know, for sure, if anyone else from Middletown was in Vietnam but he checked the lists anyway because he figured that if there really was another GI in Vietnam who *was* from Middletown, he would be OK.

"I figure it this way," he said. "It ain't in the cards for two guys from Middletown to get killed . . . not from a dinky little ol' town like that. No, sir! So, you see, if I read that one guy from Middletown is on the casualty list, well, I figure I'm safe."

Exaggeration, hyperbole (as they say) is much used in official reports of the results of war action by all armies. Ours is no exception. For example, a young Special Forces captain was telling a group of friends about an action he had participated in.

"We went out and my outfit killed three VC and freed two prisoners. The next week my commanding officer called me in and told me I'd killed sixteen VC and freed five prisoners. And I'm wearing the medal to prove it!"

"YEAH, YOU GET USED TO THE RAIN!"

Tony Zidek. CHOI OI.
Chas. E. Tuttle Co.

Tube Steak – Mess hall frankfurters.

TUIFU – The Ultimate In Fuck Ups.

Turret Head – An argumentative person.

Turtle – The GI's replacement who always seemed oh-so-slow in coming - - - like a turtle.

GiZMO and **8** **ONE SLIP**

FRED RHOA

Leatherneck Magazine.

"Can I take my finger out of
the leak now, sir?"

Oscar Charlie – Old Crow whiskey. The phonetics for O and C
are Oscar and Charlie.

A GI was showing his buddy a picture of his sweetheart, sitting in a boat back home. "What do you think of her?" the proud lover asked.

His buddy stared at the picture so long that the first one became embarrassed. Finally, he blurted out, "Well, tell me, what do you think of my darling?"

"She's a beauty," his friend said, nodding his head and smiling in appreciation. "Why, she must be at least a twenty-footer!"

During Fire Prevention Week at a base in Vietnam, the chaplain put up a sign:

DON'T GET BURNED
(Either here or in the hereafter!)

No Man's Nam – Vietnam. "You're about 10,000 miles from No Man's Nam."

One-Eyed Zipper Snake – The penis.

One In The Hangar – To be pregnant.

There's an interesting story about a sailor who had for weeks been assisting in the landing of infantry in Vietnam. The sailor was fed-up with the work. He craved action, so he attached himself to one of the combat units and soon arrived at Hill 248. There was hot action and the sailor distinguished himself so that he was decorated for outstanding bravery. But his absence was discovered back at the port. They determined where he was and wired that he be returned immediately.

The reply from the sailor's commanding officer read like this: "Your seaman is fighting on Hill 248. He's doing a helluva job, been cited for bravery and decorated. You come and get him because we're afraid to go up after him!"

At Da Nang, a tough, experienced Marine lieutenant was indoctrinating a group of men fresh in for service in his platoon. "Don't never sell these boys out here short! They're rough, tough, real blitzers! Never mind what you learnt in trainin', fergit all that jazz and remember they're battle-tough and take no shit. Don't let 'em out of your sight. If they jump fer cover, you jump, too. Don't never take your eye off 'em.

One GI piped up, "Just how near to the Viet Cong are we, Lieutenant?"

"Who the hell said anything about the VC?" the officer shouted, "I'm talking about my own gunnies!"

"How do the men feel about
going back to the States?"

Patrick. Leatherneck Magazine.

A GI wrote home from Vietnam that he didn't know what kind of work he'd be able to do when he got home. "But," he wrote, "I can tell you this much . . . I'll be able to do it 24-hours a day and 7 days a week."

There was one truly tough question asked during a quiz at an Air Force pilots' class in Vietnam. The pilots complained about the difficulty and the instructor remarked that he knew it was a tough question, but that it was intended to separate the wheat from the chaff.

One flyer moaned, "So that's it . . . we're bein' reaped."

Missing Link – A second lieutenant.

Mr. No-shoulders – A snake.

Mox Cox – "It doesn't matter," as, "Mox cox to me!"

Newfer – A new man in a unit.

91 Bed-Pans – Army medical specialist. Adapted from the official MOS-91B.

A GI was asked if there were electric dishwashers in Vietnam.

"Nope," he replied. "Don't need 'em. We just take a new arrival and plug him in!"

It was Christmas Eve and a bunch of GIs decided to celebrate with a group of Vietnamese Christians. They stood before a church and sang carols.

During a pause, one GI remarked, "Man, this is somethin' else! Here I am, a Jew, and busy singin' Christmas carols with a group of nuns in front of a Protestant church and this is Buddhist country!"

You had to have a sense of humor to make it in Vietnam. There's the story of the GI who got sick and tired of the perennial rain. But he figured a way to get a laugh out of it. He put up a sign beside one of those deep, wide, black, filthy and innumerable mud puddles. It read "Shower Before Entering The Pool."

"BUT WHAT I SAID WAS . . . CHUTE UP THE COLONEL!"

Pacific Stars and Stripes

Jesus Boy – A religious goody-goody GI; a sissy, a square, a pantywaist.

A Jug Fuck – To get drunk!

Khaki Teat – To suck the khaki teat (or tit) indicates that Uncle Sam's Army takes care of you.

Land Of The 24-Hour Generator – The United States. Also *The Land of the Round Doorknob.*

Lifer Juice – Coffee.

⚓ ⚓ ⚓ ⚓ ⚓

A GI was in basic training for several months when he received his absentee ballot just before the election. He wrote back to the board of elections in his home district: "Sure do thank you for the ballot application. It was most welcome and quite flattering and I must tell you that this is the first time in 22 months that I have been invited to express an opinion!"

⚓ ⚓ ⚓ ⚓ ⚓

The GI wrote home on his first tour in the Army. It was during basic training. "It's not so bad here. We're not totally denied our usual wine, women and song because they still let us sing while we're marching!"

⚓ ⚓ ⚓ ⚓ ⚓

The mess sergeant was lecturing about waste. "You men have got to make better use of our leftovers. For instance, what can we do with left-over carrots?"

Nothing but puzzled shrugs came from the men.

"OK, so you can't figure it. You can make carrot pie. That's what you can do with leftover carrots. Doesn't it make sense?"

The sergeant paused to let his idea take root. Then he asked, "Any questions?"

A hand was raised and a voice asked, "Sir, what can you do with the leftover pie?"

⚓ ⚓ ⚓ ⚓ ⚓

Liquid Cork – Medicine for diarrhea.

Lower Than Whaleshit – A way to express rank, as "I'm a private, lower than whaleshit."

MFWIC – Motherfucker What's In Charge, as "Listen, soldier, I am the MFWIC of thisyer MF'er outfit!"

Menopause Manor – An installation for older personnel, GIs over thirty!

"Claims it's arthritis! Says he
gets stiff in every joint."

W. Cowan. Leatherneck Magazine.

A man was serving a tour of duty in south Vietnam. He wrote home to his wife that he had received a form requesting an answer to the question "What do you plan to do upon leaving the service?" He told her that his response was four words: "Cartwheels and more cartwheels!"

The extreme dampness in Vietnam created a lot of trouble with the old style combat boot. They replaced it with a lighter, quick-drying model that had a specially designed, removable inner sole. On one sole was printed "DO NOT BOIL" under which one GI scratched "Just peel and eat."

The GIs in Vietnam are required to take a weekly pill to lessen their chance of coming down with malaria. On the last pay day before he was due to be rotated home, the second lieutenant wrote to his wife: "Dear Susie. Today I'm swallowing my last pill. I suggest that you start taking yours."

Send Up A Polka Dot Flare – A response to the hysterical question, "What do I do now?" There is no such thing as a "polka dot flare"; hence, it means "don't ask me."

Powder House – A WAC barracks.

There's more than one way to skin a cat, as this GI proved when he was questioned as to why he drove thirty miles to a tavern to drink beer that was a nickel cheaper at the the base facility.

"Look at the extra gas it costs to drive there," was the final remark.

"Not to worry," the GI replied. "I just drink till I have a profit out of the deal."

They tell of the army chaplain who, during his counseling period, hung a sign outside his door. It read "HALT! Who goes there? Advance and be reconciled."

GIs in Vietnam who are in action for a long time find that the nights are very long and that their imaginations begin to play strange tricks on them.

Unable to trust his eyes, after staring into the darkness from his foxhole, this one GI said that he kept count of the trees and shrubs in front of him. "I take a roll call about every twenty minutes," he said, "and if there are more than 15 trees, I begin to shoot."

Blow Smoke – To bamboozle, deceive, do a snow job!

To Blow Zs – To sleep and snore.

Body Shop – A mortuary. Also a word for prosthetic surgery.

"CHOI OI! NOW ME KNOW WHY YOU AMERICANS CALLED JUNGLE EXPERTS!"

Tony Zidek. CHOI OI.
Chas. E. Tuttle Co.

Six-Pack of Asskick – As, "you mess with me, man, and you'll need a whole platoon and a six-pack of asskick to come out whole."

Slick-Sleeve – A buck private, one who has no rank.

Back in a rest area, the combat troops could get a few days respite from the anguish of the advanced line. Many went to church. On this one Sunday, the chaplain chose for his sermon the perversion of language represented by profanity.

"The word hell," he told the troops, "especially, when used in such phrases as 'What the hell goes on here' and 'Get to hell and gone out of here,' and 'Just what the hell do ya think you're doing,' is disgraceful, disgusting, unchristian."

The troops seemed to receive the message gladly. After services, when the men were filing out, one GI shook the chaplain's hand and remarked, "That was a helluva sermon, sir."

One night the men were moving through dense Vietnamese cover when suddenly the patrol was surrounded by the enemy. Bullets were flying everywhere and from all directions. The captain radioed for immediate air support! In reply to his radio call, a pilot requested the exact location of his unit.

The captain spoke into his mike to the pilot: "Take a look at those tracer bullets below you. See 'em? Good! Now go right to the center of those goddam tracers and that's where I am!"

The mess sergeant on a Vietnam base was very sensitive to criticism. If there was much of it the guys found that, for a couple of days, they got nothing but coldcuts — and lousy ones at that.

But this one night, the meat was outrageously tough. One PFC found a way to say what all felt needed saying, "Gee, Sergeant, I'm sure sorry your rhinoceros died!"

The ensign was instructing a group of enlisted reserves on the potential for information about an attack transport their ship was towing. They were seated in a cramped room full of green scopes and crackling radios. The end of the lecture was concluded with these words: "Thus you can tell that there is no possible danger because nothing can approach within 2000 yards of us without our being aware of it at once."

Just then the towed ship bumped into the main vessel where the lecture was held and all were thrown off their feet. While they were struggling to get up, the duty radarman said, "Now you men must realize something the officer lecturing you did not tell you. There is a 300-yard deductible on that guarantee!"

Boomers – Officers and men of the nuclear-powered elements of the Navy.

Boy Scouts – A nasty game played by soldiers in barracks, as "What's the difference between the Boy Scouts and the Army?" "Well, for one, the Boy Scouts have adult leaders."

Brag Rags – Service stripes or hash marks.

Brown Bomber – A most effective laxative pill.

BAM – Broadass marine. The unofficial title of female marines.

"Pfc Fensterwahl, the old lady wants to see you on the double!"

Bob Fleischauer. Leatherneck Magazine.

They tell the story of a GI who had volunteered for Vietnam duty. Once there, he had an unusually rough time of it, spending most of his twelve months slogging through the interminable mud and endless rain. After return, his first remark to his father was

"Anybody who volunteers to go to Vietnam ought to have his feet examined!"

There's a wonderful story that came from Fort Bragg, N.C. It seems that during a basic airborne course for paratroopers, the men had to do push-ups until ordered to quit. There were over 200 of the lads in training and they were sweat-soaked, sunburned and "plumb wore out." After a grueling set of exercises, the men were cussing the mosquitoes, the Army, the Fort, and most of all, North Carolina.

The tough instructor got tired of hearing the endless grousing and asked the men, "How many of you guys are sick of North Carolina?"

Every hand was raised.

"Very well," said the instructor, "let's see you get down on your hands and push it away!"

Boot training was completed at a Marine training station. Assignments were handed out and there was only one objection. A Missouri farm lad objected to his assignment as a gunner on a bomber. He was then offered a job in the submarine service. That, too, was unacceptable.

"What the hell do you want?" he was asked.

"Let me put it to ya thisaway," the farmboy replied. "I want me a job that don't put me no higher than cornstalks and no lower than peanuts!"

Take Six For The Benefits – Recruiting slogan to get GIs to re-enlist: "Don't get pissed, re-enlist! Take six for the benefits."

Teeth To Tail Ratio – The proportion of fighters to men supporting them.

Tent Pegs – Totally misfit, or inadequate GIs.

A recently commissioned Navy nurse was being shown about the hospital by a corpsman. As they passed a wardroom full of men wounded in Vietnam and brought back for treatment, they were met by a fusillade of whistling that stopped them both.

"Sailor," asked the new nurse, "Are those men whistling at me?"

"I hope so, ma'am," replied the corpsman. "I sure do hope so."

Two officers were walking down the company street when they passed a GI loaded with parcels. The soldier saluted, losing, in the process, all his parcels. The officers helped him load up again.

"Thank you, sir," the GI said, saluting smartly and, of course, dropping the packages once again.

Again he was helped. The officer told him that, given the circumstances, he did not have to salute an officer.

The soldier nodded and said "Thank you, sir!" Then he threw *another* snappy salute!

YOU CAN TELL A FIGHTER PILOT

Tune: Battle Hymn of the Republic

By the ring around his eyeball
You can tell a bombardier
You can tell a bomber pilot by
    The spread across his rear
You can tell a navigator by his
    sextants, maps and such
You can tell a Fighter Pilot,
    but you cannot tell him much!

By the stormy look about him,
    you can tell a weather nut
You can tell a chopper pilot
    by the quiver of his butt
You can tell the local nurses
    by their bedroom eyes and such
You can tell a Fighter Pilot,
    but you cannot tell him much!

James P. Dunham. BULL DURHAM'S SONGS OF THE S.E.A.

Due to be rotated back to the United States, an old GI who had been in service for, it seemed forever, received this telegram from his wife: "On my 25th birthday you were away at war. On my 50th birthday, you were away at war. Now, buster, if things haven't improved by my 75th, I'm cutting out!"

A young marine who had served during the North Vietnamese encirclement of Khensanh, was having a ball at his homecoming party. Encircled, this time, by a bevy of cute young ladies, he announced, "All I gotta say is, that if I got to be surrounded, this is the way to do it.

Corpsman, Medic, Doc; the nurse with balls.

Tad Foster. THE VIETNAM FUNNY BOOK.
Presidio Press. 1980

A chief walked into the PX. He was wearing more hash marks than most of the GIs there had ever seen.

"Gee whiz, Sergeant," one man said. "You sure have been in a long time. What were you in civilian life?"

"A baby!"

After a particularly disastrous bombing raid, one of the planes resembled a sieve as it circled the home base. The pilot radioed the flight leader and told him that he'd lost all of his hydraulic fluid and couldn't lower his wheels or flaps. What should he do?

The flight leader told him to bail out and that the best way to do that was to roll the plane over on its back, loosen his seat belt and let go.

The pilot called back, "Sir, uh, sir, what's the next best way to bail out?"

At a Navy base in Vietnam, a radio station announced the time: "It is now six bells. For you Air Force guys, that's 1400 hours. And for you marines, the big hand is on . . . ."

Sound off like you've got a pain – *Make yourself known. Speak up!* Act like you've got two testicles.

Special Feces – A pun on Special Forces.

Special Forces Prayer:
    Yea, though I walk through the valley
    Of the shadow of death, I will fear
    No evil. For I am the meanest
    Motherfucker in the valley.

A ground crewman reported all of his movements during an air raid on headquarters. "The bombs exploded all around our building. I sounded the alarm, made sure all sensitive documents were secure, locked the safe, closed the security files, put on combat gear, left the office, entered the bunker outside."

"How much time elapsed between the first bomb and your final entrance into the bunker?" he was asked.

"About five seconds, sir."

The sergeant was reading instructions to a group of GIs recently arrived in Vietnam. "Where confusion exists, common sense will prevail," he read.

One old timer interrupted him. "Excuse me, Sergeant. Just one question. Isn't that a revolutionary change of policy?"

A GI was having a few drinks at the Son Nhut Airport bar. Suddenly, Vietcong terrorists bombed the place. He wrote a letter home in which he described the experience. "It finally happened. I got bombed on one beer."

Proword Or Prosign – GI slang using numbers to make a forceful statement. For example 2-4-8, shouted over the telephone, could mean: "Answer your g-damn phone!" or "Screw you! A strong letter follows." Or, the numbers 1-3-4 could mean "You eat shit, bark at the moon and chase 'coons."

The non-commissioned officers (who consider themselves the unrecognized force behind *all* military movement of importance) created this analysis of the actual, modest way things get done in the military way.

THE CHAIN OF COMMAND

Colonel

Leaps over tall buildings with a single bound,
Is faster than a speeding bullet,
Can fly higher than a mighty rocket,
More powerful than a locomotive,
Gives policy guidance to GOD.

Lieutenant Colonel

Must take a running start to leap over tall buildings,
Is just as fast as a speeding bullet,
When flying cannot penetrate the atmosphere,
Talks to GOD.

Major

Can leap over short buildings,
Not quite as fast as a speeding bullet,
Only flies as high as transports,
Loses tug-of-war with locomotive,
Listens to GOD.

Captain

Crashes into buildings when trying to leap over them.
Can shoot bullets,
Has trouble flying,
Gets run over by locomotive,
Talks with animals.

First Lieutenant

Stumbles into buildings when attempting to enter,
Wounds self with bullets when attempting to shoot gun,
Can barely walk,
Talks with walls.

Second Lieutenant

Cannot recognize buildings,
Gets all wet when playing with a water pistol,
Still crawling,
"Choo choo, daddy. Choo choo,"
Too busy sucking on pacifier.

First Sergeant

Lifts buildings, walks under,
Catches bullets, chews its ass,
Flies higher than "Champagne Charlie,"
Smashes locomotive, chews caboose,
He is GOD!!!!

Wm. Ferris, Jr. N.Y. Folklore Society. 1976

"In the beginning, I created heaven and earth. . . ."

Jake Schuffert. NO SWEAT – HERE'S JAKE.
Stackpole Books. 1983.

"I DON'T CARE WHO YOUR GREAT, GREAT, GREAT GRANDFATHER WAS, CUSTER — THE LONG HAIR AND MUSTACHE HAVE GOT TO GO!"

The platoon was practicing movement through territory guarded by barbed wire and pocked with explosive pits. They had been instructed that, on reaching the barbed wire, they were to turn onto their backs, lift the wire with their weapon, scoot under the wire and go on yet avoiding the explosives buried in the pits. They all came through, all except Corporal Edwards, the most experienced man in the platoon with three enlistments. At last Edwards came crawling up.

"Where the hell have you been, Edwards?" the sergeant-in-charge barked.

"Sergeant, I've been collecting the change the others lost out of their pockets when they rolled over on their backs to get under the barbed wire!"

To Pull The Pin – To vamoose, to depart, to go.

Fellow officers gave a farewell party at Da Nang for a GI who had been long in Vietnam. He was given a lovely gift, then invited to say a few words.

"I leave Vietnam," he began, his voice choked with emotion, "with mixed feelings of delight, joy and ecstatic happiness!"

At an impromptu chapel made out of tents and canvas, there were *five* chaplains to hear confession and *five* lines of men waiting to confess. Suddenly from the tent came the booming voice of one of the chaplains. "YOU . . . DID . . . WHAT!" Then came a telling silence and a soldier came out and slunk away.

Immediately, that line destined for the loud-voiced chaplain melted away and there were, suddenly, only *four* lines!

Buddha Belly – Fat person with a big belly.

BUFF – Big Ugly Fat Fellow (or Fucker!) An affectionate term for the B-52 strato-fortress bomber.

Buy It! – To be killed. Death.

Under intense hostile fire in Vietnam, two infantry men ("grunts") huddled behind a tree, worried at the bombs bursting on all sides of them. "Chin up," one grunt advised the other. "Don't forget that none of those shells are going to get you unless it's got your name on it."

"Yeah. Thanks. I'd forgotten that," said the other.

Just then, a Viet Cong soldier popped up behind them and said most politely, "Pardon me, sir, but exactly how do you spell your name?"

"HAVE YOU NOTICED SOME SUBTLE CHANGES IN HIM SINCE HE WAS NAMED 'DRILL SERGEANT OF THE YEAR'?"

In Vietnam, there were times when troops were not permitted to fire on the enemy without prior permission from higher authority. Frustrating? Yes! But there were ways to get the job done. Witness this. . . .

An infantry platoon of the First Cavalry Division, near An Khe, was harassed by snipers and frequent mortar fire. Finally, the men pinpointed the enemy positions and requested to return fire.

The platoon leader told the seasoned sergeant to wait for radio permission. The latter asked, "Sir, what'd you do if suddenly we had no radio communication?"

The lieutenant grinned. "Gotcha," he said and nodded. Soon a crash was heard in the vicinity of the radio. The sergeant worked his way back to the lieutenant and reported, "Sir, the radio is not working . . . at the moment."

"Whadayouknow! What happened, Sergeant?"

"Near as I can make out, one of them fallopian tubes went out."

First Hot – The First Sergeant! Other complimentary names: *first pig, first shirt, first skirt, first sleeve.*

Flagpole Leave – A leave spent at work.

Flatpeter – A GI so stupid he's always stepping on his peter.

FNG – Fucking New Guy, a replacement.

A GI wrote home about a most interesting beggar he had run across outside his military compound in Saigon. "You wouldn't believe the number of beggars we got around here," he wrote, "but this one guy seems a real nice fella. He grins and smiles and bows and it doesn't matter whether you put money in his hat or not. But the other day I passed by his usual place and he was gone. I asked another bum, just down the street from him, if the beggar was sick."

" 'No. Him busy. Him talk to stockbroker this day . . . each week,' was the reply."

"No wonder the gedunk's so crowded every night!"

Leatherneck Magazine.

One of our field artillery units at Tuy Hoa used to sing this lovely, tender melody to the tune of "On The Banks Of The Wabash."

When the lice are in the rice along the Mekong,
    And Charlie's in there shooting at you,
You can bet your ass I won't be there beside you,
    I'll be shacking with your gal in old Pleiku.

At the CPO club at Camp Tien Sha, this conversation was heard as two navy vets talked at the bar. An argument developed as to which one of them had the most time in service.

"Chief," the one said, "I bet I got more time in just standing in a shipboard chow line than you got in the entire Navy."

"Yeah? Well, let me tell you I got plenty time, served on every major type of combat ship plus a lot of support ships."

"OK. So tell me what's a C-V-S?"

"That's easy . . . Antisubmarine carrier."

"Right. Try this one. What's an A-P-A?"

"Hell, man, everyone knows that's an attack transport."

"So tell me, wise guy, what's A-P-E?"

There was a pause. Finally, the other admitted that he was stumped, saying, "I can't seem to remember. Musta forgot!"

"By god, I fooled ya! any dumb bastard knows that A-P E is your cousin, an ape five feet tall!"

Pricksmith – A GI in the medical corps.

Private Slipinshits – The lowest ranking enlisted personnel.

Prone Position – Sexual intercourse. From the prone position when firing a rifle.

Commenting in a significant way on the manner of warfare in Vietnam, a marine sergeant, just back from there, sat watching a floor show in a San Francisco night club. He remarked, "Well, here, at least, we've got a definite front and a definite rear!"

An army sergeant with nearly thirty years of service announced that he had come to Vietnam to pull a two-in-one tour of duty — His first tour and . . . his . . . last!

Flim-flam artists can be found in every culture and Vietnam is no exception. It seems that an officer noticed a beautiful small ocelot in a cage in a shop. He went in to look at it and knew that he had to own it. It was beautiful. So he bargained for the beast and finally got it for 750 piasters. The store owner cautioned him not to handle the lovely creature for a few days, not until it got used to its new master.

He took the lovely critter home in the cage. There a young soldier saw it and, unbeknownst to the owner, opened the cage and began to stroke and fondle the ocelot.

"Careful, soldier!" the officer yelled. "He isn't tamed yet. He's vicious and could bite you!"

The soldier removed his hand and closed the door of the cage. Then the officer noticed the black and yellow paint smeared on the soldier's hand. Then he heard the "ocelot" go "meow."

"OH, MY GOODNESS GRACIOUS! SAKES ALIVE! MERCY ME! GOLLY GEE WHIZ!"

They tell of a certain signal posted outside the photo lab of the Commander of Naval Forces Vietnam:

NOBODY IS PERFECT

Each man is a mixture of good and bad qualities. We must always remember that, when we go to judge our fellow man, we should recall the good qualities and know that his bad ones, his faults, only go to show that he is a human being like the rest of us. We must not make harsh judgments of such a man simply because he is a lousy, miserable, low-down, no-good sonofabitch.

Some funny, often unbelievable, things happened in Vietnam. Consider the night mortar attack at Phuoc Vinh in 1967. A chaplain, minus his pants, shirt and other impedimenta, rushed into a bunker and when he had got his breath, sang out: "Goddamit, man, that was close!"

It was very difficult for a certain newspaper correspondent —or anyone else, for that matter, given the lack of easy travel outside of Saigon — to get to Phu Vinh, in the Mekong Delta. A reporter wasted two days trying to get a ride and then happened on a seasoned noncom, a veteran in Vietnam. The newsman asked the sergeant just how to get to where he had to go.

The NCO thought a bit, then told him, "If I was to try to get where you got to go, I'd try to hitch me a ride on a beer truck. Them guys may get plumb careless with a chow wagon or an ammo truck but they ain't never gonna let anything happen to a beer truck!"

On one of the air bases in Vietnam there was a true shortage of water. As a result, the men had gone without showers for a good, long time. But one NCO seemed to have a personal solution to the problem.

"Me, I hardly ever run out of water," he said. "Only when the general is shy of water, am I without it. It seems," he added with a grin, "that we share a party line."

Di Di Mao – Vietnamese for: "Get the fuck out of here."

Diamond – Hope. The light at the end of a very dark tunnel as, "It shines like a diamond in a goat's asshole."

Diddly Shit – As with "diddly squat," it signifies worthlessness, e.g., "It ain't worth diddly shit."

Ding – To shoot, wound, kill.

A GI tried to mail home a certain type of bomb as a souvenir. This particular type of bomb can be aimed, fired at will and it's filled with a lot of small, steel balls. It's terribly lethal. The package weighed so much that the postal clerk asked what was in it.

"It's a bomb, a good one, too," was the reply.

"We can't permit you to mail home such a lethal object."

"Why not? I found it and have every right to it. So why not?"

"Because it is not allowed. Besides, what in hell would you

do with it once you got it home?"

"A buddy of mine said he'd keep it for me. Now, when I get home, I'll pick it up from him, take it to my house, set it up in the back yard, go to the front of my house, ring the bell and wait. If I hear that goddam back door slam . . . bet your boots . . . Kerpow!"

"Well, *my* boot camp was so rough we took R&R in Vietnam!"
Leatherneck Magazine

Can you imagine the laughter when the front page of the *Saigon Daily News,* on October 12, 1967, carried this headline?
LBJ LEARNS OF DAUGHTER'S ROMANCE IN BED.

Hymn – A synonym for *him* as used in a GI group chant, sung piously, to express dislike for a superior, as: "Him, him," then the troops sing out: "FUCK HIM!"

IHTFP – Scrawled on Vietnamese signs, walls, etc. It means: I Hate This Fucking Place!

One of the most unusual stories we've heard concerns a captain in the Air Force who returned from Vietnam. He landed at Kelly Field and telephoned his wife concerning his E.T.A. in Kansas City.

She was tickled pink to hear his voice and asked if there was anything at all she could get at the super market to tickle his palate.

"Only one thing," he said, "pick up five pounds of green jelly beans."

"Jelly beans? Why on earth would you want so many jelly beans?"

"Because, sweetheart, when I get home, kiss you a few times, catch my breath, I'm going out on our front lawn and pitch those green jelly beans all over the lawn. Then I'll tell the children to go outside and pick them up. Every . . . last . . . bean!"

The American soldier has a genius for tagging stupidity and noting it in terse, succinct language. For example, this notice appeared on the bulletin board of an artillery unit:

FROM HERE ON OUT THERE WILL NOT BE ANY DISTINCTION BETWEEN FIRST AND SECOND LIEUTENANTS. STUPIDITY KNOWS NO RANK."

The phrase "Remember, we're fighting for their hearts and minds" was posted on almost every bulletin board in Vietnam. But it was reported that in a bunker near Don Ha, a leatherneck put up a crude sign that was far more efficient and direct:

GRAB 'EM BY THE BALLS AND THEIR HEARTS AND MINDS WILL FOLLOW!

A group of combat veterans were about to be discharged. The base chaplain was asked to give them advice as to proper comportment, once they had rejoined civilian life.

The chaplain went through the usual banal instructions about honesty, prayer, morality, consideration of others and then, seeing that the GIs were bored, ended with this admonition: "Men do watch your language! Be careful when at home or in public. For example, when you are at a restaurant or, even, at home, and you request coffee, butter or whatever . . . don't describe it!"

Ration Of Shit – A hard time, as "I don't need your ration of shit, man!"

Records Manglement – A pun on records management.

"All I said was, 'I'd like some more.' "

Leatherneck Magazine

A lad who had been on quiet, behind-the-lines duty . . . or so he informed his parents in all his letters . . . returned from Vietnam and told his father that, in truth, he had been on helicopter duty as a gunner. When his dad reproached him for deceiving them, and asked him why he had resorted to the deception, the lad said, "Mother necessitates invention."

A GI serving in south Vietnam wrote home that he was stationed just north of Pleiku. "On the map," he wrote, "that's about three inches south of Russia, one inch this side of China, just a bit more northeast of Cambodia and straight north of Rand McNally!"

Roach Coach – A mobile snack-bar.

On Eating S.O.S

Oh buddy mine, oh dearest friend,
Oh, will you tell me true,
Is this stuff really S.O.S.,
Or a nasty kind of glue?
For it's stuck my jaws together,
And I've lost a tooth or two.
Fear not, old friend, it's dinkum stuff,
An Old Corps kind of stew;
I saw the cook a'makin it,
He was grinding up a shoe.
With a little soap, some table wax,
And a cup of milk or two.
He seasoned it with dynamite,
And a bull cockroach, all blue,
Then to make it set just right,
This maestro of the stew,
He sat down at the table and,
Tossed in his other shoe!
He stripped his feet of both his socks,
And threw them in there too;
He added salt and pepper,
Just to make a tasty brew.
He served it over first aid packs,
Of canvas nice and new.
I'll have to say, You're right, old friend,
It's too durned tough to chew.

GySgt. H.F. Hiles. Leatherneck Magazine

A ship was sunk off the coast of Vietnam and three GIs managed to stay alive by clinging to floating bits and pieces of the ship. Three days after being sunk they were picked up by a destroyer. One man had a bad compound fracture and was immediately put in sick bay. The doctor examined him and was surprised to find that the fractured leg had no infection.

"What treatment was given?" he asked.

The GI replied, "Inadvertant medication, Doc. I've been soaking that leg in salt water for three days."

A group of recent arrivals in south Vietnam were given a lecture on life in those parts and how to conduct themselves. The lecturer advised against marrying the local girls because, he said,

"You'll take them back with you to the states and, if there's a breakdown, where will you be . . . ? You'll be unable to get spare parts for them."

"And this is my buddy Tex. Tex is from Louisiana.
We call him Tex 'cause he don't
like being called Louise!"

Leatherneck Magazine

Hat Up And Head Out – To Absquatulate, leave in a hurry, depart precipitously!

Hong Kong – Anything cheap, shoddy, false. A GI squeezed a bar girl's breasts. "You Hong Kong?" he asked.
She grabbed his phallic member, "*You* Hong Kong?" she replied.

Hot Skinny – Information.

Hydrostatic Lock – As with the sky hook, stove jack and a left-handed monkey wrench, this item is to be fetched by gullible greenies.

A GI strolled into the chaplain's office and asked for a copy of the Old Testament.

"Glad to oblige you, soldier, but you have me puzzled. A week ago you asked for our Catholic Bible. Fine. I gave you a copy. Then you brought it back and asked for a Protestant Bible. Now you want a Jewish Bible. What goes on, soldier?"

"Well, sir, I heard that we were going to Vietnam," explained the GI. "Fair enough. Suits me fine. But I tell you this, chaplain, I ain't takin' no more chances than are absolutely necessary!"

Then there's the story of the officer who was playing the slot machines at the Da Nang officers club. For three hours one evening he lost roll after roll of quarters down the tube! Finally, the machine exploded quarters in all directions and the officer was tickled pink. But the club manager protested that the officer had used a slug! He had. It came out of his .45 pistol!

Major Brown, new in Vietnam, was assigned a sergeant who, upon meeting him for the first time, asked if he knew why he was in Vietnam.

"Yes, I do. We all went through an orientation course, you know."

"Then you think you know what we hope to accomplish here?"

"Of course. That's clear to me."

"Major," said the sergeant, "take my advice. You write down just exactly why you think you are in Vietnam because a year from now you probably will be damned unsure."

"And you know," the Major Brown remarked, a year after his arrival in Nam, "that sergeant was 100% right!"

The Saigon bar girls got pretty cynical about the real intentions of the GIs there. One of the most frequently heard expressions from the girls was "you *sao.*" which means "you lie."

One time, a GI was laying it on thick and heavy to a pretty young girl.

"Soldier, you *sao,*" the girl told him.

"Listen kid," the GI replied, "I'd never lie to you. Why I'd tell you the truth 500 ways just so's not to lie to you."

Slushing Oil – A light rifle oil, hence, light talk of no importance. Idle chatter.

Somewhere Between Shit And Syphilis – The same as *between a rock and a hard place.*

Someone Else's War – A remark in reply to a demand, e.g. "don't bug me about *that*! Why, that's someone else's war!"

"For cryin' out loud, don't shoot, man!"

Leatherneck Magazine.

An order was posted that, between 5:30 P.M. and 8:30 P.M., no more than two drinks per man were to be served at the NCO club at Phu Bai headquarters of the Third Marine Division.

One marine circumvented the order in a typically ingenious way. He marched up to the bar, one evening and extracted an enormous glass. The bartender hesitated, grinned and, at the GI's instructions, poured the glass nearly full of gin, 8 ounces, then added ice and orange juice to fill it to the top.

"And this one," said the GI, "is my first drink!"

A grizzled, much-decorated marine sergeant, veteran of World War II and two years in Vietnam, was hit by a V.C. rocket and badly hurt. He recovered and was given orders to return to the United States. Bidding goodbye to his buddies, he mentioned that he had just received his fourth Purple Heart. This time he had been hit by shrapnel high and inside his right thigh, very close to the groin.

"Did you get hit in the . . . ah . . . did you lose, I mean . . . "

"No! Things turned out fine. I was lucky. I was dressed *left* when I got hit."

There is the story about the colonel who was due to meet friends in Saigon's excellent Caravelle Hotel. But he was very late and not entirely dressed. He rushed to the elevator and was busily engaged in running his belt through the loops on his trousers. The elevator stopped to pick up a hotel guest who, it so happened, was a lovely and exotic performer, a sexy dancer.

She took one look at the colonel and remarked, "Well, now, honey, you sure are in a hurry, aren't you!"

A GI was arrested for fighting and then shooting another soldier. The provost marshall had him put on trial within a week.

The judge asked, "What reason did you have for shooting this man, soldier. Was it in self-defense or not?"

"Judge, that feller called me a dirty name. I couldn't take that insult."

"What did he call you?"

"He called me a mother fuckin' son-of-a-bitch, that's what!"

"Soldier, that's no excuse. You had no business shooting him for that."

"Well, Judge, what would you have done if he'd called you that?"

"He'd never had've called ME that! Mother fuckin'? Never!"

"Well, Judge, I know he wouldn't. But suppose he called you the honest-to-gawd kind of a sonofabitch you are! Then what?"

In the jungle of Vietnam, an infantry company halted to check on the situation.

"Sarge!" said a corporal, "We got enemy troops in front of us."

"And we got the bastards on our left, too," reported another man.

"They're in back of us, Sarge," said a PFC.

"And on our right, too," came the final report.

"Good! " exulted the Sergeant. "Good! Good! Good! We finally caught 'em all!"

The South seems never to forget the Civil War. As an example of that state of mind, an Alabama marine's mother wrote to tell him to send no more photos of himself dressed in marine blues. She suggested that he be photographed in white uniform because "Grandpa might not quite understand that blue outfit!"

When the GI returned from Vietnam, he was met by his wife and baby. Her hair was done up in curlers, so that it was natural to ask why she appeared before him, after such a long absence, with so little regard for her beauty.

"Maybe," one GI suggested, "that's the way she looked when he went away."

While in Vietnam, a bunch of GIs composed a letter to go to one of the nation's largest universities. Finished with the letter, they opened a college directory and mailed it to one of the large schools, addressed to the dean of women.

The GI letter read as follows: "We address you as America's most fierce, hostile warriors. We wait many moons for smoke signals from squaw friends back home in big nation. Now we feel lower than buffalo grass. No mail back comes. Big idea come to us. We send letter to college, to beautiful girls playing there. Then we pray to great Mail Spirit that girls answer our letter."

What was their surprise when they actually did get a letter back in response to their random mailing. The letter read, "Most big, brave Indians. How! Thank you for lovely smoke signal. Maybe Great Spirit fool you more than somewhat. Worried that you take on big load firewater, we must send reply anyhow. Braves, most brave, you send letter to big reservation of Catholic sisters."

AWOL – Absent without leave. Sometimes said to represent After Women Or Liquor, or, A Wolf On the Loose.

Baby Shit – Mustard.

Back Trouble – A nice, diplomatic way to phrase the condition of a pregnant WAC.

Ba-Me-Lam – A man with an insatiable sex appetite. From the Vietnamese word describing an oversexed man: *ba-muoi-lam.*

Assumption – The mother of all fuck-ups! A mistaken action taken as a result of mistaken assumption. To put another way: KNOW! DON'T ASSUME.

"It's been done!"

Leatherneck Magazine

Late one night, a brand new second lieutenant reported to his first combat assignment, an infantry battalion in Vietnam. Worn out, he requested a guide to lead him through the dark to his quarters.

"Yes sir," said the sergeant on duty. "You just select any nice muddy spot for yourself, sir. I'd suggest you bed down over there next to the colonel's muddy hole, sir."

The Vietnam veteran returned to the states and, within one week he was in church and married to the sweetheart of his dreams. As they walked out of the church, now man and wife, she hoped for some endearing words from him but got, "You're out of step!"

Your Ass Is Grass – "Buddy, you've had it!"

Cut A Huss – Give a guy a break, cut him some slack.

Armpit Sauce – An ultra strong Vietnamese sauce smelling like "a garbage truck that has run over a skunk in front of a fish factory in a slaughter house town."

_____ _____ _____ _____

It was reported that at the Higher Educational Aid Board of the State of Wisconsin, the administrator of student loans, received this letter:

I regret that your debtor, Mr. J.M. Sweitzer, is no longer a student simply because he was forced to take arms against a sea of Oriental troubles. Further, it is to be doubted that he can make the expected payment of $144.38 a month since his employer of the moment only pays him $122.28 a month. The moral to this rejoinder is . . . never work for relatives, especially an uncle. Mr. Sweitzer began his present job on 29 June 1969. His contract is scheduled for conclusion 28 June 1971, assuming no further problems such as parcels of schrapnel, a passel of bullets or an occasional viper sting.

Thanking you for your concern, he remains,

Pvt. J.M. Sweitzer, U.S. Marine Corps.

_____ _____ _____ _____

YOU'LL NEVER MIND

Come and join the Air Force
We're a happy band they say
We never do a lick of work
just fly around all day
While others work and study
and soon grow old and blind
We take to the air without a care
and you will never mind

Chorus

You'll never mind, you'll never mind
So come and join the Air Force
and you will never mind

Come and get promoted
As high as you desire
You're riding on a gravy train
If you're an Air Force flier
And when you get to General, you will surely
    find
Your wings fall off, the dough rolls in

But you will never mind.

You rake it up and spin it
And with an awful tear
Your wings fall off, the ship spins in
but you will never care
For in about two minutes more
another pair you'll find
You'll dance with Pete in an Angel's suit
But you will never mind

While flying the Pacific
You hear the engine spit
You watch the tach come to a stop
The goddamn thing has quit
The ship won't float, and you can't swim
The shore is far behind
Oh, what a dish for crabs and fish
But you will never mind

James P. Durham.
BULL DURHAM'S SONG OF S.E.A.

They tell of a sign just outside the gate at the outer perimeter of Duc Lap Special Forces Camp. Quite close to the Cambodian border, in South Vietnam was one: REMEMBER THE ALAMO! Down the road, there was yet another: REMEMBER THE PUEBLO. And, as the road wound up the hill, there was a third: REMEMBER THE MAIN! And still another greeted GIs as they entered the inner perimeter: TRY NOT TO THINK ABOUT DUC LAP.

A physician was examining a GI hurting from a painful wound suffered during his first week in Vietnam. "So you got shrapnel in that leg, eh?" the doctor remarked.

"I sure do," replied the wounded GI. "There's been an awful lot of it going around lately."

An army officer in full dress, medals and all, attended a cocktail party. He was approached by a civilian, a stranger who was pretty well-oiled. The civilian put his arm over the officer's shoulder and told him that he, too, had been in the service. Then his eyes drooped and he suddenly saw the array of medals on the officer's chest.

"Holy smokes, sir!" he gasped. "You're in this thing mighty deep, aren't you!"

Round Brown – Another name for the "Smokey the Bear hat."

Rubber Bitch Or Lady – An inflatable rubber air mattress for use by field troops.

Saigon Quickstep – Diarrhea.

Sandpaper – Issue toilet paper.

"What's this I hear about you knocking the promotion system, Airman Hemlock?"

Jake Schuffert. NO SWEAT – HERE'S JAKE.
Stackpole Books. 1983.

After a very tough day, a group of worn-out recruits were sacking out in their barracks and talking about how nice it would be if they were once again back in civilian life. "I'll tell you one good thing about this life, though," one recruit remarked. "There's one thing sure. Here, we don't have to worry about the draft!"

A group of wounded soldiers were recovering in the hospital. With much time on their hands, they amused themselves by wheeling their chairs to the desk of the prettiest nurse in the hospital. They had such a good time talking and kidding her until one day, as they wheel-chaired to the desk, they noticed that the staff had posted a sign: "UNAUTHORIZED PERSONNEL NOT ALLOWED. IF FOUND HERE THEY WILL BE TOWED AWAY!"

At an air base in Vietnam, stood a sign over the coffee counter. "Coffee ten cents. Please pay. Ali Baba had less trouble with his 40 thieves."

And underneath it some GI had printed "Yes, for sure. But then, Ali Baba had GOOD coffee."

Whitewall – Completely bare sides of a white marine's head, startlingly bright under his cap.

Wire Hangers – Rear echelon troops who are so comfortable, they hang their clothes on a wire hanger rather than sleeping in them, like combat troops.

The World – The United States, as thought of by GIs in Vietnam.

There was a sign posted in the pilot's ready-room on an aircraft carrier. It read:

THE LAW OF GRAVITY

Sir Isaac Newton created this law: "Everything that goes up must come down." That's The Law of Gravity. And our commanding officer says, "Everything That Comes Down Had Better Be Able To Go Up Again." AND THAT IS *THE* LAW!

Water Walker – A GI who gets a maximum rating on his efficiency report.

When In Doubt, Whip It Out – If it's a possible superior officer, salute (just to be safe).

"YOU WANTED TO TALK TO ME ABOUT YOUR UNIFORM? WHAT'S WRONG WITH IT?"

When The Balloon Goes Up – When things begin to happen. A variant of "when the shit hits the fan."

A second lieutenant, married only a few hours before he and his outfit were shipped to Vietnam, was a very tough, demanding, relentless officer.

One night while censoring outgoing mail, he was surprised to see a letter addressed to his own wife. When he opened it he found:

Dear Susan,

True, he did marry you but we are the ones taken on the honeymoon. Let us tell you, Susan, you haven't missed a damned thing.

Love,
"The Company."

A witty surgeon, stationed in a naval hospital, had a sign above his door: WIZARD OF GAUZE.

To Raise Five – To salute.

"Look at that, Elroy. As if we don't have enough to do around here already."

Jake Schuffert. NO SWEAT–HERE'S JAKE
Stackpole Books. 1983.

They tell about the arrangement of tents during a field exercise. The chaplain's tent was set between the sick bay and the company headquarters.

One afternoon, the chaplain came to hear confession. He paused to read the sign in front of the sick bay: SICK CALL: 0830.

He moved onto another sign in front of headquarters: MAIL CALL: 1200.

The chaplain returned to his own tent and came out to hang up a sign: SIN CALL: 1530.

A most revealing experience came to the Kiwanis Club of Springfield, Illinois, when a high ranking officer was asked to speak about the planned integration of the three military services into one defense establishment. He gave a very good talk, summarizing the advantages of the union. After his talk, during the question period, one man asked "Why if marrying the services one to another, is such a good idea, then why is the military fighting it so fiercely?"

The speaker said, "We have never disagreed about the wisdom or the advantages of the marriage. The only problem has been . . . which one is going to be the bride."

FIAP – Fuck It And Press (onward). Get on with the business at hand!

Puzzle Palace – A military headquarters, especially the Pentagon.

RAMF – Rear-Area Mother Fucker or REMF that uses Echelon instead of Area! Support and non-combat troops.

A report came back from Vietnam that the chaplains at the Phu Cat Air Base in South Vietnam came up with a great sign to identify their unity: THE GOD SQUAD.

A woman called at the gynecological clinic requesting medication. The clerk, on Form 234, took the data concerning her medical needs and asked for her husband's rank and service serial number. "One more question," the clerk said, "is your husband active or retired?"

"If he wasn't so damned active I wouldn't be coming here for birth control pills!" she replied.

An Air Force captain returned from Vietnam and, at a bull session, told this story.

"I was approaching the target of this particular mission, when anti-aircraft fire began and we were quickly into heavy, heavy, flak. While coping with the danger by evasive action, my base radioed me for my exact position. I replied, 'Kneeling!' "

At a stateside base, three lieutenants were walking down the street when they passed a very cute young WAC. She smiled sweetly at them but failed to show military courtesy, with a salute.

One officer stopped her. "Hold on there, soldier. Haven't you yet learned you're supposed to salute officers?"

"Yes, sir! I know that, sir! But this is my lunch hour!"

When the body was first made each part wanted to be the boss. General Brain said, "Since I control it all and do all the thinking, I should be boss."

Colonel Feet said, "Since I carry men where they want to go and get them in line to do what General Brain orders, well, I should be boss."

The Major Hands spoke, "Since I do all the work to keep all you men moving, I oughta be boss."

Thus it went with each part of the body demanding that it be the boss. Finally Sergeant Asshole spoke up and demanded in no uncertain terms that he be made boss. Of course, all the other parts laughed at this silly notion. Sergeant Asshole boss? Haw! Haw! Haw!

This made the sergeant mad as hell and he shut every-thing off and refused to function. Well! Soon General Brain went wacky, the captain's mouth got dry and his eyes crossed. Colonel Feet got so weak he had to hit the sack. And Major Hands went limp and was totally out of order. First Lieutenant Heart and Second Lieutenant Lungs gasped and gurgled and choked, just to keep up.

They all pleaded with General Brain to give up his authority, to relent and let Sergeant Asshole be boss. And that is how it all came to be . . . Sergeant Asshole was the BOSS and gave out all the shit.

The moral of this beautiful story: YOU DON'T HAVE TO BE A BRAIN TO BE BOSS. JUST BE AN ASSHOLE SERGEANT.

5/18/69

The Porcelain Dream.

Tad Foster. THE VIETNAM FUNNY BOOK.
Presidio Press. 1980.

A GI was invited over to his girl's house for dinner, to meet the folks just a few days before departure for Vietnam. He arrived looking like a million dollars. Things went well until they sat down at the table. The soldier started by spilling a glass of water. Then he dropped a fork in the soup. Later he singed his napkin with a careless move of a cigarette lighter.

After he had departed, the girl's father remarked that he liked the lad but that he seemed awkward, clumsy.

"'That worries me, too, Daddy," said his daughter."He's in the bomb-disposal unit!"

Spoons – Cooks and all mess personnel.

Squat – A cipher, a nothing as in "It don't mean diddly squat."

Squelch, A Box Of Squelch – An imagined box for which naive recruits are sent. Something like a tent wrench.

To Stack Pencils – To loaf on the job.

There was a contest to name a new officers club on Taiwan. The winning name for it was . . . "TAI-ONE-ON!"

A troop ship pulled up to the dock in San Francisco with a load of GIs long in Vietnam. When the ship was fast to the dock, the yelling from GI to girlfriend and reverse was deafening.

One GI yelled to his wife, "FF" and she'd yell back, "EF" again and again.

A soldier next to him asked, "What's the trouble between you two?"

And the GI replied, "No trouble. Just argument. She wants to eat first."

The GI returned to his base outside Saigon, thoroughly swacked. It was not the first time, so his CO ordered him to report for interrogation the next day.

Came the next day, "Jones," his CO said, "you're still a PFC. Been one for many months. Your drinking is the cause of no promotion and I got to tell you that if you don't quit it, you're in for a lot of trouble. But if you do quit, get on the wagon, you could make corporal and even sergeant. There's no limit for a good man like you. So quit drinking! You'd like a promotion, wouldn't you?"

"Sir," replied the GI, "I got to tell you that when I get lit, swacked, really high, I already feel like a colonel!"

Groundpounders – The infantry.

Gunge – Also *crotch rot*. A mythical disease said to cause a GI to decay, to rot from his genitals on back.

Hanoi Hannah – The woman broadcaster who nightly aimed her propaganda at American GIs.

"I don't care where they are . . old Ace'll find 'em!"

Hal Atkins. Leatherneck Magazine.

Pinups

Oh, pinups on my bunker wall,
How dearly that I love you all,
The best collection to be found
In Vietnam and parts around.
I gaze at you until I think
Of you as more than printed ink,
And in my dreams you all please me
In partying and revelry.
But though, my pinups, I love you
I'm sorry, but it's very true:
A photograph, however cute,
For flesh-and-blood can't substitute.

Cpl B. Keith Cossey
Leatherneck Magazine.

To Get A Steam And Cream – A steam job where you get a massage AND sex.

Stockade Shuffle – The peculiar, bouncing, dancing kind of half-march used by military prisoners.

Straddle Trench – A field latrine or toilet.

To Strike – To go bar-hopping.

They tell a cute story about news coverage during the Tet offensive. The report was that the Communists were hanging on in two areas, the Phu Tho race track and the Tan Son Nhut golf course.

"Hell fire," blustered a newspaperman, "We had just as well go on home and let *Sports Illustrated* cover the damned fight."

The chaplain at a rear base in Vietnam was asked about his capacity for shelter if the base was ever bombed. Just how many GIs could sleep in his church?

"I'm not real sure," the chaplain answered. "But on a good Sunday morning, if things are fairly quiet around here, we manage to sleep about 150."

At a USO dance, a much-decorated veteran from Vietnam was asked where he had been raised. He replied, "I was born in Chicago . . . but I grew up in Vietnam!"

A group of recruits were listening to a lecture on propaganda and its purposes. One of the questions that followed the lecture was "Who is responsible for armed forces propaganda?"

The reply from the audience was "The recruiter, sir."

COMMFU – Completely Monumental Military Fuck-Up.

Cuntsville – The United States where live the only beautiful, desirable girls in all the world. Dreamsville!

Cycle Boy And Cycle Girl – A pimp and his whore.

Scarf-Up – To eat, gobble up. Also, to steal.

Sewer Trout – Fish served in the mess hall.

Shot At And Missed But Shit At And Hit – Signifying that one has come through combat only to be downed by official shit.

"*CHOI OI! THIS IS BIG PONCHO!*"

Tony Zidek. CHOI OI.
Charles E. Tuttle. VT.

Choi Oi – Equivalent to Oh boy! Great! Holy smokes!

GI Number 1 – Used by Vietnamese when American troops did something good or when Vietnamese wanted to ingratiate themselves to Americans, also a form of *thank you.*

GI Number 10 – Used by Vietnamese when they disliked Americans, GIs were never in-between; you were either 1 or 10.

Take A Burst Of Six – To reenlist for six years (re-up).

F.U.B.A.R. – Fucked up beyond all recognition.

F.T.S. – The most frequent saying among the troops, Fuck the Service. This was written as a slogan almost everywhere.

Nuc Mau 100s – Marijuana cigarettes.

Two Step Charlie – A snake, the Bamboo Viper, it was rumored (incorrectly) that you only took two steps after being bitten by one.

SAIGON CITY

Here's to 'ole Saigon
What a hell of a place
The way that it's run
Is a friggin disgrace
There's Captains and Majors
And Light Colonels, too
With their thumbs up their asses
And nothing to do.

They stand on the flight line
They yell and they shout
Yelling of things
They know nothing about
For all the good they do
They might as well be
Shoveling shit on
The Isle of Capri

It's up in the morning
And to the latrine
It hurts when I (he) pea (s)
Cause I've (hes) been with the Queen
Oh I've (hes) got it bad, boy
And I'm telling you
If you don't quit short-timin
You'll have it too!

When this war is over
We'll all go back home
Back to our Round-eyes
And never more roam
To Hell with 'ole Saigon
And her misery
To Hell with 'ole Saigon
and all her V.D!!!

James P. Durham. BULL DURHAM'S SONGS OF S.E.A.

Chicken Shit – The same as *owl shit*. Meaning: of absolutely no use, a complete cipher!

Clean Sleeve – The basic soldier. A buck private.

The security officer was making the rounds of a Vietnam base, checking on its condition. Suddenly he heard the metallic click of a gun bolt sliding into place. "Halt!" came the sentry's command.

The officer froze, then identified himself and demanded to know why the sentry didn't give the proper command, "Halt! Who goes there!"

The sentry replied, "Sir, when I says 'HALT!' there ain't nobody goin' nowhere. Period!"

A marine captain and a WAVE were having a drink together. The marine mentioned that one of the best materials for shining shoes was a silk stocking. The WAVE promised to bring him one the next day.

True to her word, the next day, the WAVE presented the marine with one of her abandoned silk stockings.

The soldier thanked her, then said, "Shucks, girl, you've taken all the fun out of it!"

There was a large sign just outside the Ground Controlled Approach radar facility: Welcome to Quang Tri Marine GCA. You can depend on us to let you down.

The chaplain was holding services close to the Cambodian border. Near the end of his sermon, rifle fire burst out near the area and the chaplain, trying to put the men at ease, remarked, "All right, Charlie! Come on now! My sermon wasn't that bad!"

It worked and the men laughed uproariously. Then a voice broke through the laughter: "What makes you think those were enemy rounds, sir?"

Clerks And Jerks – GIs not faced with combat, such as clerks and all types of rear echelon personnel.

Grunt – Infantryman, usually spoken with some degree of pride.

F.N.G. or Newby – Fucking new guy, a replacement.

Gook, Slope, Dink, Zips, Slant Eyes – Name for Vietnamese. Gook meant foreigner in Vietnamese.

Dink Pusher – Supervisor for a Vietnamese work force, filling sand bags, etc.

Boom Boom Girl – Vietnamese prostitutes.

Round Eyes – American women.

Peons – E.M. referred to themselves as peons.

Ha, ho ho, these boots thinking there's a Charlie behind every bush.

"CLICK-CLICK"

END

Tad Foster. THE VIETNAM FUNNY BOOK.
Presidio Press. 1980

Off the coast of Vietnam, a large fleet of Navy ships was moving toward shore. The very difficult admiral of the one ship, part of a set of three, was nervously pacing the bridge, terribly distraught. He was one tough hombre, at best, and his men were in constant fear of his vicious tongue. None of them dared ask why he was so nervous.

Finally, he threw up his arms and blared out to the men around him, "There are supposed to be three aircraft carriers with me as we approach shore. I see only two. Where in hell is the other one?"

Complete silence met his demand. None dared say a word!

"Somebody answer me, I say, by god, or else . . . or else . . . "

Finally, the tiny seaman at the helm said, very softly, "Sir, you're standing on it."

A group of 35 recruits were seated in the reception center, preoccupied with filling out information cards as to their personal status. Finished, the sergeant in charge collected the cards, returned to his desk and began to examine them. Finished, he put the cards aside and stood to make his welcoming speech.

"Your group is one of the most interesting, even fascinating we have seen here. I note from the cards you just completed that two of you were never christened and are without names, and four of you have no sex or a lot of sex or are of the wrong sex.. Then I note that one gentleman was born just two months ago. Now, before we conclude this session, I'm curious to see the gentleman who is 135 feet tall and weighs in at 43-5. Will he please try to stand?"

A young paratrooper had just returned from Vietnam and was having a few drinks with his buddies and their girlfriends. One of the girls asked him, "Where do you find the guts, the courage to jump out of an airplane moving at such terrific speeds, and so high up in the air? How can you do it?"

"It ain't so tough, Mary," the paratrooper replied. "I just make believe that the plane is about to blow up . . . say in thirty seconds or so. After that, it ain't a bit hard to jump."

Dip – Same kind of term as *dink*.

Donut Rollers – American Red Cross volunteers, more than 600 of them, who dispensed coffee, confections and sympathy to American Vietnam troops.

Get Your Ducks In Line – "Straighten out your thinking, man, you'd better straighten things out!"

Our First Sergeant had an interesting billeting system. If you were a troublemaker, he placed you on the first floor where he could watch you himself. If you did not make trouble, you slept on the second floor. When I arrived, we had the following exchange:

"Go to church on Sunday?"

"Yes."

"Send some money home?"

"Yes."

"Drink?"

"Just a little."

"Do you like to stay up late, play cards, read a lot, listen to music or get into noisy arguments?"

"No."

Apparently pleased by the answers, he turned to his clerk – and snapped, "He's a liar! Put him on the first floor!

–Alfred J. O'Donnell
APO San Francisco, CA

"JEEP? WHY YES, IT MEANS 'GENERAL PURPOSE,' SO IT'S O.K. TO BE HERE!!"

Tony Zidek. CHOI OI.
Charles E. Tuttle. Vt.

"You spend month after month holding the leash
of a hundred and ten pound scout dog,
and your arm'd look like this."

Leatherneck Magazine

A doting mother was trying to get information out of her son who had telephoned her from his army base a week after induction. "So tell me about yourself," she said. "How do you feel? Is it fun out there? What have you been up to?"

On and on, she continued to throw questions at him. But he would only mumble almost inarticulate replies. Finally she asked him about bathing and such. He did admit to having received a haircut.

"Wonderful," she said. "You certainly did need one when you left here. Was it a crewcut?"

"Well!" he replied, "I sure hope it grows into one."

"Fess up girls, who hid the gunny's girdle?"

Bob Fleischauer. Leatherneck Magazine.

Going Downtown – A flyer's expression for his mission against Hanoi.

Golden Flow – A urinalysis!

Grab 'em By The Balls (and their hearts and minds will follow). – The philosophy that sweet talk and gentle hands will never win the Vietnamese to a love for us.

To Get The Green Banana – To get shafted.

Fort Fumble – The Pentagon.

Gas Attack – To break wind, fart.

Gink – A nasty word for a Vietnamese.

GIs, GI Shits – Diarrhea, as, "your youth drops out your asshole within two weeks of arrival in Vietnam" Also the *Vietshits*.

"There now, Zilch, feel more confident?"

Leatherneck Magazine.

"This is Willy's war souvenirs from
his days in the Marine Corps."

Leatherneck Magazine.

At a bar, very late at night, a drinker with a speech impedi-
ment announced, "If they r-r-really w-w-w-wanted t-to end the-the-
the war in V-V-Viet N-N-Nam, they c-could do it in a-a-a-about t-t-
three w-w-weeks."

"Yeah. Yeah," said a companion. "That's easy enough for you
to say."

Leatherneck Magazine.

During an interview in Vietnam, a pilot, married with three kids was asked how high he generally flew his jet on combat missions. His reply: "I notice the flak exploding around me. That's the first thing I do. That means I'm flying too low. I just add 1500 feet for my wife and 500 feet more for each of my kids."

After Sunday service at Scott Field, Illinois, a tall, lean soldier handed the chaplain a white envelope. It was a donation.

"Mighty fine, soldier," said the chaplain. "We can use this to repair the chapel." Then he opened the envelope and was surprised to take out of it four twenty-dollar bills. "My! This is the largest contribution I've ever received! Tell me, why did you do this?"

"Well, sir, I confess. I won it."

"Don't you think it the Christian thing to give it back to whomever you won it from?"

"No sir, I don't," murmured the soldier. "Anyway, them geeks has shipped out.

"Well, then, I'll accept it. I can sure use it," the chaplain said."

Twice more, the GI appeared at church and gave the chaplain a donation that he accepted. But when the GI showed up with a $500 contribution, that was too much. The chaplain determined to end what was growing to be an unsavory and suspicious series of contributions.

"Now you listen to me, soldier," he said to the GI, "This is too much. You've a mighty bad habit in your gambling and you must stop it. The fact that you give all you won, to the church, is no excuse at all!"

"Excuse me, Chaplain," the GI broke in to say, "But I'm not giving it all to you. Heck no! You get a tenth only. But after that wonderful sermon of yours where you told us that the Lord provides for people who tithe, well, I tried it. Man, you told it like it was. It works! Pastor, it really works."

"That's not what I meant when I told you to get a photo of a fighter pilot going into a dive."

Jake Shuffert. NO SWEAT – HERE'S JAKE.
Stackpole Books. 1983.

A pilot was disgusted with the amateurish efforts of his navigator. They wandered all over the area looking for the air base.

Finally, he called the navigator forward and said, "Soldier, I'm convinced that when you die you'll go to heaven. 'Know why? Because you'll be so far off course!"

A mechanic was being reprimanded for ruining the transmission of a helicopter. He caught pure hell, a reprimand that was heard by the angry officer's squadron commander who suggested that he was unduly harsh on the mechanic.

"After all, Lieutenant, just a week ago I made the same mistake and ruined a transmission. Do you think, had our positions been reversed, that I should have been reprimanded so harshly?"

"Oh, no, sir," the officer hastened to reply. "But he's an enlisted man! He should know better!"

The men of this particular infantry company had been working on Charlie for some time. During that time, their CO had not required them to salute since the salute identified officers.

But new officers had joined and they very much wanted the usual discipline to be observed. The men simply would not regain the habit of saluting. Several times they were reprimanded until, one day, the seasoned first sergeant told the CO that he'd handle it.

The next day the men saluted as required. "What did you do, Sergeant?" the CO demanded to know.

"Come here, sir. I'll show you."

There, near each foxhole, was a small sign" "Salute your officers *because* Charlie may be watching!"

Military personnel are wonderfully shrewd. Witness the sailor who tried to get past a tough deck officer so as to catch the last liberty boat. The officer sent him back to get a haircut. But the sailor found that the barber shop was closed. He hesitated only a moment, brightened, returned to the spit-and-polish officer with the remark, "Request permission to leave the ship, sir. How do my shoes look *now*, Sir?" he asked.

The officer glanced at the high polish on the black shoes, then said, "Much better. Permission granted."

A Two-Digit Fidgit – The state of nervous apprehension of a soldier who had only 10-99 days left before going home.

"That's no excuse. Next time you're working on something that's too high to reach, use a stand or ladder!!"

Jake Schuffert. NO SWEAT – HERE'S JAKE.
Stackpole Books. 1983.

Sign on a Dak Ao brothel wall:

PLEASE PAY WHEN SERVICED

Conversation overheard between a pair of Boonie Rats on a Nha Trang street corner as a Vietnamese peddler passed by:

"Imagine that. Two thousand years of progress and they've learned to pick up one grain of rice with two sticks, and two buckets of shit with one."

Bang - Clap – Self-explanatory GI word for Bangkok, Thailand.

Bare-Ass – A pun on barracks.

Bent Whore – A pun on the city Bien Hoa, South Vietnam.

Bird Farm – An aircraft carrier.

The following interview, a spoof of the thousands of actual interviews in Southeast Asia, is a classic of GI wit and humor in the Vietnam War . . . or any of our wars. As Major Joseph F. Tuso said, about profanity, "Anyone who finds it in poor taste, I'm afraid, misses the point. During my combat tour I found profanity, on the lips of those who faced death cleanly every day, seemed more a blessing than a curse.

This particular interview occurs in 1967 between a reporter and a jet fighter pilot. To keep all in order, a Wing Information Officer is present as monitor so that the "real" Air Force story can be told. The pilot is first asked his opinion of the F4C phantom.

Captain: "It's so fuckin' maneuverable you can fly up your own ass with it."

IO: "What the captain means is that he has found the F4C Phantom highly maneuverable at all altitudes and he considers it an excellent aircraft for all missions assigned."

Corr.: "I suppose, Captain, that you've flown a certain number of missions over North Vietnam. What did you think of the SAMs used by the North Vietnamese?"

Captain: "Why those bastards couldn't hit a bull in the ass with a bass fiddle. We fake the shit out of them. There's no sweat."

IO: "What the captain means is that the Surface-to-Air Missiles around Hanoi pose a serious problem to our air operations and that the pilots have a healthy respect for them."

Corr.: "I suppose, Captain, that you've flown missions to the South. What kind of ordnance do you use, and what kind of targets do you hit?"

Captain: "Well, I'll tell you, mostly we aim at kicking the shit out of Vietnamese villages, and my favorite ordnance is napalm. Man, that stuff just sucks the air out of their friggin' lungs and makes a sonovabitchin' fire."

IO: "What the captain means is that air strikes in south Vietnam are often against Vietcong structures and all operations are always under the positive control of Forward Air Controllers, or FACs. The ordnance employed is conventional 500 and 750 pound bombs and 20 millimeter cannon fire."

Corr.: "I suppose you spend an R and R in Hong Kong. What were your impressions of the Oriental girls?"

Captain: "Yeah, I went to Hong Kong. As for those Oriental broads, well, I don't care which way the runway runs, east or west, north or south — a piece of ass is a piece of ass."

IO: "What the captain means is that he found the delicately featured Oriental girls fascinating, and he was very impressed with their fine manners and thinks their naiveté is most charming."

Corr.: "Tell me, Captain, have you flown any missions other than over North and South Vietnam?"

Captain: "You bet your sweet ass I've flown other missions. We get scheduled nearly every day for a place where those fuckers over there throw everything at you but the friggin' kitchen sink. Even the goddam kids got slingshots."

IO: "What the captain means is that he has occasionally been scheduled to fly missions in the extreme Western DMZ, and he has a healthy respect for the flak in that area."

Corr.: "I understand that no one in your Fighter Wing has got a MIG yet. What seems to be the problem?"

Captain: "Why you screwhead, if you knew anything about what you're talking about — the problem is MIGs. If we'd get scheduled by those peckerheads at Seventh for those missions in MIG Valley, you can bet your ass we'd get some of those mothers. Those glory hounds at Ubon get all those missions while we settle for fightin' the friggin' war. Those mothers at Ubon are sitting on their fat asses killing MIGs and we get stuck with bombing the goddamned cabbage patches."

IO: "What the captain means is that each element in the Seventh Air Force is responsible for doing their assigned job in the air war. Some units are assigned the job of neutralizing enemy air strength by hunting out MIGs, and other elements are assigned bombing missions and interdiction of enemy supply routes."

Corr.: "Of all the targets you've hit in Vietnam, which one was the most satisfying?"

Captain: "Well, shit, it was when we were scheduled for that suspected VC vegetable garden. I dropped napalm in the middle of the fuckin' cabbage and my wingman splashed it real good with six of those 750 pound mothers and spread the fire all the way to the friggin' beets and carrots."

IO: "What the captain means is that the great variety of tactical targets available throughout Vietnam make the F4C the perfect aircraft to provide flexible response."

Corr.: "What do you consider the most difficult target you've struck in North Vietnam?"

Captain: "The friggin' bridges. I must have dropped 40 tons of bombs on those swayin' bamboo mothers, and I ain't hit one of the bastards yet."

IO: "What the captain means is that interdicting bridges along enemy supply routes is very important and a quite difficult target. The best way to accomplish this task is to crater the approaches to the bridge."

Corr.: "I noticed in touring the base that you have aluminum matting on the taxiways. Would you care to comment on its effectiveness and usefulness in Vietnam?"

Captain: "You're fuckin' right, I'd like to make a comment. Most of us pilots are well hung, but shit, you don't know what hung is until you get hung up on one of the friggin' bumps on that goddam stuff."

IO: "What the captain means is that the aluminum matting is quite satisfactory as a temporary expedient, but requires some finesse in taxiing and braking the aircraft."

Corr: "Did you have an opportunity to meet your wife on leave in Honolulu, and did you enjoy the visit with her?"

Captain: "Yeah, I met my wife in Honolulu, but I forgot to check the calendar, so the whole five days were friggin' well combat-proof — a completely dry run."

IO: "What the captain means is that it was wonderful to get together with his wife and learn first-hand about the family and how things were at home."

Corr: "Thank you for your time, captain."

Captain: "Screw you — why don't you bastards print the real story, instead of all that crap?"

IO: "What the captain means is that he enjoyed the opportunity to discuss his tour with you."

Corr.: "One final question. Could you reduce your impression of the war into a simple phrase or statement, captain?"

Captain: "You bet your ass I can. It's a fucked up war."

IO: "What the captain means is . . . it's a FUCKED UP WAR."

TERMS AND DEFINITIONS

Have you ever looked over your Evaluation Report and asked yourself, "I wonder just what he means by this phrase?" Well perhaps the following list will help.

Term	Definition
Exceptionally well qualified	Has committed no major blunders to date
Active Socially	Drinks heavily.
Character and integrity above reproach	Still one step ahead of the law.
Wife is active socially	She, too, drinks.
Zealous attitude	Opinionated.
Unlimited potential	Will retire or be kicked out shortly.
Quick thinking	Offers plausible excuses for errors.
Takes pride in his work	Conceited.

Takes advantage of every opportunity to progress.................	Buys drinks for OIC and NCOICs
Forceful and aggressive	Argumentive.
Outstanding	Frequently in the rain.
Indifferent to instructions	Knows more than superiors.
Tactful in dealings with superiors..	Knows when to keep his mouth shut.
Approaches difficult problems with enthusiasm...........................	Finds someone else to do the job.
A keen analyst.............................	Thoroughly confused.
Definitely not a desk man	Did not go to college.
Often spends extra hours on the job..	Has a miserable home life.
A true southern gentleman	A hillbilly
Meticulous in attention to detail	A nit picker.
Demonstrates qualities of leadership......................................	Has a loud voice.
Judgement is usually sound	Lucky.
Maintains a professional attitude ..	A snob.
Strong adherence to principles.....	Stubborn as a mule!
Career minded.............................	Hates reservists.
Gets along extremely well with superiors and subordinates alike..	A coward.
Average Officer of NCO................	Not too bright.
Slightly below average	Stupid.
A very fine officer of great value to the service	Usually gets to work on time.
Develops a good "Team feeling"...	Has everybody mad at him.
Outstanding ability to get the maximum out of his men and all available resources	A slavedriver.
Exceptionally effective in the utilization of resources.................	Cheapskate.
Correctly interprets rather difficult instructions	Spell it out for him.
Has mastered all duties with knowledge or related positions	Jack of all trades.
Hesitates to ask for clarification	Doesn't speak English too well.
One of the few outstanding Airmen I know...............................	In this two man Detachment?
Exceptional flying ability	Has an equal number of take-offs and landings.

PATRICK'S
LEATHERNECK
LAFFS
in
BLACK
and
WHITE..

"This is the deepest latrine I
wuz ever ordered to dig!"

"You'll see something if you
take the lens cover off your
binoculars, Wells!"

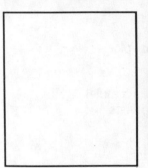

"Excellent job on winter
camouflauge men! Now,
where are you?"

"Twenty years in the Corps
and this is the dirtiest rifle
barrel I've ever seen!"

"It's Crenshaw in the base
laundry,- he's using too much
soap again!"

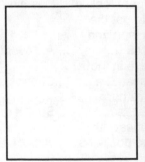

"Read what eye chart, Doc?"

"I think we're lost, men!"

"Aim that flame thrower at me
again and I'll throw the book
at you!"

ACKNOWLEDGMENTS
AND BIBLIOGRAPHY

Argosy Magazine. Blazing Publications, Inc. New York.
American Legion Magazine. Daniel S. Wheeler, Editor-in-Chief. Indianapolis, IN.
George Baker. *Sad Sack* © 1944; renewed 1971 by George Baker. Simon & Schuster, Inc. New York.
Max Barsis. *They're All Yours, Uncle Sam*. 1943. Stephen Daye Publishers. New York.
Don Blanding. *Pilot Bales Out*. 1943. Dodd Mead & Co. New York.
Dave Breger. *Pvt. Breger in Great Britain & Pvt. Breger's War, His Adventures in Britain and At The Front*. "Reprinted with special permission of King Features Syndicate, Inc." New York.
Tuck Boys. Ben Hoa Productions. Fayetteville, AR.
George Cornell. *GI Slang In Vietnam*. Journal of American Culture. Vol. 4:2, Summer 1981. Bowling Green, Ohio.
James Dankey. State Historical Society of Wisconsin. Madison, WI.
William Davidson, Editor. *Tall Tales They Tell In The Service*. 1943. Thomas Y. Crowell Co.
Marione R. Derrickson, Editor. *Funny Business & Laugh It Off*. Whittlesey House, Philadelphia, PA.
Sylvia G. L. Dannett. *A Treasury of Civil War Humor*. 1963. Thomas Yoseloff. New York.
James P. "Bull" Durham, USAF. *Bill Durham's Songs of the S.E.A.* Jackson, TN.
John R. Elting, Dan Cragg, Ernest L. Deal. *A Dictionary of Soldier Talk*. 1984. Reprinted with permission of Charles Scribner's Sons, an imprint of Macmillan Publishing Co. New York.
James Estes. Artist. Amarillo, TX.
Lydia Fish. Dept. of Anthropology. Buffalo State College. Buffalo, New York.
Tad Foster. *The Vietnam Funny Book*. 1980. Presidio Press. If you would like a permanent hardcover edition of the entire works from The Vietnam Funny Book: An Antidote to Insanity, please send $9.95 plus $2.50 postage and handling (pbk. $6.95) to Black Pearl Publishers, 109 Minna St., #209, San Francisco, CA 94105.
Marion Hargrove. *See Here, Private Hargrove*. 1943. Henry Holt & Co. New York.

Harold Hershey. *G.I. Laughs*. 1944. Sheridan House. New York.
Sid Hoff. *Mom, I'm Home*. 1945. Doubleday, Doran & Co., Inc. New York.
Illinois Historic Preservation Agency. Springfield, Illinois. Tom Schwartz,
    Curator, Abraham Lincoln Collections.
The Illinois State Library. Springfield, Illinois. Sondra Hastings. Interlibrary
    Loan Department. Larry Weyhrich, Reference Department.
John Rogers Inkslinger. *Paul Bunyan in the Army*. Tom O'Brien, Illustrator.
    1942. Binford & Mort Publishing. Portland, OR
Lariar, Lawrence. Whitttlesey House. Philadelphia, PA.
The Lincoln Library. Springfield, Illinois. Interlibrary Loan Department.
    Jeanne Kains, Director. Jean Ann Long, Processor. Reference
    Department: Gerri Whitaker, Head. Cleris Wagner,Classie Murray,
    Jenny Holmberg, Marie Ellen Halcli, Pat Blenn, Laurie Bartolini.
Bill Mauldin. *Up Front*, Henry Holt & Co. *Bill Mauldin In Korea*; W. W.
    Norton Co. New York. *This Damn Tree Leaks*; Stars & Stripes,
    Mediterranean. *Bill Mauldins Army*; Presidio Press, Novato, CA. *The
    Brass Ring*; W. W. Norton Co., New York.
Judge Richard Mills, United States District Court. Bridadier General -
    Illinois Militia. Federal Building. Springfield, Illinois
Out of Line; Pacific Stars & Stripes. 1962. Tokyo, Japan
Sgt. Norval E. Packwood, Jr. *Leatherhead in Korea*. Marine Corp.
    Gazette. Quantico, VA.
Virgil Franklin Parch. *Here We Go Again*. 1964. Duell, Sloane & Pearce.
    New York.
Don Pratt and Lee Blair. *Salmagundi: Vietnam*. 1970. C.E. Tuttle Co.
    Rutland, VT.
Leonard Sansone. *The Wolf*. 1945. United Publishers. New York.
John H. "Jake" Schuffert. *"No Sweat" "Here's Jake"*. *A Collection of
    Military Cartoons*. 1983. Stackpole Books. Harrisburg, PA.
Stars & Stripes. Wm. Bartman. New York.
Joseph F. Tusco, USAF, from Folklore Forum. V.1 (January, 1972) 25-27.
The Leatherneck Magazine. William V. H. White, Editor. Marine Corp.
    Assn. Quantico, VA.
The Best from YANK, the Army Weekly, 1945. The World Publishing
    Company. New York.
Tony Zidek. Choi-Oi: *The Lighter Side of Vietnam*. 1965. Charles E. Tuttle
    Co., Inc. Tokyo, Japan.
Edwin N. Appleton. "The Navy Explained". 1918. Edwin N. Appleton, Inc.
    New York.

Here is a list of the current books of superb-humor published by the Lincoln-Herndon Press, Inc.

The humor in these books will delight you, brighten your conversation, make your life more fun, and healthier, because "Laughter Is The Best Medicine."

*Grandpa's Rib-Ticklers & Knee-Slappers $8.95
*Josh Billings —
    America's Phunniest Phellow $7.95
Davy Crockett —
    Legendary Frontier Hero $7.95
Cowboy Life on the Sidetrack $7.95
A Treasury of Science Jokes $8.95
The Great American Liar — Tall Tales $9.95
The Cowboy Humor of A.H. Lewis $9.95
The Fat Mascot . . .
    22 Funny Baseball Stories & More $7.95
A Treasury of Farm & Ranch Humor $10.95
Mr. Dooley . . . We Need Him Now!
    The Irish-American Humorist $8.95
*A Treasury of Military Humor $10.95
Here's Charley Weaver, Mamma and Mt. Idy $9.95
*These books are also available in hardback.

Order From:
    Lincoln-Herndon Press, Inc.
    818 S. Dirksen Parkway
    Springfield, IL 62703